INTO HIS PRESENCE

A THEOLOGY OF
INTIMACY WITH GOD

T0339223

INTO HIS PRESENCE

A THEOLOGY OF
INTIMACY WITH GOD

Tim L. Anderson

To My Wife Barbara

God's gracious provision
of the best partner in this life
I could ever have.

CONTENTS

ACKNOWLEDGEMENTS

When it is claimed, "It takes a village to raise a child," I would also add, "It takes a village to write and publish a book." I have been blessed by the Lord not only with His Word and guidance throughout this project, but He has blessed me with many people whose help has been invaluable.

Corban University has been the greenhouse for significant aspects of this book. I am so grateful for the sabbatical to write the proposal and the bulk of the manuscript. Dr. Greg Trull's support is immeasurable. He originally suggested that I teach my Intimacy with God course, worked with my teaching schedule to make research easier, provided help in framing certain chapters, and also provided the ability to take time off from teaching for my sabbatical. Several of my Corban colleagues helped in many different ways. Dr. Gary Derickson put me in contact with Kregel, and has been very reassuring throughout. I cannot thank David Sanford enough for his unending support, advice, and help with the book proposal. Dr. Ryan Stark sacrificially read a large portion of the original manuscript and helped me be a better writer. Any inadequacies in the book are solely mine. My dear colleagues Dr. Sam Baker, Dr. Leroy Goertzen, and Dr. Marty Trammell have been so helpful and encouraging in all the parts of the process. My students in my Intimacy with God classes helped me clarify the concept as well as its depth and breadth.

Dr. Erik Thoennes has been a dear friend and supporter for two decades. He encouraged me to find my voice as an author. His example has inspired me along this journey.

I'm so grateful to be on Kregel's team of Herb Bateman, Dennis Hillman, Laura Bartlett, and Shawn Vander Lugt. They have made this book more than I ever thought it could be.

Finally, the continuous support, sacrifice, excitement, and encouragement of my wife Barbara, and each of my children, David, Jonathan, Emily, and Stephen, has been vital and precious to me.

Thank you, Village.

INTRODUCTION

AS WE BEGIN . . .

When I was a freshman in college, I made the decision to follow the Lord wholeheartedly. One of my initial desires was (and still is) to relate to God as He has proscribed in the Bible. One Sunday I was listening to my pastor preach, and I was struck to my spiritual core by a thought that had never even remotely occurred to me in all my years of growing up in the church: "Who do I pray to?" This was not a venture into other religions; rather, I was simply asking, "Do I pray to the Father only? To the Son, Jesus Christ? To the Holy Spirit? Am I slighting or disrespecting any one of Them when I am praying to one of the Others? Is it possible to pray to only one of Them?" In my growing faith, I simply had a desire to pray right. This was accompanied by the realization that what I believed about intimacy with God had profound implications.

That same year, a friend gave me his own personal copy of A. W. Tozer's *The Pursuit of God*. Tozer began to open my world to the understanding that the rightness of my relationship with God is to be combined with my closeness to Him. Specifically, Tozer makes this astounding assertion: "God wills that we should push on into His Presence and live our whole lives there."[1] Like entering into the biblical temple's Holy of Holies, rightness is combined with closeness. Maybe you can relate to that in your spiritual journey as well. There are times when I still feel like a freshman in my understanding and close-

---

1. A. W. Tozer, *The Pursuit of God* (Harrisburg, PA: Christian Publications, 1948), 36–37, italics his.

ness to God in Three Persons, Blessed Trinity. Furthermore, when discussing intimacy with God with my students, in small groups at church, at retreats and conferences, and during counseling sessions, I have heard a variety of perspectives—some cogent and some very peculiar, some derived from bits and pieces of Scripture understood in isolation, some derived from sitcoms and Disney films. A study on what the Bible says about intimacy with God, to me, seems to be crucial for our day.

WHAT THIS BOOK IS *NOT* ABOUT

So as we begin, it would be helpful to make clear what this book is *not* about. This book will not be a narrative of someone's personal experience with God, on his or her own journey from distance or loneliness to a feeling of closeness with Him, though I would validate many such narratives. Indeed, it would be tragic if, after reading this book, readers were not moved toward God one iota. As Ron Brackin pointedly advises, "We can read a good spiritual book in search of information or in search of God. We will find only what we're looking for."[2] Reading this book does not have to be one or the other, either. In fact, I hope it is both.

This book will also not be a "how-to" devotional guide, providing ten steps to a better intimacy with God, or some such formulation. At the same time, we are certainly examining the Bible's theology on intimacy with God, and so we should expect transparent principles to rise to the surface and function as assessment points for us to tell, for example, if we truly are any closer to God today than yesterday or last year. Additionally, this book cannot hope to address all of your favorite passages, or pursue every corollary theme related to intimacy with God in the Bible. I apologize straight away, but the basic topic at hand is more than enough to keep me busy throughout. Keep in mind, too, that what may seem to be a direct correlation or implication may not be addressed because I simply have not noticed it, or perhaps I chose other themes to develop that were, in my mind, more germane. In other words, there are undoubtedly missed opportunities in my pursuit of the topic, but I hope that my fundamental aim has been achieved: to explain intimacy with God in a way that answers fundamental questions about who God is and how we are to relate to Him.

Let me add at this point that this is not a book that claims to be written by someone who has all the answers, nor does the book want to sound preten-

---

2. Ron Brackin, "Reading Skills Quotes," Goodreads, http://www.goodreads.com/quotes/tag/reading-skills.

tious, and so if you take it that way, I am sorry—please allow me the chance to explain, and then you can make a judgment.

WHAT THIS BOOK *IS* ABOUT

So what *is* this book about? In short, this study will develop what the Bible says about intimacy with God. However, before we get into specific definitions and concepts, let me start by addressing its purposes. First, it is an *affirmation*. When Christians study the Scriptures, there will be a shared agreement over basic and most important truths because of the promised Holy Spirit's work (John 14:26; 1 Cor. 2:12; 1 Thess. 4:9; 1 John 2:26–27). Believers have always sought to draw near to their God. While sin separates, trust in the salvation God provides by faith has been a rallying point throughout the ages. It is a glorious reality that Abraham, Moses, David, Daniel, the disciples, Paul, John, Peter, Antony, Augustine, Aquinas, John of the Cross, Teresa of Avila, Luther, Calvin, Owen, Edwards, Wesley, Parham, Nee, Tozer, Lewis, Merton, Nouwen, etc. have all drawn near to the God of their salvation. They all have something to teach us as well. The significance of recent classics should never be minimized. They are profoundly enriching works, yet they are a product of their time, culture, worldview, philosophy, theology, and human limitations. Their theological method is often less precise and more devotional in thrust. For example, Tozer's *The Pursuit of God* is a classic text on intimacy with God; and as I have already shared, I am indebted to him on a profound level. However, as important as this work is, it is broader than what I am attempting. Also, a more thorough biblical theology needs to be done to provide a more substantive grounding in scriptural data and specific biblical themes. J. Oswald Sanders's *Enjoying Intimacy with God* is another classic book on this topic.[3] It includes concepts that I will also develop, and yet it includes broader Christian life issues; again, the key difference is that his is more of a devotional, practical, how-to book, not a robust systematic/biblical theology.

The other purpose of this book is to attempt an *intervention* of sorts. By its very nature, an intervention into someone's life, ideas, and experience is emotional and challenging, and yet necessary and affirming. This book's intercession will seek to address head-on the foundational assumptions and imprecise theologies of intimacy with God that appear to be addictive. These assumptions are quite evident in the sheer amount of books that have been written with "intimacy with God" in the title in the last two decades. There are

---

3. J. Oswald Sanders, *Enjoying Intimacy with God* (Grand Rapids: Discovery House, 2000).

three categories of the types of works and issues: Catholic Mystical, Pentecostal Experiential, and Evangelical Devotional.

Catholic Mystical

Contemporary Catholic mystical writers like Thomas Merton and Thomas Keating are part of a tradition that dates back to the early monastic movements. Their passion to mortify the sins of the flesh is commendable. Their spiritual self-discipline is in itself exemplary. Their desire to connect with God as a two-way experience is a crucial corrective to a one-way—we talk and He listens—approach. So I haltingly bring anything negative against these deeply sincere spiritual giants. However, one challenge for them is that they tend to follow aspects of a tradition born out of a Neoplatonic view of reality and humanity from Augustine and St. John of the Cross.[4] This simply means that the body and flesh are less valuable than the spiritual and rational. One problem with this is that they can also drift toward an Eastern mysticism that tries to free the self from fleshly hindrances. While this may be commendable, such attitudes can focus less on immersion in truth of what God has revealed in the Scriptures, and more on escaping the confines of our earthly existence and emptying ourselves of our rational humanity. Their goal is the achieving a union with God that has us being absorbed into Him[5]—that is, His spirit, will, and essence—rather than having a relational unity that preserves our personal human identity.[6]

---

4.   Pearcey rightly notes, "Partly because Augustine was such a towering figure in church history, a kind of Christianized Platonism remained the *lingua franca* among theologians all the way through the Middle Ages." Nancy Pearcey, *Total Truth: Liberating Christianity from Its Cultural Captivity*, Study Guide Edition (Wheaton, IL: Crossway, 2005), Loc. 1740; José C. Nieto, *Mystic, Rebel, Saint: A Study of St. John of the Cross* (Genève: Librarie Droz, 1979), 126.

5.   One type of example of this union can be found in Thomas Merton, *New Seeds of Contemplation*, introduction by Sue Monk Kidd, Kindle ed. (New York: New Directions, 1961, 2007), loc. 257.

> Contemplation is also the response to a call: a call from Him Who has no voice, and yet Who speaks in everything that is, and Who, most of all, speaks in the depths of our own being: for we ourselves are words of His. But we are words that are meant to respond to Him, to answer Him, to echo Him, and even in some way contain Him and signify Him. Contemplation is this echo. It is a deep resonance in the inmost center of our spirit in which our very life loses its separate voice and re-sounds with the majesty and the mercy of the Hidden and Living One. He answers Himself in us and this answer is divine life, divine creativity, making all things new. We ourselves become His echo and His answer. It is as if in creating us God asked a question, and in awakening us to contemplation He answered the question, so that the contemplative is at the same time, question and the answer.

6.   See Thomas Keating's book, *Intimacy with God: An Introduction to Centering Prayer* (New York: Crossroad, 2009), for a modern mystical Catholic perspective. Alex Aronis's *Developing Intimacy with God: An Eight-Week Prayer Guide Based on Ignatius' "Spiritual*

Pentecostal Experiential

The Pentecostal experience writers find their roots in the Methodist Holiness movements of the late nineteenth-century America. Their practical and transformative Christianity has rightly found fertile ground around the world. The resurgence of experiencing the Holy Spirit's ministry has been a necessary intervention into the church. The expectation of experiencing the true and living God is important for any age of the church. However, this experiential emphasis, coupled with an unassailable American individualism and existentialism, has resulted in some having the mindset that everything intimate and miraculous with God that believers experience in the Bible can and should be the norm for all Christians today.[7] Thus experiential claims, no matter how bizarre, cannot be challenged. Claims of intimacy with God through visions and experiences of Jesus are becoming more common. David Taylor, in his *Face-to-face Appearances from Jesus: The Ultimate Intimacy*, assumes that since Jesus has supposedly appeared to him on more than one occasion, seeing Him "face-to-face" is normative for believers today. In addition, these visions bring intimacy, prosperity, and a clear destiny for one's life.[8]

Evangelical Devotional

The evangelical devotional writers often find their foundations in the Puritans, the Great Awakening, the fundamentalist/modernist controversies, and the broadening of the evangelical movement. Like most evangelicals, the personal conversion experience is necessary, but must be followed with a discipleship based upon studying the Bible's teachings on the broader issues

---

Exercises" (Bloomington, IN: Author House, 2003) is an interesting Catholic approach based upon an early church father, though this is not rooted in a biblical theology but in elements of a Neoplatonic philosophy.

7. Phillip H. Wiebe, "The Pentecostal Initial Evidence Doctrine," *Journal of the Evangelical Theological Society* 24, no. 7 (1984): 465–72; Beni Johnson, Sue Ahn, Ann Stock, DeAnne Clark, Heidi Baker, Sheri Hess, Winnie Banov, and Nina Myers, *Beautiful One: A Walk in Deeper Intimacy with the One Who Created Us*, ed. Shae Cooke (Shippensburg, PA: Destiny Image, 2010).

8. David Taylor, *Face-to-face Appearances from Jesus: The Ultimate Intimacy* (Shippensburg, PA: Destiny Image, 2009). We will later examine the claims of Matthew Robert Payne, in his *Finding Intimacy with Jesus Made Simple* (Litchfield, IL: Revival Waves of Glory Books & Publishing, 2016). In *Experience the Power of God's Presence: A Call to Intimacy with God, Volume 1* (Royal Center, IN: Exson Publishing, 2012), Harry Muyenza focuses on defining worship and experiencing Pentecostal phenomena for intimacy with God. Joyce Meyer, in her *Knowing God Intimately: Being as Close to Him as You Want to Be* (New York: FaithWords, 2008), uses "Scripture and powerful real life examples" in her Pentecostal approach, focusing mainly on the baptism of the Holy Spirit and gifts.

of the Christian life. Thus intimacy with God is a topic associated with learning to practice the Christian life. The clearest evidence of this is by doing one's devotions. Their literature tends to focus on an American pragmatism of how to achieve intimacy with God.[9] Others incorporate psychology into their approach to a close relationship with God. This can be very useful, and yet they do not provide substantial theological grounding for its elements.[10]

Planning for Precision

So what's my plan? One cannot pursue an affirmation and an intervention without a plan. As a minimum, we need to work toward a precise definition of intimacy with God. This is especially important when it appears that our culture faces the temptation to reduce intimacy with God to an experiential narrative and to spiritual how-to lists. Thus, precise definitions seem to be an afterthought at best. J. Gresham Machen in *What Is Faith?* pointed out liberalism's aversion to precision. He noted:

---

9. Steve Korch, *My Soul Thirsts: An Invitation to Intimacy with God* (King of Prussia, PA: Judson, 2000), has good elements in its approach to intimacy with God, but is more of a how-to book for a more popular audience. It is also more conceptual at points than biblical (for example, see sections on joy [for the "humor-impaired"], prayer/spiritual power ["overcoming life's obstacles"], knowing the Bible ["hearing God's voice with your whole being"], and authentic passion for God ["dancing in the Arms of God"]), and much broader in scope than the present volume. Malcolm Macdonald, *Set Me on Fire: Being Filled with the Presence of God* (Venice, CA: Monarch, 2015), is classified under Christian Living on Amazon, and under Christian Life and Devotionals on Kregel (http://www.kregel.com/christian-living-and-devotionals/set-me-on-fire). Randy Madison's *Pursuing Intimacy with God: Life's #1 Priority* (Las Vegas: Next Century Publishing, 2010) is a book based in his sermon series on this topic. It is therefore limited in scope to certain passages and themes, and lacks theological depth, clarity, and precision. Christian Paul Osburn's *The Key That Unlocks the Door to Intimacy with God* (Kindle ed., Amazon Digital Services, 2014) is a "how-to" that is more of a basic theology booklet about being able to be right with God/justification. Dr. Benjamin Sawatsky's *Intimacy with God: Drawing Ever Closer to the Almighty* (Colorado Springs: Book Villages, 2011) develops theological themes in practical ways (i.e., "Intimacy with God and the Holy Spirit"), yet it is broader than intimacy with God as it ventures into other areas of God's role in the Christian life (e.g., "The Holy Spirit as My Resident Rabbi"). Eddie Snipes's *Simple Faith: How Every Person Can Experience Intimacy with God* (Carrollton, GA: GES Book Publishing, 2011) is a basic introduction to Christian faith that appears to be intended for newer believers and lacks theological development.

10. Dr. Anthony J. Fischetto, *Transformed: Intimacy with God* (Reading, PA: Alpha Omega Counseling Center, 2000). This book, written by a psychologist, centers on avoiding the stress of life through Christian meditation and psychobiology. Dr. Norm Wakefield's *Living in God's Presence: Pursuing Intimacy with Our Heavenly Father* (Loveland, CO: Walking Carnival, 2013) is not theological but psychological and devotional.

> This temper of mind is hostile to precise definitions. Indeed nothing makes a man more unpopular in the controversies of the present day than an insistence upon definition of terms. . . . Men discourse very eloquently today upon such subjects as God, religion, Christianity, atonement, redemption, faith; but are greatly incensed when they are asked to tell in simple language what they mean by these terms.[11]

First, I would add that for many in our era it isn't simply an aversion to precise definitions, but an inability to see the need for them on a substantive level. If intimacy with God is personal, then it is subjective and relative. To claim a precise definition could alienate people, invalidate their experiences, and thus come across as imperialistic and hostile. Second, men and women are speaking very eloquently on the subject of intimacy with God but we find that there is a hesitancy to claim some definitions and approaches as being out of bounds. This reluctance is motivated in part by viewing intimacy with God as a means to spiritual and emotional health. And there are many paths and practical ways to that end for the individual. Yet, this kind of posture is precisely why we need to have a robust and clear theological development of the concept of intimacy with God from the source of truth God has revealed, in the Scriptures to His creations.

We also face the temptation to absolutize intimacy with God. The Achilles heel of any worldview or theological position is when it either makes too much of its theological importance or reduces its complexities to something too simple.[12] For example, I have had students absolutize God's sovereignty even in His gift of free will, to the point that they claim that God is the ultimate author of evil. In the past some hyper-Calvinists have absolutized God's sovereign choice in election to the point that they have denied the need for evangelism. Similarly, some Baptists have absolutized religious liberty to the point that they have allowed in their churches and seminaries the denial of certain fundamentals of historic orthodox Christianity. Some of my students, because of cultural and theological forces, have absolutized God's love to the extent that when I ask them what the Bible is all about, they say almost without thinking, "It's God's love letter to mankind." All I have to do is ask them how they would fit the Bible's kingdom theme and the judgments of Revelation into that and their foreheads begin to wrinkle. Intimacy with God is not

---

11. J. Gresham Machen, *What Is Faith?* (New York: Macmillian, 1925), 13–14.
12. Steve Wilkins and Mark Sanford, *Hidden Worldviews: Eight Stories That Shape Our Lives* (Downers Grove, IL: IVP, 2009).

the theme of the Bible. However, it is a significant theme and, as we will see, it does overlap with other important scriptural themes and foundations.

Some define intimacy with God by absolutizing one Bible verse. For example, Fischetto bases his approach to intimacy with God around Psalm 46:10, "Be still and know that I am God." To him, this passage teaches us "how to be still and know God personally, passionately, and powerfully." Thus spiritual and physical meditation is absolutized as the key to intimacy with God.[13] I am not dismissing the fact that there are key passages that function as parts of the foundation to key biblical concepts (Eph. 2:11–22; Heb. 4:16; 10:19–22; James 4:8; etc.). Absolutizing, however, funnels all other experiences and biblical data through one main and defining passage. It is as if the gospel itself can be fully explained by writing John 3:5 on a sign at an NFL football game for all to see. The gospel is more than the phrase "being born again." Intimacy with God is more than "Be still and know that I am God."

AGAIN . . . WHAT THIS BOOK IS ABOUT

I have developed this book as a biblical and theological affirmation of the profound teaching on intimacy with God in the Scriptures. These sacred Writings not only describe coming into authentic and safe contact with the high and holy Creator and Redeemer of the human race, but they invite us to be a part of a relationship that is nothing short of epic. Think of it! The movement of God toward the beings He has made in His image is an epic drama that is as real as any national or personal history. In order to capture as much of the teachings of Scripture as possible, I have framed this book primarily around how biblical and systematic theology work. In other words, a theology of intimacy with God should address many of the structural issues important to theology, its categories and terms, as such a theology should go where the biblical data leads. Moreover, it must address some current issues and trends. Thus I hope that this theology will serve as an example and model for doing theology on other relevant topics.

Chapter 1 introduces the concept of intimacy with God. Much like the beginning of a college course, this is where the instructor provides focus to the students as to what they will be studying all semester long. What is geology, educational philosophy, Christology, etc.? Here I provide a definition of intimacy with God as *the movement of God and Christians toward a place of true knowledge and close contact*. Imbedded in this definition are

---

13. Fischetto, *Transformed: Intimacy with God*.

the four key scriptural elements of intimacy with God, which are the yarn that knits the whole intimate sweater together. The sweater metaphor, incidentally, is optional.

Chapter 2 focuses on what theologians call "theological prolegomena," that is, the preface to doing theology. When Tolkien wrote the preface to the *Lord of the Rings*, he simply stated that it is "largely concerned with hobbits."[14] J. I. Packer positions his classic work *Knowing God* on His attributes as a book for travelers on a journey, rather than simply for those who watch the journey and ask questions and make observations from a balcony above.[15] With the same intent, I will try to show where intimacy with God fits into the broader concepts of philosophy and theology in order to show where it is, where we are, and where we should go. Therefore, at the outset, we must recognize God as the source of our very existence, consciousness and delights, the indispensible human elements for an intimate relationship with Him. Our very personal expressible and inexpressible knowledge of Him is also a gracious divine gift and responsibility for us. This focuses our study and pursuit upon God's self-revelation in the Bible, and thus we form our theology primarily from it. That theology reveals our God as the immanent and yet transcendent One who is omnipresent, omniscient, *and* condescending. His nature and attributes will help us assess other examples of approaches to intimacy with God such as those situated within the three camps listed above. We will examine how their presuppositions undergird and thus shape and limit them.

Chapter 3 provides an understanding of the fall of humanity and its effects on intimacy with God. The Bible claims that the human condition is one of brokenness. We are beings fully culpable for cultivating estrangement from God. Without reckoning with the radical effects of the fall of humanity, we may cultivate illegitimate expectations for intimacy with God. We may expect it to be easy, long-lasting, and unassailable, or feel that our movement away from Him is not really our responsibility. Therefore, this chapter develops the backstory of how it was supposed to be and what went wrong. It describes the continuing barriers to intimacy with God in wickedness, spiritual adultery, Satanic opposition, arrogant self-sufficiency, distraction, hiding, and fear.

Chapter 4 seeks to interpret the biblical symbols for God's communication of intimacy. We will delve into the beautiful arena of the figures of speech, or anthropomorphisms, used by the writers of Scripture to express intimacy

---

14.   J. R. R. Tolkien, *Fellowship of the Ring* (New York: Random House, 1965), 19.
15.   J. I. Packer, *Knowing God* (Downers Grove, IL: IVP, 2009), 11–12. ·

with God. We will examine the profoundly rich symbols of God's face, ears, hands, voice/mouth, bosom, and how we are to interpret them.

Chapter 5 will interpret the biblical image of God our Father. Too often the church gives congregants a simplistic view of God, which paints Him only as an angry or disappointed judge, and so circumvents a lasting relational intimacy with Him.[16] For those who struggle to approach God because of the shame they suffer from past sins and current temptations, the Bible's teaching on God as a good and intimate Father coupled with recent psychological research provides tremendous insights. In this chapter I demonstrate that those who agonize over feelings of shame need new "cultural scripts" and "life scripts" by which to flourish—new narratives wherein a healthier view of God, self, and community might emerge. The starting point is a proper biblical script of God as our Father, a vision of Him that resists one-dimensional notions of divine anger and disappointment. A more robust and grace-filled concept of God the intimate Father, in other words, provides relief to the sufferers of unhealthy shame.

Chapter 6 interprets Christ and the marriage images. This is one of the most profound images of intimacy with God in the Bible with Christ and His people as husband and wife and bride and bridegroom. However, the church has struggled interpreting these metaphors and how these marital images apply to us today. Do they correspond to contemporary Western ones? Are we to seek some sort of divine romance with Christ? This chapter answers these questions, so that the Christian's conception of and quest for an intimate relationship with God will not only be freed from the burden of misconceptions and perhaps idolatrous errors, but wonderfully enriched.

In Chapter 7 we examine the Holy Spirit's intimate provisions for believers. We see that as the *parakletos* He provides intimate disclosure of the truth of Christ's sustaining presence and indwelling leadership over sin and his life-giving influence. He intimately intercedes for us in our prayers amidst our deep suffering and gives us hope that He will clearly communicate the depth of our longings to the God who holds our destinies.

Chapter 8 is perhaps the most relationally intense one. It grapples with the seemingly uncaring hiddenness of God that appears to be glued to many instances of suffering. This is why we will seek to understand the sufferer's feelings and perspectives toward God in the scriptural data. We will then

---

16. This has been going on for a while. See David Van Biema, "Behind America's Different Perceptions of God," http://content.time.com/time/nation/article/0,8599,1549413,00.html (accessed April 25, 2019).

examine how God not only has intimate knowledge of our trying circumstances, but how He provides in Himself the necessary intimate place of security and safety amidst suffering.

The last chapter will put into practice the biblical and theological themes of the book in assessing our songs of intimacy with God. The church has a long history of expressing the theme of intimacy with God with music. First, I will provide a brief survey of some of these songs, while focusing on contemporary Christian songs that communicate the intimate nature of God's movement, presence or place, His knowledge, and His contact or touch. Then I will assess some for biblical and theological accuracy, precision, and clarity. I hope to do this while avoiding being judgmental of the songwriter's motives and emotions.

At this point, I must admit that crafting a theology of intimacy with God is a risky endeavor. I must return to the wise counsel of one of our mentors. Tozer was surely correct in his recognition of the risk of rightness without closeness.

> Sound Bible exposition is an imperative *must* in the Church of the Living God. Without it no church can be a New Testament church in any strict meaning of that term. But exposition may be carried on in such a way as to leave the hearers devoid of any true spiritual nourishment whatever. For it is not mere words that nourish the soul, but God Himself, and unless and until the hearers find God in personal experience they are not the better for having heard the truth. The Bible is not an end in itself, but a means to bring men to an intimate and satisfying knowledge of God, that they may enter into Him, that they may delight in His Presence, may taste and know the inner sweetness of the very God Himself in the core and center of their hearts.[17]

Our approach must not merely be a sound exposition of the biblical theme of intimacy with God. Our knowledge must be intimate and move us toward Him to an intimate place of close contact with Him.

So how should we come to this? Another one of our mentors, Jonathan Edwards, calls us to the way of affections.

> I am bold to assert that no change of religious nature will ever take place unless the affections are moved. Without this, no natural man will earnestly seek for his salvation. Without this, there is no wrestling with God in prayer for mercy. No one is humbled and brought to the feet of God unless he has

---

17. Tozer, *The Pursuit of God*, 9–10.

seen for himself his own unworthiness. No one will ever be induced to fly in refuge to Christ as long as his heart remains unaffected. Likewise, no saint has been weaned out of the cold and lifeless state of mind, or recovered from backsliding, without having his heart affected. In summary, nothing significant ever changed the life of anyone when the heart was not deeply affected.[18]

Notice his call not only for feelings from the heart, but also an intimate knowledge and internal desire that move us to God. The unconverted must move by seeking salvation and mercy. Everyone must move to a place before God in humility, must come to a deep knowledge of their own unworthiness, and move as a bird flies from danger, to seek Christ, their place of refuge. We Christians must cease sliding back away from God by redirecting our hearts by the gradual replacement of a "cold and lifeless state of mind." May this book be a map and guide for this movement of our hearts and minds ever closer to the true and living God.

WHAT DO YOU THINK ABOUT INTIMACY WITH GOD?
Initial Personal Reflections

1. What do you want out of this study on intimacy with God?

2. What do you think you should want out of it?

3. What does God have to say about what you want?

4. Do you believe He will provide that for you? If so, how? If not, why not?

5. What is your responsibility in it?

6. What resources do you need for it?

---

18. Jonathan Edwards, *Faith beyond Feelings: Discerning the Heart of True Spirituality*, ed. James M. Houston (Colorado Springs: Victor/Cook Communications, 2005), 46.

CHAPTER 1

DEFINING INTIMACY WITH GOD

The old Chinese proverb, "The journey of a thousand miles begins with the first step," invites us to ask some questions: Why is this person taking this journey in the first place? Who will they meet? Whom or what do they seek? Where they are going? When we as Christians reflect on intimacy with God, we may not know where to step, at least not always, and should admit it is a journey to "God knows where and why." And yet we should admit we nonetheless have an intuitive desire to move closer to God even if we catch a glimpse of God's glory far off on the horizon. C. S. Lewis surely knew of this when in *The Horse and His Boy* he described the boy Shasta's sense that there is something more out there. Reflect on how Lewis recounts how even the established practical authority in Shasta's life could not explain away his thirst to know and experience a distant voice that called to him:

> Shasta was very interested in everything that lay to the north because no one ever went that way and he was never allowed to go there himself. When he was sitting out of doors mending the nets, and all alone, he would often look eagerly to the north. One could see nothing but a grassy slope running up to a level ridge and beyond that the sky with perhaps a few birds in it.
>
> Sometimes if Arsheesh was there Shasta would say, "O my Father, what is there beyond that hill?" And then if the fisherman was in a bad temper he would box Shasta's ears and tell him to attend to his work. Or if he was in a peaceable

mood he would say, "O my son, do not allow your mind to be distracted by idle questions. For one of the poets has said, 'Application to business is the root of prosperity, but those who ask questions that do not concern them are steering the ship of folly towards the rock of indigence.'"

Shasta thought that beyond the hill there must be some delightful secret which his father wished to hide from him. In reality, however, the fisherman talked like this because he didn't know what lay to the north. Neither did he care. He had a very practical mind.[1]

Little did Shasta know that his journey would not just lead him to a place, but to a Person . . . "the Voice," "the Lion."[2]

In this chapter we will study a definition of what our compass (i.e., the Bible) reveals of this "delightful secret"—intimacy with God. A crucial first step in our quest for understanding and developing intimacy with God is to establish a definition. In other words, what do we mean by intimacy? What are its synonyms and its opposites? With what is it associated? What tools, besides *Roget's Thesaurus*,[3] can we use to clarify some corollary concepts: close-

1. C. S. Lewis, *The Horse and His Boy* (New York: Macmillan, 1954), 2–3.
2. Lewis, *The Horse and His Boy*, 157–60.
3. "Intimacy," *Roget's Thesaurus*, http://www.roget.org/scripts/qq.php (accessed July 6, 2017).
    #163 Reproduction: Nn. copulation, copula, coupling, mating, coition, coitus, venery, intercourse, commerce, congress, sexual intercourse, sexual commerce, sexual congress, sexual union, sexual relations, relations, intimacy, connection, carnal knowledge, aphrodisia.
    #533 Secret: Nn. intimacy.
    #888 Friendship: Nn. nearness, thickness, familiarity, intimacy, closeness.
    #892 Sociality: Nn. intimacy, familiarity.
"Intimate," http://www.roget.org/scripts/qq.php (accessed July 6, 2017).
    #43 Junction: Adj. hand-in-hand, hand-in-glove, intimate.
    #79 Speciality: Adj. personal, private, intimate, esoteric.
    #189 Abode: Adj. comfortable, friendly, cheerful, peaceful, cozy, snug, intimate.
    #197 Nearness: Adj. near, nigh, close, intimate.
    #199 Contiguity: Adj. near, nigh, close, intimate.
    #221 Interiority: Adj. innermost, inmost, intimate.
    #225 Clothing: Nn. shirt, shirtwaist, intimate, sark, shift, waist.
    #526 Latency, Implication: Vb. hint, intimate.
    #527 Information: Vb. hint, intimate, suggest, insinuate, imply, indicate, signify.
    #531 Publication: Vb. notify, intimate, give notice.
    #533 Secret: Adj. intimate, inmost, innermost, inner, interior, inward.
    #888 Friendship: Adj. on familiar terms, on intimate terms, familiar, intimate, close, near.
    #890 Friend: Nn. intimate, familiar, close friend, intimate friend, familiar friend.
    #892 Sociality: Adj. intimate, familiar, cozy, cosy, chatty.

ness, nearness, familiarity, connection, etc.? How does the Bible frame what we should be examining as we formulate a biblical and systematic theology of it?

At the outset, we might observe the obvious: intimacy is a relational concept. Relationships in general have certain elements or characteristics. Intimacy stresses a certain quality of relationships themselves. Therefore, one careful step we will be taking is to investigate how psychology and relational science provide clarification as to what intimacy is and is not. This will help us to identify its synonyms and antonyms. Otherwise, if we simply look in a concordance (and doing theology is definitely more than this, but not less) to find the term "intimacy" related to God in the Bible, we would have little if any data with which to work.[4] Once we have a basic idea of concepts associated with intimacy, however, we can examine, compare, and contrast them with the biblical data. To put it another way, the term "intimacy" does not occur in most translations of the Bible. That does not mean we should proclaim intimacy with God a nonstarter, an illegitimate concept foisted upon Him and the Bible. If that were the case, then we would have no justification for studying biblical concepts like the Trinity or inerrancy, clearly terms chosen to summarize a large amount of scriptural data in a coherent manner. So let me announce up front that the biblical patterns associated with intimacy with God form the following working biblical definition: *the movement of God and Christians toward a good place of true knowledge and close contact.* This will be the hub from which the spokes of the rest of our study will emerge.

WANTING INTIMACY

If this definition is to be valid and helpful, we must grapple with what people want out of intimacy. Dr. Phil, on his television show, will often listen to two sides of an argument and then ask one of the family members involved, "What do you want?" He tries to get them to state the heart of the matter from their perspective. We should be asking what God wants out of our relational intimacy, and only then can we understand what we should want. As with our definition above, we should be saying something like the following: "I

---

4. In the New American Standard translation, "intimate" with reference to God is used in the entire Bible twice (Ps. 139:3; Prov. 3:32), only once in the New International Version (Job 29:4), and not at all in the King James Version, New King James, the English Standard Version, and the Christian Standard Bible. It is interesting to note these translations only use "intimate" for sexual relations (except for the KJV, which doesn't use it at all; and the ESV, which uses it twice and only for close friends).

want God to move toward me and I want to move toward Him, so that in full disclosure we can meet in a good place of close contact."

However, what do we actually mean by intimacy? We often rely on what we know and experience, and so we connect intimacy to our family relationships. Often it is minimized to or substituted entirely with romance and sexual intimacy (we will address this more in Chapter 6). Yet it is broader than the category to which we assign it today. That is why the Bible uses a significant range of images and metaphors for intimacy with God. However, the common denominator concerning intimacy is that it is a relational concept of a certain quality.

Psychological and sociological studies of relationships describe intimacy as a close bond or attachment.[5] This actually seems to have become intimacy's common cultural designation, including even bonding with our animals.[6] Parsing this a bit, notice the overlap with and yet differences from our working definition. For example, closeness logically speaks of a place or location of intimacy and is tied to being near. Thus we can say, "We experience closeness," and "They are near and dear to my heart."[7] Closeness is also a movement within the relationship.[8] Since closeness is a directional goal, it requires

---

5. Debra J. Mashek and Arthur Aron, eds., *Handbook of Closeness and Intimacy* (Mahwah, NJ: Lawrence Erlbaum Associates, 2004); Harry T. Reis and Caryl E. Rusbult, eds., *Close Relationships: Key Readings in Social Psychology* (New York: Psychology Press, 2004); Stanley O. Gaines, Jr., *Personality and Close Relationship Processes* (Cambridge: Cambridge University Press, 2016); Jeffrey A. Simpson and Lorne Campbell, eds., *The Oxford Handbook of Close Relationships*, Oxford Library of Psychology, 1st ed. (Oxford: Oxford University Press, 2013).

6. Penelope Smith, *When Animals Speak: Techniques for Bonding with Animal Companions* (New York: Simon and Schuster, 2009); Victoria Schade, *Bonding with Your Dog: A Trainer's Secrets for Building a Better Relationship* (Hoboken, NJ: Howell/Wiley, 2009); Bonnie Ebsen Jackson, *From Herdmates to Heartmates: The Art of Bonding with a New Horse* (Bradenton, FL: Booklocker.com, 2015); etc.

7. An intimate location in American culture is associated with a wedding venue, a place just the right size to accomplish the union of two people in holy matrimony. An NFL stadium does not have an intimate feel for most, because the intimate connection between the two would be lost in the magnitude of the location. Intimate concerts allow the audience actually to be or at least feel like they are participants, that they have some connection with the artist. Intimate restaurants capture the need for quiet privacy to allow for personal communication in the dining experience.

8. Henri Nouwen argues for closeness as movement from his spiritual-psychological perspective: "This 'first and final' movement is so central to our spiritual life that it is very hard to come in touch with it, to get a grasp on it, to get hold of it, or even—to put a finger on it. Not because this movement is vague or unreal, but because it is so close that it hardly allows the distance needed for articulation and understanding. Maybe this is the reason why the most profound realities of life are the easiest victims of trivialization." Henri J. M. Nouwen, *Reaching Out: The Three Movements of the Spiritual Life* (New York: Image/Doubleday, 1986), 114.

our movement, prompted by vulnerability and trust, to achieve it.[9] It is not static, but grows and deepens. So we say, "We are growing closer . . . more intimate." The opposite of this movement toward closeness is a sense of abandonment and aloneness.[10] Therefore, intimacy or closeness is a movie depicting a long-term relationship, as well as momentary selfie with both people in it. Research attempts to help us assess how far we are in our "relational intimacy satisfaction." This is the difference between our idealized intimacy (how I wish things could be) and our realized intimacy (how things are now).[11] This cultural description does tell us that it is important to assess the level of closeness we have with God, and this satisfaction survey approach can help us ask important questions and see patterns in our thoughts and feelings. However, as we will see in a theology of intimacy with God, this approach fails to have an ultimate or objective standard for true intimacy. God must be the One we turn to for the essential elements of closeness with Him and with others.

Furthermore, bonding, like closeness, is also a journey and a destination.[12] Yet studies show it is more than simply a close connection with someone, but an attachment.[13] A popular perspective is that bonding is mainly emotional. While the affective bond between people is very strong, bonding includes the mental, intellectual, and spiritual. So we can say, "Our hearts are bound together," "We are kindred spirits," "We are so close, we think alike," and "We finish each other's sentences." This means that intimate knowledge as a result of observation and self-disclosure is essential for this bonding, and communicating personal feelings and information is the best way to achieve this knowledge.[14] Thus we can

---

9. Jonathan S. Gore, Susan E. Cross, and Michael L. Morris, "Let's Be Friends: Relational Self-construal and the Development of Intimacy," *Personal Relationships* 13 (2006): 83–102.

10. This will be discussed in Chapter 5.

11. Lauren M. Walker, Amy Hampton, and John W. Robinson, "Assessment of Relational Intimacy: Factor Analysis of the Personal Assessment of Intimacy in Relationships Questionnaire," *Psycho-Oncology* 23, no. 3 (2014): 346–49 (348). For them, the two main features of intimacy are: engagement—the degree to which one feels connected to another, and communication—the degree to which one experiences understanding from one's partner and the ability to freely express one's emotions and beliefs to another through an open and fluent exchange of ideas.

12. Cindy Hazan and Mary I. Campa, eds., *Human Bonding: The Science of Affectional Ties*, 1st ed. (New York: Guilford, 2013).

13. For a helpful overview of attachment theory, see David Wilkins, David Shemmings, and Yvonne Shemmings, *A–Z of Attachment*, Professional Keywords Series (New York/London: Palgrave Macmillan, 2015).

14. H. T. Reis and P. Shaver, "Intimacy as an Interpersonal Process," in *Handbook of Personal Relationships*, ed. S. W. Duck (Chichester, UK: Wiley. 1988), 367–89; H. T. Reis and B. C. Patrick, "Attachment and Intimacy: Component Processes," in *Social Psychology: Handbook of Basic Principles*, eds. E. T. Higgins and A. W. Kruglanski (New York: Guilford, 1996), 523–63.

say, "They truly know me," "They know me best," or "I know them intimately" and "Our interaction is on an intimate level" or "We share intimate things." As a result, a bond or identity is formed and thus we can say, "We possess an intimate relationship," "I am their intimate . . .," or "We have an inseparable bond." Therefore, in some psychological sense, intimacy with God is the believer's bonding with or attachment to the Triune God through growing close interaction.

The important part about intimacy with God is that its essence is intricately tied to what we want: results. In other words, how can we say we have intimacy with God without enjoying its benefits? If the essence of intimacy is relational bonding or attachment, then it makes sense that the research on attachment has recognized that the primary concerns in bonding relationships between children and adults are care and protection.[15] Thus, intimacy provides what we all really desire: security, safety, acceptance, belonging, identity, loyalty, love, and support.

FOUR BIBLICAL ELEMENTS OF INTIMACY WITH GOD

So let's return to our working biblical definition of intimacy with God as *the movement of God and Christians toward a good place of true knowledge and close contact.* This is basically the result of asking how, where, and what. The Bible answers how we may obtain intimacy or closeness with God by showing the need for movement to a location or place where this intimacy occurs. The most common elements associated with this intimacy are intimate knowledge or understanding and contact or touch. It is best now to take a tour of the orchard of the Bible and point out some of the dense, rich, ripe clusters of these fruitful themes.

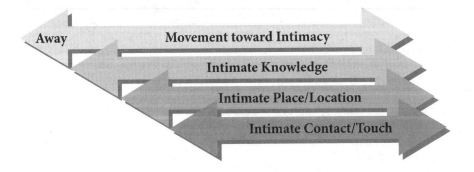

---

15. Wilkins, Shemmings, and Shemmings, *A–Z of Attachment*, viii.

Movement toward Intimacy

The Bible describes the basic element of intimacy with God as a movement of God and the believer towards one another. As we will see, movement within this relational dynamic is in the advancement or the changing of location of God and/or a human's consciousness or attitude. In other words, it is an attempt to encounter—or avoid—an exchange between these two parties. Both sides move, but not necessarily at the same time, at the same rate, and even in the same direction. In the Bible we observe this movement in God's initiation of it and also through a variety of human activities. Let's examine a couple of substantial scriptural themes as examples, to give some substance to this first element.

One common movement to or away from divine intimacy is *seeking*. Most of the data on this concerns the human seeking after God. Nevertheless, God initiates moving toward the lost by seeking them out. In restoring Israel, the Lord promises to "search for My sheep and seek them out. As a shepherd cares for his herd in the day when he is among his scattered sheep, so I will care for My sheep and will deliver them from all the places to which they were scattered on a cloudy and gloomy day" (Ezek. 34:11–12). He then declares, "I will seek the lost, bring back the scattered, bind up the broken and strengthen the sick" (Ezek. 34:16). Jesus Christ fulfilled this because His very mission on earth has been to "seek and to save that which was lost" (*zēteō*, Luke 19:10). Furthermore, the Father rejoices over the lost being found (Luke 15:1–32; cf. Matt. 18:12).

We also witness this seeking movement in a variety of human activities. It is searching God out or striving after Him in trust and worship (*baqash* and *darash*). It is seeking an audience with God in order to place our innermost feelings and needs before Him. Eliphaz claims, "But as for me, I would seek God, and I would place my cause before God" (Job 5:8; cf. 8:5; Pss. 9:10; 10:4; 34:4; 69:32–33; 105:4; Dan. 9:3, 4). When David brought the ark to Jerusalem, he called the people to "let the heart of those who seek the LORD be glad. Seek the LORD and His strength; seek His face continually" (1 Chron. 16:10–11). Even though seeking other gods would cause Israel to be banished (Lev. 19:31; Deut. 4:25–28), God promises, "But from there you will seek the LORD your God, and you will find Him if you search for Him with all your heart and all your soul" (Deut. 4:29; cf. Isa. 55:6; 65:1, 10; Hos. 3:5; 5:15). This seeking heart is the gold standard for the kings of Israel's history (1 Chron. 28:9; 2 Chron. 12:14; 15:2; 19:3; 20:3; 26:5; 34:3) and the prerequisite in order for God's people to be forgiven and their land healed (2 Chron. 7:14; 20:4; 30:19; Ezra 4:2; 6:21; 8:21–22; Hos. 5:14; Zeph. 2:3; Mal. 3:2). The seeker does not escape the notice of God. David claims, "The LORD has looked down from heaven upon the sons of men to see if there are any who understand, who seek after God" (Ps. 14:2). Tragically, the fool does not have the trait of being this kind of seeker (Ps. 14:1–3; Rom. 3:11). Many seek with wrong motives in order merely to have their physical needs met or their curiosity satisfied (*zēteō*, John 6:26; 7:35; 8:21). However, Christ's disciples followed Him because of who He is (John 1:38). James witnessed the seeking and turning of Gentiles toward God (Acts 15:17 of Amos 9:12). Paul appealed to the general revelation in creation that causes Gentiles to seek God, even to "grope for Him and find Him, though He is not far from each one of us" (Acts 17:27). This search is the manifestation of the faith of those who come to God believing "that He exists and that He is a rewarder of those who seek Him" (Heb. 11:6).

Another common movement to or away from intimacy with God is that of *turning*. God also initiates movement toward His people by turning to us. In the midst of trial the believing heart's great desire is that God would turn to face us with His presence and blessing. David implores the Lord in Psalm 25:16 to "turn to me and be gracious to me, for I am lonely and afflicted." Notice for him what the movement of God is associated with when He turns to us in Psalm 69:16–18:

> Answer me, O LORD, for Your lovingkindness is good; according to the greatness of Your compassion, turn to me, and do not hide Your face from Your servant, for I am in distress; answer me quickly. Oh draw near to my soul and redeem it; ransom me because of my enemies! (cf. also 86:16; 119:132)

The Lord blesses the obedience of His people in His turning toward them (Lev. 26:9). He has even made an everlasting covenant with them to "not turn away from them, to do them good" (Jer. 32:40; cf. Ezek. 36:9).

Our movement toward nearness to God also requires our turning to Him. It is not only a conscious choice to position ourselves in His direction, but also to follow Him. This is not just turning to follow His rules, but follow closely where He personally leads us. We are to trust His desires for our lives. In Israel's history, the Lord made this clear. Their hearts turned aside (*pana*) from the Lord (Deut. 29:18; 30:10; cf. Jer. 17:5; Ezek. 6:9), and because this vacuum would be filled, He had to warn them against turning aside to idols, mediums or spiritists (Lev. 19:4, 31). If they did, He would set His face against them (Lev. 20:6; Deut. 7:4; 11:16, 28; 23:14; Ezek. 7:22). It makes sense that He viewed this as spurning Him (Deut. 31:20) and hostility toward Him (Lev. 26:23), which would cause Him to abandon them in the wilderness (Num. 32:15) and hide His face from them (Deut. 31:18). It is sad that they would do this so "quickly" after His saving them (Deut. 9:12, 16; cf. Acts 7:41–42), which would be the theme of the period of the Judges (Josh. 24:20; Judg. 2:17). At the dedication of the Temple, Solomon prayed that when Israel sinned she would turn to the Lord for forgiveness and restoration (1 Kings 8:33, 35). Again, it is a tragedy that Solomon's many wives turned his heart toward other gods so that was no longer wholly devoted to the Lord (1 Kings 11:2–4, 9). This pattern continued with all the people of Israel (2 Chron. 29:6; Isa. 9:13; Jer. 2:27; 50:6; Hos. 3:1; 7:14; 11:7; Zeph. 1:6) unless the Lord turned their hearts back to Him (1 Kings 18:37–39; 2 Chron. 15:4; Jer. 31:19; 32:40) or certain kings like Josiah remained faithful and encouraged faithfulness (2 Kings 22:2; 23:25; 2 Chron. 30:9; Isa. 45:22).

Nevertheless, the power of the Holy Spirit through the gospel causes people to turn to God from sin (*epistrephō*). Luke recounts this at various points in the book of Acts when those in Lydda and Sharon (9:35) and Antioch (11:21), as well as the Gentiles of Paul's ministry (15:19), turned to the Lord. This also occurred in Corinth (2 Cor. 3:16), Galatia (Gal. 4:9), and Thessalonica (1 Thess. 1:9). The early missionaries summoned everyone to to turn away from sin and idolatry and toward God (Acts 14:15; 26:20) according to the Lord Jesus's instructions (Acts 26:18).

A final example of a common movement to or away from intimacy with God is that of *coming*. We can celebrate that our God is one who comes to His people and wants us to come to Him. The foundational instance of "coming" in the Old Testament is when the Lord came down near to Moses in a thick cloud (*bo'*, *yarad*, Exod. 19:9, 11) and allowed him to come up Mount Sinai (*alah*, Exod. 24:12; 34:2). The Lord only usually allowed people to come to the foot of Mount Sinai (*nagash*, 19:13, 22, 23; *alah*, 24:1–2; 34:3) to meet Him (19:17), to test their fear of Him (Exod. 20:20), and to bless them (Exod. 20:24).

God's people are to come near to Him in sacred ways. He established the holy pattern for this in the tabernacle and temple (*qarab*, Lev. 10:3). People presented certain cleansing offerings when they came "before the LORD to the doorway of the tent of meeting" (*bo' paniym*, Lev. 15:14; cf. also 21:21, 23). The Lord even met certain people there (Num. 12:4–5).[16] David connects coming before the Lord with bringing Him an offering, glorifying His name and worshiping Him (1 Chron. 16:29; cf. also Pss. 66:13; 96:8). The psalmist calls all of God's people to "come before His presence with thanksgiving" and

---

16. Balaam expected the Lord to come and meet him when he presented his burnt offerings (Num. 23:1–4).

"Come . . . worship and bow down . . . kneel before the LORD our maker" (Ps. 95:2, 6). This would be true of those coming to the baby Jesus Christ (Matt. 2:2). It is tragic that His people would come to Him with impure motives and deeds (Jer. 7:10; 26:1–6; Ezek. 20:3; 44:13; Mic. 6:6–8; Matt. 2:8). However, David assumes that one day all nations will "come and worship" before Him (Ps. 86:9; cf. Isa. 2:3–6; 66:18; Jer. 16:19; Mic. 4:1–2; Zech. 8:22). The Lord calls upon those who trust him to come and follow him (Matt. 19:21; Mark 10:21; John 1:39, 46) to the point of taking up their own cross (Matt. 16:24). He even called Peter to come to Him in trust by walking on water (Matt. 14:28) and the Samaritan woman to come with her "husband" (John 4:16).

Often God's people come close to Him because of their needs. David puts this principle simply: "O You who hear prayer, to You all men (*basar* or flesh) come" (Ps. 65:2). The Lord came down (*yarad*) to deliver His people from the Egyptians because their cry came to Him (*bo'*, Exod. 3:8–9). Boaz blessed Ruth by saying, "May the LORD reward your work, and your wages be full from the LORD, the God of Israel, under whose wings you have come to seek refuge" (*bo'*, Ruth 2:12). It was self-evident to Job that the suffering could argue their case before God, but that "a godless man may not come before His presence" (Job 13:16). Amidst his groaning, he exclaimed, "Oh that I knew where I might find Him, that I might come to His seat!" (Job 23:3). The psalmist insatiably longs for God and His deliverance: "My soul thirsts for God, for the living God; when shall I come and appear before God?" (Ps. 42:2). Asaph asks the Lord to "let the groaning of the prisoner come before You" (Ps. 79:11). Therefore, the psalmist pleads with the Lord, "Let my prayer come before You; incline Your ear to my cry!" (Ps. 88:2; cf. 102:1; 119:169, 170; 144:5; Jer. 36:7). David boldly asks the Lord, "When will You come to me?" (Ps. 101:2). Later, the Lord assured those far off in exile about His plans: "Then you will call upon Me and come and pray to Me, and I will listen to you" (Jer. 29:12; cf. 50:5; Hos. 3:5). Similarly, some came to Jesus and implored Him to come to meet the need of another person close to them: Jairus for his daughter (Mark 5:22–23) and the nobleman for his son (John 4:46–49). The centurion came to Jesus for his paralyzed servant, though he knew Jesus didn't need to come but could simply heal him from a distance (Matt. 8:5–9; Luke 7:1–10). Jesus's expressed desire has been for people to come to Him to have their needs met by letting children come close to Him (Mark 10:14), and by coming to drink of the Spirit (John 7:37–39), to have life (John 5:40; 11:47), and to find rest for their souls (Matt. 11:28–29).

The coming of God is a grand expectation among the people of the Bible. Asaph implores God to "come and save us!" (Ps. 80:2). Therefore, David called for Zion to be ready to receive the King of glory when He comes in triumph into the holy city (Ps. 24:7; cf. Isa. 59:19–20; Zech. 14:4–5). Like many who expected His powerful delivering presence, Asaph exclaims, "May our God come and not keep silence; fire devours before Him, and it is very tempestuous around Him" (Ps. 50:3; Isa. 66:15; Mic. 1:3–4; Mal. 3:1–3). When the Lord does come, His compassion (Pss. 79:8; 119:77) and lovingkindness (Ps. 119:41) are assumed to be present as well. In Psalm 121:1–2, a psalm of ascent sung while heading up the paths toward Jerusalem, the psalmist asks, "I will lift up my yes to the mountains; from where shall my help come?" The expectation of the Lord's coming deliverance is apparent in the next line: "My help comes from the LORD, who made heaven and earth." Jesus Christ is the glorious fulfillment of this grand expectation. He came out of Bethlehem to be "a Ruler Who will shepherd" God's people (*exerchomai*, Mic. 5:2; Matt. 2:6). Furthermore, He has promised not to leave His followers as orphans (John 14:18) and has sent the Holy Spirit to call upon His followers to be His witnesses (Acts 1:8). He also stands and knocks at the door of self-sufficient lukewarm churches, and out of love promises to the repentant to "come in to him and dine with him and He with Me" (Rev. 3:20). However, at the event of His return to earth, everyone will see His "coming on the clouds of the sky with power and great glory" (*erchomai*, Matt. 24:30). He will come again to gather His followers to Himself and to the place He has prepared for them to take up residence with Him (John 14:3, 23). And so we who trust in the Lord Jesus Christ's promise that He will come quickly, echo the words of the Apostle John, "Amen. Come, Lord Jesus" (Rev. 22:20; cf. 1 Cor. 16:22).

Intimate Knowledge

A second biblical element of intimacy with God is intimate knowledge. God does not merely know information, but has understanding, awareness, and familiarity with us. He has deeply personal knowledge of us that we can keep secret or private from everyone else but Him. Thus He has a thorough and detailed knowledge of our lives, that is, our experiences, conduct, and behavior, as well as our inner workings, thoughts, ambitions, motivations, desires, etc.[17] At the same time, we can have an element of intimate knowledge

---

17. God's movement and His intimate knowledge are connected. One example is in the use of term *paqad*. It is variously translated as when He visits, numbers, cares for, has concern for, takes note of, etc. We can see the common idea of God being on the move, visiting His people to take careful note of their situation and concerns. In Genesis 21:1, the Lord "*took note* of Sarah," and in Exodus 4:31 was "*concerned* about the sons of Israel." Job expressed his impression of God's constant visitation and careful notation questioning Him in Job 7:18–19: "You *examine* him every morning and try him every moment? Will you never

of God. We will discuss in more detail the important issue of our epistemology of intimacy with God as well as how it fits theologically in Chapter 2. Nevertheless, let me give some biblical examples of intimate knowledge.

We should join the people of the Bible in being convinced that God knows our intimate and personal thoughts and motives. He clearly knows every human heart. When dedicating the temple, Solomon implored the Lord to "forgive and act and render to each according to all his ways, whose heart You know, for You alone know the hearts of all the sons of men" (*yadah*, 1 Kings 8:39; 2 Chron. 6:30).[18] When choosing the disciple to replace Judas, the apostles prayed, "You, Lord, who know the hearts (*kardiognostēs*) of all men, show which of these two You have chosen" (Acts 1:24).[19] Nathaniel was shocked at Jesus's knowledge of his sarcastic reaction to the news about Him being the Messiah before they even met (John 1:48).[20] Christ personally addresses each letter to the Seven Churches with "I know . . . (your deeds . . . your tribulation . . . where you dwell . . . etc.)" (Rev. 2:2, 9, 13, 19; 3:1, 8, 15) and then gives them specific instructions like "do not fear" (2:10), "repent" (2:16), "hold fast (to what you have)" (2:25), etc. He can do this simply because He discerns the thoughts and motives of the churches and responds to each accordingly. Therefore, He admonishes Thyatira, the fourth and center of the list of churches, with the words, "And I will kill her children with pestilence, and all the churches will know that I am He who searches the minds and hearts; and I will give to each one of you according to your deeds" (Rev. 2:23).

---

turn your gave away from me, nor let me alone until I swallow my spittle?" Jeremiah could trust the Lord's careful investigation of his trial when He said, "You know, O LORD, Remember me, *take notice of me*, and take vengeance for me" (Jer. 15:15, emphasis added).

18. It is foolish to refuse to acknowledge and trust in God's intimate knowledge of everyone. Psalm 73:11 recounts the arrogantly wicked as saying, "They say, 'How does God know? And is there knowledge with the Most High?'" Proverbs 24:12 reminds the fool that "If you say, 'See, we did not know this,' Does He not consider it who weighs the hearts? And does He not know it who keeps your soul?" Furthermore, God's intimate knowledge of everyone includes the seemly untouchable, the foreign king. In Genesis 20:6, God said to Abimelech in a dream, 'Yes, I know that in the integrity of your heart you have done this." In Exodus 3:19 the Lord told Moses, "But I know that the king of Egypt will not permit you to go, except under compulsion (*yad*, hand)." In 2 Kings 19:27, the Lord told Sennacharib, "But I know your sitting down, and your going out and your coming in, and your raging against Me" (cf. Isa. 37:28).

19. The apparent conviction behind their prayer is reminiscent of the reciprocal intimate knowledge they have with Jesus Christ, when He said, "I am the good shepherd, and I know My own and My own know Me" (John 10:14) and "My sheep hear My voice, and I know them, and they follow Me" (John 10:27).

20. "Nathaniel said to Him, 'How do You know (*ginōskō*) me?' Jesus answered and said to him, 'Before Philip called you, when you were under a fig tree, I saw you'" (John 1:48).

We should also recognize that God's intimate knowledge is capsulized when men pleaded with God concerning their integrity. Jeremiah simply claimed, "But You know (*yadah*) me, O LORD; You see me; And You examine my heart's attitude toward You" (Jer. 12:3; cf. 17:16).[21] David also said, "O LORD, You know," referring to the integrity his heart (Ps. 40:9–10; cf. 2 Sam. 7:20). He could say this because he knew the Lord desired "truth in the innermost being (*tuchah*, or kidneys), and in the hidden part You will make me know wisdom" (Ps. 51:6). He trusted that God knew his troubled feelings when he said, "You know my reproach and my shame and my dishonor; All my adversaries are before You" (Ps. 69:19). When Jesus asked Peter if he loved Him three times, he responded, "Yes, Lord; You know that I love you" (John 21:15, 16) and finally, "Lord, You know all things; You know that I love You" (John 21:17).

In Psalm 139:1–4, David provides us with a comprehensive view of God's intimate knowledge. White is probably correct when he says, "This psalm represents the peak of the Psalter, the maturest individual faith in the Old Testament, and the clearest anticipation of the New."[22] Immediately note how David uses a series of synonyms to describe the fullness of God's intimate knowledge:

> O LORD, You have searched me and known *me*.
> You know when I sit down and when I rise up.
> You understand my thought from afar.
> ³ You scrutinize my path and my lying down,
> And are intimately acquainted with all my ways.
> Even before there is a word on my tongue,
> Behold, O LORD, You know it all.

He acknowledges that the Lord "searches" us (from *chaqar* used for what spies do), in that He penetrates into and explores essential secrets of our hearts (Pss. 44:21; 139:23). His knowledge of us is comprehensive and includes our daily activities ("sit down," "rise up"). He perceives and considers (*bin*) our inner thoughts, purposes, and intentions. He does this "from afar," from the transcendent perspective of His dwelling place (139:2b; cf. Ps. 138:6), "contradicting the delusion (Job 22:12–14) that God's dwelling in heaven prevents

---

21. Job's frustration was in God's clear knowledge of His integrity, but "According to Your knowledge I am indeed not guilty, yet there is no deliverance" (Job 10:7).
22. R. E. O. White, "Psalms," in *Evangelical Commentary on the Bible*, vol. 3, Baker Reference Library (Grand Rapids: Baker Book House, 1995), 3396.

Him from observing mundane things."[23] He "scrutinizes" (*zarah*, that is, winnows or sifts like grain) our life's journey and days' endings. Furthermore, like a nurse He is "intimately acquainted" (*sakan*) with all our ways and whole lifestyle.[24] David wraps up this section with the fact that the Lord even knows our thoughts before we verbalize them. How he closes the psalm should not surprise us:

> Search me, O God, and know my heart;
> Try me and know my anxious thoughts;
> And see if there be any hurtful way in me,
> And lead me in the everlasting way. (vv. 23–24)

Thus, as a tremendous example for future generations, David opens himself up completely for the Lord to transform and redeem his innermost self (cf. Ps. 26:2).

May we have a thirst for intimate knowledge of God. May we have Moses's desire for knowledge when he prayed, "Now, therefore, I pray You, if I have found favor in Your sight, let me know Your ways that I may know You, so that I may find favor in Your sight" (Exod. 33:13). May we have David's desire: "Make me know Your ways, O LORD, teach me Your paths" (Ps. 25:4). We can seek this because God's knowledge of Himself is a gift. He invites worshipful believers into His secret counsel and knowledge of Him (Ps. 25:14; Prov. 3:32; John 7:17; 17:25–26). He has promised through the new covenant, "I will give them a heart to know Me, for I am the LORD; and they will be My people, and I will be their God, for they will return to Me with their whole heart" (Jer. 24:7 cf. also Isa. 52:6). And again, "Call to Me and I will answer you, and I will tell you great and mighty things, which you do not know" (Jer. 33:3). Thus we should heed Hosea's call to Israel, "So let us know, let us press on to know the Lord. His going forth is . . . certain. . . . And He will come to us like the rain" (Hos. 6:3). As Christ's sheep we are given the ability to know His voice (John 10:4; cf. Acts 22:14). Our pursuit will not be in vain, because knowing the Son of God means eternal life (John 17:3). It is not in vain because the Holy Spirit powerfully mediates this deep personal knowledge when we pray (Rom. 8:26–27). And Daniel claimed that if we know our God, then we "will display strength and take action" (Dan. 11:32).

---

23. John Peter Lange, et al., *A Commentary on the Holy Scriptures: Psalms* (Bellingham, WA: Logos Bible Software, 2008), 647.
24. J. A. Motyer, "The Psalms," in *New Bible Commentary: 21st Century Edition*, eds. D. A. Carson, et al., 4th ed. (Downers Grove, IL: Inter-Varsity, 1994), 578.

Thus from what we have seen so far, J. I. Packer is right that knowing God is a matter of personal dealing and involvement, not just of theology and facts. He states:

> Knowing God . . . is a matter of dealing with Him as He opens up to you, and being dealt with by Him as He takes knowledge of you. Knowing about Him is a necessary precondition of trusting Him . . . but the width of our knowledge about Him is no gauge of our knowledge of Him.[25]

He adds an important note, stressing that we must do this with our whole being: "We must not lose sight of the fact that knowing God is an emotional relationship as well as an intellectual and volitional one, and could not indeed be a deep relation between persons were it not so."[26] Again, we must know enough about God to trust Him, and know Him deeply enough to hold nothing back from Him and for Him.

Intimate Place/Location

A third vital image of intimacy with God is the place or location where God meets with or connects with His people. There is truth in the old adage "Absence makes the heart grow fonder," but it is also true that "Absence makes the heart go yonder." Intimacy with God cannot survive and grow without a sense of God's actual presence with His people in the here and now. Location of this intimacy is associated with His nearness in a relational and spatial sense. It also overlaps with His movement toward us in relationship to time or how quick He is to respond to our cries for help. Moses proclaimed, "For what great nation is there that has a god so near to it as is the Lord our God whenever we call on Him?" (Deut. 4:7; cf. Ps. 148:14). Thus His intimate nearness is a tremendous source of hope and comfort, as Psalm 34:18 clearly demonstrates: "The Lord is near to the brokenhearted and saves those who are crushed in spirit." This source is likened to a place of refuge and salvation, and so the psalmist Asaph declares, "But as for me, the nearness of God is my good; I have made the Lord God my refuge, that I may tell of all Your works" (73:28; cf. Ps. 85:9). Therefore, as His people we are enjoined to move toward God's intimately safe place because He is never far off.[27] Listen to Isaiah's words: "Seek

---

25. Packer, *Knowing God*, 39.
26. Ibid., 40.
27. Because God's location is always intimately near, the opposite that He is never far way is also true. The Lord Himself sums this up in Jeremiah 23:23: "'Am I a God who is near,' declares the

the Lord while He may be found; Call upon Him while He is near" (Isa. 55:6). May the place where God is near be our constant delight as in Isaiah 58:2: "Yet they seek Me day by day and delight to know My ways, As a nation that has done righteousness And has not forsaken the ordinance of their God. They ask Me for just decisions, They delight in the nearness of God."

Tozer grapples with this concept and is right not to limit God to one place:

> Our pursuit of God is successful just because He is forever seeking to mani-fest Himself to us. The revelation of God to any man is not God coming from a distance upon a time to pay a brief and momentous visit to the man's soul. Thus to think of it is to misunderstand it all. The approach of God to the soul or of the soul to God is not to be thought of in spatial terms at all. There is no idea of physical distance involved in the concept. It is not a matter of miles but of experience.
>
> To speak of being near to or far from God is to use language in a sense always understood when applied to our ordinary human relationships. A man may say, "I feel that my son is coming nearer to me as he gets older," and yet that son has lived by his father's side since he was born and he has never been away from home more than a day or so in his entire life. What then can the father mean? Obviously he is speaking of experience. He means that the boy is coming to know him more intimately and with deeper understanding, that the barriers of thought and feeling between the two are disappearing, that the father and son are becoming more closely united in mind and heart.[28]

He overstates his point by limiting God's nearness only to an experience of relational distance without accenting how He seems to "move" the "location" of His presence. Even if the biblical writers were only speaking metaphori-cally about God being near, they still experienced relational distance during their trials and/or their sinful rebellion. They longed for God to be "spatially" close to them right where they were. Thus Tozer is correct when he claims, "We need never shout across the spaces to an absent God. He is nearer than our own soul, closer than our most secret thoughts."[29]

Lord, 'And not a God far off?'" God's distance from the biblical writers was in space and time. David beseeches the Lord in Psalm 22:11, "Be not far from me, for trouble is near; For there is none to help" and again in 22:19, "But You, O Lord, be not far off; O You my help, hasten to my assistance" (cf. Pss. 35:22; 38:21; 71:12; Prov. 15:29; Isa. 46:13). Thus, to lack intimacy with God is have a heart that is far from Him (Matt. 15:8; Mark 7:6; Luke 16:23; Acts 17:27; Eph. 2:13, 17).

28. Tozer, *The Pursuit of God*, 65–66.
29. Ibid., 66.

The Bible is clear that God's location is "with" us. When God is "with" someone, His powerful gracious presence is with them in order to watch over them and bless them. God was with "the son of Hagar" (Gen. 21:20), Abraham (Gen. 21:22), Isaac (Gen. 26:24), Jacob (Gen. 28:13), Joseph (Gen. 39:2, 21), Moses (Exod. 3:12), etc. However, "with" is also used when God is with certain people in an intimate way. On Mount Sinai, the Lord descended in a cloud and met with Moses, "and stood there with him as he called upon the name of the LORD" (Exod. 34:5). David claims that he will not fear death and evil "for You are with me; Your rod and Your staff, they comfort me" (Ps. 23:4). Psalm 46 connects God being with His people to His being a stronghold and place of refuge. It underscores this as it repeats, "The LORD of hosts is with us; the God of Jacob is our stronghold" (Ps. 46:7, 11). God rewards the one who loves Him and knows His name with the promise of His presence: "He will call upon Me, and I will answer him; I will be with him in trouble; I will rescue him and honor him" (Ps. 91:15). David recognized God's continual thoughtful presence when he said, "When I awake, I am still with You" (Ps. 139:18). When God's people struggled with trusting in kings and political alliances to deliver them, He promised, "Do not fear, for I am with you; Do not anxiously look about you, for I am your God. I will strengthen you, surely I will help you, Surely I will uphold you with My righteous right hand" (Isa. 41:10; cf. 42:3, 5).

God's presence with His people isn't only stationary, however. The Bible profoundly describes walking with God, a theme emphasizing the closeness of God's location as we move with Him through this life. It is striking that Adam and Eve customarily walked with their Creator in the garden in the cool wind of the day (Gen. 3:8). Amidst the depressing repetition of "and So-and-so became the father of So-and-so . . . and he died" in the genealogy of Genesis 5, we find the interruption of "Enoch walked with God, and he was not, for God took him" (Gen. 5:22, 24). Then after the description of the Lord's grief over the legacy of human rebellion, Moses inserts the first *toledot* of Genesis, "These are the records of the generations of Noah," and describes Noah as one who "walked with God" (Gen. 6:9). Thus the standard of true biblical religion is "to walk humbly with your God" (Mic. 6:8), and heaven will consist of "walking with" the Lord Jesus "in white" (Rev. 3:4). Thus, God's people are not only to walk in God's "ways" or "laws" (Deut. 5:33; 10:12; Josh. 22:5; Neh. 10:29; Jer. 7:23; Luke 1:6; 1 Cor. 7:17; Phil. 3:17; 1 Thess. 4:1; 2 John 1:6), but to walk "before" or in light of the place of His presence (1 Kings 8:23, 25; 2 Kings 10:31; 2 Chron. 6:14, 16; see also 2 Cor. 6:16).

A final example of themes of divine location or place is God's dwelling among His people.[30] Initially, the holy of holies containing the ark of the covenant was the place where God would meet with the high priest (Exod. 25:22) and meet with His people at the tabernacle (Exod. 29:43). The people were to view the ensuing temple as His lovely dwelling place and long to be within its courts (Ps. 84:1). This was because it was the location on earth where God graciously came close to His people. Psalm 65:4 declares, "How blessed is the one whom You choose and bring near to You to dwell in Your courts. We will be satisfied with the goodness of Your house, Your holy temple." However, Jesus Christ is Immanuel or "God with us" (Matt. 1:23; see Isa. 9:6), who "dwelt among us" or "tabernacled among us" (*skēnoō*, John 1:14). As the great high priest of His people, Christ has intimate knowledge of His churches as He walks through them as lampstands (Rev. 1:13). Furthermore, we as the church individually and corporately are the temple of the Holy Spirit (1 Cor. 3:16; 6:19). And yet, there will be an ultimate intimate safe place where there will no longer be a need for a temple structure because all of God's people will dwell with Him in the New Jerusalem (Rev. 21:2–3).

God's intimacy with us is not limited to our quiet times or brief periods of concentration in prayer. John White calls us to remember, "you do not leave God when you go from the quiet place any more than He leaves you. . . . You may leave the room where you pray, but you do not leave the inner sanctuary deep inside your being."[31] Like Brother Lawrence's *The Practice of the Presence of God*,[32] God calls us to make our knowledge of His intimate location with and in us a continuous integral part of our lives.

Intimate Contact/Touch

The fourth basic element of intimacy with God is contact or touch, as the Bible suggests. I look forward to exploring this aspect more carefully in chapter 4, which examines the metaphors used to describe God's body parts and how He touches us in some sense. Nevertheless, we see, for example, that God upholds or lifts up His people when they are weak (Ps. 145:14). We see His intimate touch and location when He promises, "Nevertheless I am continu-

---

30. For a helpful broader and more Reformed study on the biblical theme of God's dwelling, see Greg K. Beale and Mitchell Kim, *God Dwells among Us: Expanding Eden to the Ends of the Earth* (Downers Grove, IL: IVP, 2014).
31. John White, *The Fight* (Downers Grove, IL: IVP, 1976), 35.
32. Brother Lawrence, *The Practice of the Presence of God the Best Rule of a Holy Life*, Kindle ed. (New York: Fleming H. Revell, n.d.).

ally with You; You have taken hold of my right hand" (Ps. 73:23). Similarly, God makes intimate contact with His people as their shepherd when He carries them in His arms close to His heart (Isa. 40:10–11). Thus we are deeply moved when Jesus describes the Father's returning with His lost sheep on His shoulders (Luke 15:5) and His embracing and kissing his prodigal son upon his return (Luke 15:20). Christ's intimate touch was often a means of healing people when He knew their fear and need for compassion (Matt. 8:3, 15; 9:25, 29; 20:24; Mark 1:31; 7:33; Luke 7:14; 22:51).[33] With this in mind, we look forward to when God will, with an intimate touch, wipe away the tears of mourning and pain from the faces of His oppressed but faithful people at the beginning of the new heaven and earth (Rev. 21:4).

At this point my hope is for us to revel in the richness of intimacy with God as it is revealed in these four biblical elements. We can now go on to explore them further as they relate to God as our Father, Christ as the Bridegroom, the Holy Spirit, etc. Hopefully, it has become clear as a result of this journey that the elements of intimacy are not isolated from each other but work in concert together. They may not all four be found in the same context, but often two or more are. Movement toward intimacy is often coupled with intimate knowledge of another. Movement can be to an intimate location. These may culminate in intimate contact.

To be fair to the biblical record, we must also be ready to address the opposites of intimacy with God. Avoidance and abandonment, for example, provide a couple of necessary contrasts to the closeness and security of the scriptural reality of intimacy with God. Much of this will be developed in succeeding chapters. Nouwen, like all of us, knows that our existence in this world is often not a connected one:

> We probably have wondered in our many lonesome moments if there is one corner in this competitive, demanding world where it is safe to be relaxed, to expose ourselves to someone else, and to give unconditionally. It might be very small and hidden. But if this corner exists, it calls for a search through the complexities of our human relationships in order to find it.[34]

---

33. By contrast, this is one reason why the false kiss of intimacy Judas showed Him as he betrayed Him is such a contrast to Jesus's touch (Luke 22:47–48).

34. Henri J. M. Nouwen, *Intimacy: Essays in Pastoral Psychology* (San Francisco: HarperCollins, 1969), 23.

How much more do we need a place with God like this and how much more effort should we expend to navigate the complexities of our minds, hearts, experiences, and cultures to find it with Him?

Nevertheless, intimacy by nature has elements that are intuitive to us. Gina Cloud, a radio talk-show host, author, and self-help guru, makes this claim:

> Real Intimacy isn't the nakedness of the body, but the vulnerability of the heart. This is why we run towards it and also run away from it. Intimacy requires vulnerability and surrender. It demands that we reveal ourselves to each other, naked, exposed, raw, real, honest. It requires that we be willing TO BE SEEN—FULLY.[35]

She understands the movement to and away from intimacy to a place of intimate knowledge and contact. These intuitive elements are very similar to our intimacy with God and why pursuing intimacy with Him is not optional. Brother Lawrence called it "our profession" and "if we do not know it, we must learn it."[36] But we must know what it truly is and how to find it. Our next chapter will try to lead us further down that path.

NOW WHAT?

1. What do you want concerning intimacy with God?

2. What biblical passages or images would you add as examples of the biblical elements of intimacy with God?

3. How do you think the four biblical elements will help you pursue intimacy with God?

4. Ask God to weave these images into your mind and heart to bring you closer to Him.

---

35. Gina Cloud, "Are You Longing for and Afraid of Intimacy?," GinaCology, http://www. ginacology.com/are-you-longing-for-and-afraid-of-intimacy. Emphasis in original.
36. Brother Lawrence, *Practice of the Presence of God*.

CHAPTER 2

THE PLACE OF INTIMACY WITH GOD IN PHILOSOPHY AND THEOLOGY

Where does intimacy with God fit? I mean, what are we assuming and even presuming about it? Most of us assume elements concerning closeness to God that give us a strong measure of comfort, control, and contentment. It seems counterintuitive to assume any sort of discomfort and chaos.

It often takes a visceral or powerfully existential experience to get us to question our assumptions. A gracious pilot recently gave me a ride in his aerobatic plane, and for me it was an exercise in assumptions. From the ground I watched this competitive flying that consists of spectacular maneuvers of rolls and dives choreographed much like an ice-skating performance. I had accumulated certain positive assumptions from my own observation of pilots who made it look so easy, the testimony of two of my children who enjoyed their rides with immense pleasure (and were even allowed to fly the planes for part of it), and my experience of roller coasters and swings (and I'm not really comfortable in either). At takeoff, immediately I was no longer thinking about how they could make the plane do these amazing things, but how they (and I) could withstand what it does to your senses! You literally have to grit your teeth and grunt as you tighten your core muscles just to fight the nausea and disorientation due to the gravitational or G-forces from the sharp turns and rolls. I assumed from the ground there would be some comfort and control, yet from the cockpit there was more discomfort and chaos than I had assumed going into it. However, there was the beauty and thrill of it that got me into the plane in the first place.

So it is with assessing our assumptions about intimacy with God. It takes an amount of deep personal reflection to grasp what we are assuming and even presuming about being close to God. That is what this book is about. Let's look at some aspects of what we should assume philosophically, biblically, and theologically.

PHILOSOPHICAL ASSUMPTIONS

Our examination of our Christian philosophical assumptions can be viewed from various elevations. We may stand on a hill, overlooking a valley and its surrounding hills and mountains, without recognizing our limited perspective. An aerobatic plane's altitude is limited by its design, whereas a satellite, while limited, can take in a much more immense view of what we assume from the ground looking up. When it comes to a close relationship with the Christian God of the Bible, we need to take in all that we *do* assume, and build upon that to grasp all we *should* assume. It is here where our bearings can give us comfort, pleasure, necessary caution, and transformation, while our presumptions can hinder our approach, blind us to our location, and put us off course into idolatry.

God Gives Us Existence

The philosophical starting point for intimacy with God for Christians is with our metaphysics, and specifically our ontology or existence.[1] We must begin with the beginning, a satellite view. Where does a movement toward a place of intimate contact with God begin? Our existence in this universe is simply fortuitous at best, as we reckon with the lack of any inherent necessity for our being at all.[2] However, Western secular culture is programmed to assume that our existence came from an infinite regress of causes. This assumption

---

1. Ontology focuses on the nature of existence itself, the general features of being consistent with things that exist (for humans that would be coming-to-be, perishing, etc.), and the classification of the types or ways things exist (substances, properties, etc.). J. P. Moreland and William Lane Craig, *Philosophical Foundations for a Christian Worldview* (Downers Grove, IL: InterVarsity, 2003), 175, 187–94, 220.
2. David Bentley Hart, *The Experience of God: Being, Consciousness, Bliss* (New Haven, CT: Yale University Press, 2013), 90.

has an infinite sequence of causes/events that logically wouldn't actually ever begin. Having everything begin with the Big Bang is also flawed, because it is just another contingent physical occurrence; most importantly, it has no God tied to our existence. Assumptions that allow a compromise of a sort of naturalism with theism tend to lessen God to a ghost behind the material machine of nature, who simply used the existing eternal materials or created the existing materials with certain laws with which to function in harmony. Theistic evolution, progressive creation, intelligent design, and deism must all be careful to not only focus on what God leaves to nature. The metaphysical point is that God's being is necessary, as the unconditioned source of all things, while ours is wholly derivative and contingent.[3] Not only is He the creator, "In the beginning God created . . ." (Gen. 1:1; John 1:1–3), but the self-existent One who needs and lacks nothing as the "I AM that I AM" (Exod. 3:14).

This appears to be exhilarating for philosopher types, who need reasons for things. However, our being contingent or dependent upon God's noble generosity for our existence must move us to the inescapable conclusion that we are responsive and responsible beings to this metaphysical Reality. Hart eloquently states, "one's meditations on the world's contingency should end more or less where they begin: in that moment of wonder, of sheer existential surprise. . . . It can be a fairly taxing spiritual labor, admittedly—it is, in the end, a contemplative art—one should strive as far as possible for a simple return to that original apprehension of the gratuity of all things."[4] And so, he rightly claims, "The highest vocation of reason and of the will is to seek to know the ultimate source of that mystery. Above all one should wish to know whether our consciousness of that mystery directs us toward a reality that is, in its turn, conscious of us."[5] In other words, our contingency as beings calls us to wonder, worship, and approach the One who gave us our very existence. We are so tied to Him as the wellspring of our being that we are like the light to a candle or lamp's flame.[6] Extinguish the Absolute Source and Sustainer, and all else falls into the darkness of nonexistence. Paul told the Colossians that not only is Christ before all things as our Creator, but He is the sustainer of our existence (Col. 1:17). He summarized this to the Athenians. God "Himself gives to all mankind life and breath and everything" (Acts 17:25), and this is common knowledge since their own poets said, "In

---

3. Ibid., 109.
4. Ibid., 150.
5. Ibid., 151.
6. Ibid., 104.

him we live and move and have our being" (17:28). This should prompt us all to "seek," "grope for," and ultimately "find" the Source who "is not far from each one of us" (17:27).[7]

God Gives Us Consciousness

Where does the relational interaction with the intimate knowledge of and contact with our Creator originate? Our assumptions concerning His gift of our human consciousness provide structure to our philosophy of mind, the next philosophical foundation for intimacy with Him. What is it that actually relates to and draws close to God? It is our consciousness, that is, our mind and/or soul.[8] However, Western secular culture's dogma is that consciousness can be explained by materialist/physicalist or naturalist causes. There is no unity of consciousness, only chemical and electrical processes in the brain. It is like an image in a pointillist painting or pixels on a screen; it does not have any real existence. However, it is also reasonable to conclude that the points of paint or pixels have been arranged by some agency or formal principle outside of their material components and physical creation.[9] Consciousness is the site of intrinsic, subjective, introspective, and qualitative personal experience, something that "the alleged aimlessness and mechanistic extrinsicism" cannot produce.[10] Thus Dickerson is quite clear as to the failure of physicalism's attempt to explain consciousness or the mind as merely a machine:

> If there is no individual *self*, then there is no individual *other*. If there is no *other*, then there is nothing and nobody *else* to care for, and also no real *ecology* to speak of—no interactions of distinct beings.[11]

---

7. At the same time, how can I possibly communicate the utter impossibility of grasping God as Creator and Sustainer? His infinity and eternality? His omnipotence and immutability? His omniscience and wisdom? His holiness and goodness? How He is not made in our image? He is not some demiurge. We are in many ways the opposite: finite, temporal, limited, changing, fickle, foolish, stained, selfish. We are not devoid of the blessedness of nature. That is why we need to look further into what we should assume.

8. The Old Testament refers to the mind with *rēsh* or head (Dan. 2:28; 4:5). The New Testament terms for mind are *nous* (Matt. 22:37; 1 Cor. 16), *dianoia* (Eph. 2:3) and *phronēma* (Rom. 8:6–7). Other terms related to human consciousness and its feelings and thoughts include: *lebab* (Isa. 21:4); *lēb* (Eccl. 1:17); *nephesh* (Deut. 6:5); *ruach* (Gen. 41:8); *pneuma* (Matt. 26:41); *psyche* (Matt. 22:37); *kardia* (Matt. 22:37).

9. Hart, *The Experience of God*, 170.

10. Ibid., 179.

11. Matthew Dickerson, *The Mind and the Machine: What It Means to Be Human and Why It Matters* (Grand Rapids: Baker/Brazos, 2011), 83.

In short, we assume our consciousness to be derivative, just like our existence. God has not only given us our being, but the capacities for interaction with Him. He is the source of our intentionality, reason, subjectivity, and freedom, each of which are crucial to conscious relational intimacy.

Even children find this self-evident. I know I am one of many who can still remember the first time they realized, "I am me." I am the one looking out of my eyes. I am not some Oz wizard or ghost behind my body pulling levers, but I am myself and can be by myself even in a crowded room. I reflect on things in my mind, experience joy and sorrow even when I hide it, and make plans for my own subjective intentions. I also remember my own conversion. When I was five years old, I was invited to interact with God about crucial issues. It was one of my first "a-ha moments" as I realized I was actually talking to God, just Him and me. We talked about important things and I have continued to do so freely until this day. This is something that we Christians assume we are able to do, due to our consciousness, as opposed to every other member of the natural world. It is truly fortuitous.[12]

God Gives Us the Delightful Good

This brings us to the culmination of our philosophical assumptions in our axiology or the justification of our values, which provide understanding of our delight in the goodness of intimacy with God. We should place an extremely high value on our intimate knowledge of God and our contact and location with Him. This is not simply due to its personal, cultural, or instrumental worth, but it is intrinsic.[13] Because our existence and consciousness are contingent and derivative from our benevolent God, so our values should be.[14] Christians traditionally have held to the simple equation that what is good is an eternal reality and transcendental truth that is ultimately

---

12. Thus Arthur Holmes could claim that we are "not isolated individuals, but relational beings through and through," because "We are not self-made, but draw from him our very existence, every good thing we are and have, our purpose, our meaning, our hope." Arthur Holmes, "Toward a Christian View of Things," *The Making of a Christian Mind: A Christian World View & the Academic Enterprise*, ed. Arthur Holmes (Downers Grove, IL: IVP, 1985), 23.

13. Garrett J. DeWeese, *Doing Philosophy as a Christian* (Downers Grove, IL: IVP, 2011), 179.

14. Because He transcends our finite existence and world, what is true and good are rightly known as "transcendentals." I use this term not merely in an analytic sense for defining universal concepts (*contra* Lando and Spolaore). Giorgio Lando and Giuseppe Spolaore, "Transcendental Disagreements," *The Monist* 97, no. 4 (2014): 593–94. Transcendentals are not only universal ontologically, but transcendent in origin. However, they can be known (*contra* Kant). See Josef Seifert, "Ontological Categories: On Their Distinction from Transcendentals, Modes of Being, and Logical Categories," *Anuario Filosofico* 47, no. 2 (2014): 324 n.14.

identical with the very essence of God Himself. Hart rightly notes, "God is not some gentleman or lady out there in the great beyond who happens to have a superlatively good character, but is the very ontological substance of goodness."[15] He then appropriately adds, "The good is nothing less than God himself, in his aspect as the original source and ultimate end of all desire: that transcendent reality in which all things exist and in which the will has its highest fulfillment."[16] In other words, God is simply the end in Himself as the contingent and sustaining wellspring of our existence and consciousness. Thus intimacy with Him is the transcendent good in which we as His creations find our chief and highest purpose, delight, and pursuit. This is the ethics of intimacy with God. Anything other than our intimacy with Him as our ultimate good and delight is not only bad, but wrong.

God Gives Us Our Knowledge of Him

Where does our intimate knowledge of God come from and what does it consist of? Answers to this come through our epistemological assumptions about intimacy with God, which are parallel to our metaphysical ones above. We underscore our knowledge of the gifts of our existence and consciousness. However, there is more to knowledge of God than reason. Christians have recognized that our means to knowledge of the what, how, when, and whys of intimacy with God is "faith seeking understanding" (*fides quarens intellectum*) and that "I believe that I may understand" (*credo ut intelligam*). Yet knowledge itself is a gift to us as it grasps God's revelation through our consciousness. Further, He reveals Himself in creation (Ps. 19:1–6; Rom. 1:19–22) and conscience (Rom. 2:14–16). His most specific revelation is found in His written Word and in Jesus Christ. Thus knowledge of and intimacy with God is derivative and contingent upon Him. Lints calls this "epistemological grace," as we are invited to listen in on the conversation in Scripture and become part of that very conversation.[17] God, others, me, and then us, which includes my culture, family, Christians, church. All

---

15. Hart, *The Experience of God*, 253–54.
16. Ibid., 254.
17. Richard Lints, *The Fabric of Theology: A Prolegomena to Evangelical Theology* (Grand Rapids: Eerdmans, 1993), 57–59. Moser calls this "cognitive grace" that comes from God who is all-loving and "not from human ways that are self-crediting, manipulative, or selfishly exclusive." See Paul K. Moser, "Reorienting Religious Epistemology: Cognitive Grade, Filial Knowledge, and Gethsemane Struggle," in *For Faith and Clarity: Philosophical Contributions to Christian Theology*, ed. James K. Beilby (Grand Rapids: Baker, 2006), 72.

of these help us know God in a way that is basically consistent with what is true, and help us to make contact with what is real.[18]

Analytic philosophy helps us, with its stress on the intelligibility, accuracy, coherence, and truthfulness of the expression of our religious knowledge. Without these goals and parameters, we cannot trust our experiences alone and cannot communicate them to others in any biblically meaningful way. However, there are those in the analytic movement like Hume, Ayer, and Flew, who challenge whether we can understand and communicate "religious knowledge," let alone intimacy with God, in any sense. Yet, there is a serious problem with this philosophy's assumptions. It presupposes that if, say, intimacy with God exists, in order to be able to communicate anything about it, it must exist out in the real world in exactly the same sense. This means there must be at least one instance of it out there somewhere. However, notice the way this problematic claim is set up by analytic philosophers.[19] Many of these analytical philosophers are naturalists and atheists, and so closeness to God cannot exist and language that attempts to explain it is meaningless. This simply reveals their blind pride. However, their influence causes many Christians to doubt whether intimacy with God is verifiable or communicable. This even leads some to doubt their relationship with God overall. Others rebel against this philosophy and simply make claims to intimacy with God that are ultimately based upon pure subjectivity and irrationality. They view God's intimate relationship with His people as patterned only after our intimate relationships in our own culture and context, just maybe better. This demotes God's intimacy to what we know and experience with other humans and often borders on presumption and idolatry. We will assess an example of this later in the chapter.

Secularism and Cultural Knowledge of God

On a more popular level, philosophical assumptions of many Christians about intimacy with God come from the prevailing secularism of Western culture. They are borrowing capital from another worldview, rather than the biblical one.[20] As an epistemological issue, rather than viewing reality holistically, many divide what can be known and experienced about reality into two spheres: the upper story of sacred/spiritual values and the lower story of

---

18. Esther Lightcap Meek, *Longing to Know: The Philosophy of Knowledge for Ordinary People* (Grand Rapids: Brazos/Baker, 2003), 135.
19. Hart, *The Experience of God*, 123–27.
20. Paul Copan, *Loving Wisdom: Christian Philosophy of Religion* (St. Louis: Chalice, 2007), 16.

scientific/empirical facts.[21] As a result, Christians have filtered intimacy with God through this default understanding. Wells is correct in arguing that a baseline truth of the Bible is that *God is before us*. Yet our culture is pushing us toward the opposite—we must go *into* ourselves to know God.[22] This results in the paradox of transcendent deism or immanent psychology. His recognition of this secular influence is summarized in Figure 1.[23]

Figure 1

Secular Knowledge of God

God is out there, somewhere

Transcendent Deism	Practical Atheism
Immanent Psychology	Individual Subjectivity

God disappears within

Transcendent deism answers the question, "Does God ever intervene in my life?" with a "no" and a shrug. This does not mean that these Christians are atheists or are not spiritual. God is "out there, somewhere" but takes a "hands-off" approach to their private lives. Christian Smith's research into the religious and spiritual lives of emerging adults, the life stage of those approximately 18–25 years of age,[24] shows a significant group of them hold to what he has entitled "Moralistic Therapeutic Deism."[25] They are "spiritual" but shy away from a reli-

---

21. Pearcey, *Total Truth*, 20–21.
22. David F. Wells, *God in the Whirlwind: How the Holy-love of God Reorients Our World* (Wheaton, IL: Crossway, 2014), 18.
23. Adapted and expanded from Wells, *God in the Whirlwind*, 19–28.
24. For the research on this demographic see Jeffrey Jensen Arnett, *Emerging Adulthood: The Winding Road from the Late Teens through the Twenties*, 2nd ed. (New York: Oxford University Press, 2015), and his *Adolescence and Emerging Adulthood*, 5th ed. (London: Pearson, 2012); see also David P. Setran and Chris A. Kiesling, *Spiritual Formation in Emerging Adulthood: A Practical Theology for College and Young Adult Ministry* (Grand Rapids: Baker Academic, 2013); and Rita Žukauskienė, *Emerging Adulthood in a European Context* (New York: Routledge, 2016).
25. Christian Smith with Melinda Lundquist Denton, *Soul Searching: The Religious & Spiritual Lives of American Teenagers* (New York: Oxford University Press, 2005), 118–71. For Smith's assessment of what has happened to MTD five years after his initial research in *Soul Searching*, see Christian Smith with Patricia Snell, *Souls in Transition: The Religious*

gious orientation unless it helps them with their personal needs or recovery. This spirituality is rooted in the assumption that no one ultimately knows what is true, right, or good.[26] Among emerging adults this epistemology has significant effects on their feeling close to God. Smith notes that

> minorities of most religious types of emerging adults feel quite close to God, and even smaller minorities feel quite distant from God. Significant chunks of emerging adults state that they feel only somewhat close or distant from God. . . . But the overall trend over the half decade between the teenage and emerging adult years is clearly away from feeling close to God and toward either feeling distant from God or not believing in God at all.[27]

Paradoxically, we have unprecedented access to freedoms, education, affluence, technology, and healthcare, but with a prevalence of depression, loneliness, and dissatisfaction. And God is distant and thus rarely, if ever, moves toward or makes intimate contact with them.

At the same time, God's transcendence is dissolving into an immanent psychology in which "God disappears within." Wells describes this as a place where God's holiness gives way to His love, and human nature is redefined only as the self, as "simply an internal core of intuitions."[28] The supposed logic of this view begins with "our own unique biography, gender, ethnicity, and life-experience" all coming together "in a single center of self-consciousness." This then implies that "every self is unique because no one has exactly the same set of personal factors." Thus many in the West are now "inclined to see life, to understand what is true, to think of right and wrong, in uniquely individual ways."[29] Therefore, because "each perspective on life and its meaning are equally valid," one's private intuitions and experiences about intimacy with God are not only primary from an epistemological and phenomenological standpoint, but are inviolable by church or doctrinal standards.[30]

& Spiritual Lives of Emerging Adults (New York: Oxford University Press, 2009), 154–64. See also Jonathan P. Hill, Emerging Adulthood and Faith (Grand Rapids: Calvin College Press, 2015), and Carolyn McNamara Barry and Mona M. Abo-Zena, eds., Emerging Adults' Religiousness and Spirituality: Meaning-Making in an Age of Transition, Emerging Adulthood Series (New York: Oxford University Press, 2014).

26. Smith with Snell, Souls in Transition, 287.
27. Ibid., 121.
28. Wells, God in the Whirlwind, 25.
29. Ibid.
30. Ibid., 27.

However, this "perspectivalism" is inherently flawed.[31] We can grant that, in one sense, the perspectives described above do shape our knowledge in positive ways.[32] Yet to claim the existence of incommensurable or immeasurable perspectives on intimacy with God is incoherent or illogical. To make such a claim one must know something of each perspective, use the same language to describe them and plot them on the same plane in order to make such an assessment. Attempting to demonstrate they are radically different shows how impossible and hopeless it is to attempt to claim their immeasurability. It is then also self-defeating, since it has to appeal to some sort of objective perspective to claim incommensurability.[33]

Perspectivalism also overstates what it can actually claim. While it is true that different paradigms, descriptions, and perspectives of intimacy with God exist, it does not mean that they cannot be analyzed from an external source. That is the point of having the Scriptures as our "norming norm" and the Holy Spirit's guidance with it. While exhaustive knowledge of the divine view of intimacy with Him is impossible, we have enough information in Scripture and in the history of God's people to formulate a simple yet true knowledge of it. Furthermore, not all truth about intimacy with God in the Bible is comprised of narrative perspectives (Moses at the burning bush, Martha washing Jesus's feet, etc.). There are propositions and/or principles given to guide and interpret those phenomena and our experience of God (James 4:8; etc.). We will discuss the role of the Scriptures shortly.

Our only hope to avoid conforming to our secularized epistemology of intimacy with God must be with an allegiance to the truth and authority of Scripture as it relates to the basis and parameters of it. We need a qualified Guide to knowledge.[34] We must entrust ourselves to God's epistemological grace as the

---

31. I am indebted here to David K. Clark's three main criticisms of strong versions of perspectivalism in his *To Know and Love God: Method for Theology* (Wheaton, IL: Crossway, 2003), 147–52.

32. In this sense I would agree with many of the benefits Frame delineates concerning an evangelical perspectivalism that has God as lord over all knowledge. Thus God reveals Himself through the Scriptures, reason, and experience. These are one body of knowledge seen from different perspectives. We can appreciate this diversity of knowledge gained from all of the cultural communities of faith, rightly interpreted by the Scriptures under the guidance of the Holy Spirit. These can free us from our own blind spots and prejudices. See John M. Frame, *The Doctrine of the Knowledge of God* (Phillipsburg, NJ: Presbyterian and Reformed Publishing, 1987).

33. See Clark's helpful response to what he calls the "ingenious" appeal to the incommensurability of second order propositions vs. first-order ones in *To Know and Love God*, 148–50.

34. Meek, *Longing to Know*, 100.

source of our existence, consciousness, and intimacy with Him by His Word and His Spirit. He has revealed to us what is necessary for us to have a blissful, intimate relationship with Him. Thus His transcendence and His immanence are equal aspects of His nature and relationship with us as His creations.

Knowing and Not Knowing

What kind of intimate knowledge of God can we have? Because we are finite creatures, our knowledge is somewhere between the univocal (straightforward, precise, and exact), and the equivocal (ambiguous, imprecise, and inexact). Because intimacy with God is also experiential, our knowledge is kataphatic and apophatic[35]—what God is like, what God isn't like. Kataphatic stresses what can be known and articulated about God and our experience of Him, whereas the apophatic stresses not only what cannot be known, but what is inexpressible.[36] Thus the Bible and Christians use metaphors and concepts within religious language to express revealed truth in a kind of mystery.[37] In the Orthodox tradition this is expressed in icons, through which worship of the infinite God of mystery is achieved by faith. Prokhorov comes closer to the target when he stresses that nothing in our Christian experience is like heaven:

> Thus, starting from cataphaticism, which is usual for most people, we gradually move to the apophatic way, which was already meditated on by some of the church fathers, a way which fearlessly proclaims the superiority of a person's ignorance.[38]

While stronger forms of apophaticism face the same problems as perspectivalism above, we must not claim too much for our knowledge of intimacy with God. Furthermore, the conversation is muted because of our natural sinful bent. Paul states in 1 Corinthians 2:14, "But a natural man does not accept the things of the Spirit of God, for they are foolishness to him; and he cannot understand them, because they are spiritually appraised." These lines from

---

35. William Franke, *On What Cannot Be Said: Apophatic Discourses in Philosophy, Religion, Literature, and the Arts: Volume 1: Classic Formulations*, 1st ed. (Notre Dame, IN: University of Notre Dame Press, 2007), 1–7.
36. Constantine Prokhorov, "Apophaticism and Cataphaticism in Protestantism," *European Journal of Theology* 23, no 1 (2014): 73–81.
37. I am in basic agreement here with Harrison's expression of the goal and tension of metaphors and concepts. Verna E. F. Harrison, "The Relationship between Apophatic and Kataphatic Theology," *Pro Ecclesia* 45 (1995): 322–23.
38. Prokhorov, "Apophaticism and Cataphaticism in Protestantism," 74.

Ieromonach Roman's poem capture the challenges of intimacy with God's univocal and equivocal nature: "I pity people who do not know God; I pity people who know all about Him."[39]

At the same time, we need to recognize the profound difference between what is unknown about God and the mystery of Him. William Hordern has captured this distinction when he states:

> We may say that a man faced with the unknown has the sense of being igno-
> rant. But the man faced with mystery is not properly described as ignorant.
> He is aware of being humbled and awe-inspired. He becomes aware of his
> finiteness.[40]

This again is why knowledge of the mysteries of God prompts us to worship. We can neither be "humbled and awe-inspired" nor draw near to what we are ignorant of. We may fear or attempt to propitiate the unknown,[41] but we can only know the gracious and merciful presence of a God who knows us and allows us to know Him. May we not be enslaved to the unknown or what we think we know, but draw close to the true and real God, in the way that Paul reminds the Galatians to do:

> However at that time, when you did not know God, you were slaves to those
> which by nature are no gods. But now that you have come to know God, or
> rather to be known by God, how is it that you turn back again to the weak
> and worthless elemental things, to which you desire to be enslaved all over
> again? (Gal. 4:8–9)

Loving to Know

What should motivate our quest for intimate knowledge of this God, who is beyond the boundary of our ultimate understanding? It is and should be out of a loving desire for knowledge of Him. When we say, "I would love to know . . ." it is self-evident that there is a natural connection between what we care about most deeply and what we want to know the most about.[42] Harrison rightly states:

---

39. Ieromonach Roman as cited in Prokhorov, "Apophaticism and Cataphaticism in Protestantism," 75. The poem is in Russian. See http://tropinka.orthodoxy.ru/zal/poezija/roman/index.htm.

40. William Hordern, *Speaking of God: The Nature and Purpose of Theological Language* (Eugene, OR: Wipf & Stock, 2002), 115.

41. Ibid.

42. David K. Naugle, *Philosophy: A Student's Guide* (Wheaton, IL: Crossway, 2012), 68.

The soul is moved by this love to desire more than what it already contains and thus go out of itself beyond its own capacity into the incomprehensible. This movement outside the receptacle's boundary is what enables it to expand.[43]

Tozer echoes this loving pursuit of the God who is beyond our understanding:

In Christ and by Christ, God effects complete self-disclosure, although He shows Himself not to reason but faith and love. Faith is an organ of knowledge, and love an organ of experience. God came to us in the incarnation; in atonement He reconciled us to Himself, and by faith and love we enter and lay hold on Him.[44]

Again, we are really moved to know the most about what we care about most deeply. This should stir us to the greatest pursuit of our lives.

Knowing Personally

What kind of knowledge of God should we pursue? We must remind ourselves that we seek more than just knowledge of facts about God's movement and location, but an intimate personal knowing. What Meek calls a "substantival approach" to knowledge tends to view humans as merely reasoning animals, as humans who possess the attribute of rationality. We supposedly mainly know things by reason and proofs. Television's Spock, Data, Dr. Gregory House, Dr. Temperance "Bones" Brennan, and Sherlock Holmes exemplify this view.[45] However, even these characters are not left without their relational component, and their knowledge is shaped by interpersonal interaction.[46] This full-orbed understanding of the acts of knowing not only makes us better people, but draws us closer and outside of our selves and minds.

---

43. Harrison, "The Relationship between Apophatic and Kataphatic Theology," 328.

44. A. W. Tozer, *The Knowledge of the Holy* (San Francisco: Harper & Row, 1961), 17.

45. Diane Duane, *Spock's World* (New York: Pocket Books, 1986); Stanley Grenz, "Star Trek and the Next Generation: Postmodernism and the Future of Evangelical Theology," *Crux* 30, no. 1 (1994): 24–32; J. Z. Long, "Mediated Genius, Anti-Intellectualism and the Detachment(s) of Everyday Life," in *Genius on Television: Essays on Small Screen Depictions of Big Minds*, ed. Ashley Lynn Carlson (Jefferson, NC: McFarland & Co., 2015), 40–41; Kate Rufa, "A Sherlockian Scandal in Philosophy," in *Sherlock Holmes and Philosophy: the Footprints of a Gigantic Mind*, ed. Josef Steiff (Chicago: Carus, 2011), 3–14.

46. Meek, *Loving to Know*, 28.

Personal knowledge is more than the knowledge about a person. In one sense, it is more than propositions, that is, facts about someone. In another sense, it transcends mere knowledge by acquaintance or, as DeWeese calls it, "recognition-knowledge." Here there is no mutual sharing, respect, or personal care. Knowing God is more than either the rational understanding of a person or the casual recognizing of them. It is person-knowledge.[47]

Moser rightly claims the same thing, but from God's perspective. Our first question concerning knowledge of God should be:

> What kind of human knowledge of God would an all-loving God seek? The most direct answer is that God would seek the kind of knowledge that advances God's kind of love among human knowers. In particular, an all-loving God would seek *filial knowledge of God*, whereby humans become loving children of God and thus know God, in sacred relationship, as their loving Father.

Meek uses similar language with "covenant epistemology." This is interpersonal as it installs the believer's vibrant relationship with God as the central paradigm for all knowing, and thus knowing is not mere information but transformation.[48]

However, because knowledge of God is so very relational, it reveals the human tendency to move away from Him and knowledge of Him. Paul states in Romans 1:19–32 that humans do this out of suppression of the truth about God. Moser reiterates our chosen epistemological dimness by rightly claiming that we avoid God often times out of self-protective fear:

> We fear that God will rob us of something good for us or at least something we rightfully want. As a result, we refuse to take seriously the available evidence of God's reality. We might even completely shut down some frequency ranges on our scanner, thereby trying to suppress the issue of whether there is available evidence of God's reality.[49]

Our love of our self and our knowledge of God, then, repel each other like reversing the polarity of two magnets. We have all felt this in our lives and yet

---

47. DeWeese, *Doing Philosophy as a Christian*, 174–75.
48. Meek, *Loving to Know*, 63.
49. Moser, "Reorienting Religious Epistemology," 69.

may not have connected it to our knowledge of God. But our epistemology of intimacy with God is personal and propositional, in Whom and in which we should find our greatest good and delight.

THEOLOGICAL ASSUMPTIONS

So where does intimacy with God fit within our theological assumptions? First thoughts about theology itself often revolve around our systems and methods. However, the grand assumption for our doing theology as a whole and thus knowing is not mere information but transformation with God should be hearing God's voice through our theological interpretation of the Bible's overall message and its various topics. We are to listen in order to receive His communication. We rely on the fact that Scripture has an inherent potency because it is the transcript of the divine will. We reckon with the reality that "what God discloses as He speaks is *himself*," and since He is the Creator this opens up His communication to us about the "whole of life."[50]

God's Wisdom for Us

This should remind us of the foundational biblical teaching concerning wisdom and knowledge of God. This is seen in wisdom vs. foolishness. There is a right way and wrong way to understand intimacy with God. Solomon declares in Proverbs 2:5 that our discernment of the fear of the Lord is the means by which we discover the knowledge of God. The Hebrew word for knowledge (*daat*) here and throughout the Wisdom Literature refers to experienced understanding of God. It is not mere facts but close and deeply respectful knowledge of God's ways and motivations. In Proverbs 9:10, wisdom and understanding are parallel to "the fear of the Lord" and the "knowledge of the Holy One." Delitzsch, more than a century ago, captured this idea well: "He who strives after wisdom earnestly and really, reaches in this way fellowship with God."[51]

Constructing Our Theology

So what actually is the bridge from reading what the Bible reveals about intimacy with God to constructing our theology of it? Our passionate quest

---

50. Heath A. Thomas, "The Telos (Goal) of Theological Interpretation," in *A Manifesto for Theological Intepretation*, eds. Craig G. Bartholomew and Heath A. Thomas (Grand Rapids: Baker, 2016), 199.

51. F. Delitzsch, "Proverbs, Ecclesiastes, Song of Solomon," in *Commentary on the Old Testament in Ten Volumes*, eds. C. F. Keil and F. Delitzsch, trans. James Martin (Grand Rapids: Eerdmans, 1872, 1975), 77.

begins with identifying what God has revealed about intimacy with Him. We have already begun to define what the intimacy is we are actually looking for, but the key will be gathering that information that is encased in the language of the Bible. As we saw in the last chapter, a fruitful launching point will be identifying biblical terms related to intimacy with God (e.g., near, close, etc.) and its elements (movement, knowledge, location, and contact). Yet this also needs to include their full semantic fields (word groups, synonyms, etc.), as well as descriptions of intimacy with God in narratives and prophecy, which may or may not include certain terms we may look up in a concordance. Since God is the author of all of Scripture, we can take His consistent revelation of intimacy with Him and synthesize it into a clear, comprehensive, and consistent understanding of this concept. In constructing this system, it is necessary to continue to test our elements in an upward hermeneutical spiral of progress.[52]

Potential weaknesses exist in what some call the concordance model of theology. For Franke, this is the evangelical tendency to do theology by viewing the Bible as a rather loose and relatively disorganized collection of factual, propositional statements. This theological task, then, is to collect and rearrange the varied statements, revealing the eternal system of timeless truths they point to.[53] While this is overstated, I understand what he wants us to avoid. Many in our evangelical tradition need more refined methodological assumptions. However, the concordance model, as he calls it, can be part of our starting point. It fosters a deeper understanding of the themes of Scripture. Obviously, we must be guarded against assuming that just because we have looked up a word, we have mastered all of the data of that theme in the Bible. Semantic field analysis is a helpful corrective for this. We must also recognize the importance of discourse analysis, genre studies, and speech act theory. Without these contextual parameters, we can amass piles of Bible verses that proof-text our presumptions and cultural biases. Yet to abandon a nuanced foundationalism or realism is unjustified as well.[54] The biblical writers used repetition as a literary device to underscore their key ideas. By simple observation of the first half of Romans we can clearly identify Paul's emphasis on justification through his repetition of the *dik-* word group (righteous, just, justify, etc.). Let's not project the limitations of the inductivism of our evangelical forefathers (Warfield, Hodge, Ryrie, etc.) on this generation of evangelical theologians. While the Bible communi-

---

52. Grant R. Osborne, *The Hermeneutical Spiral* (Downers Grove, IL: IVP, 1991).
53. Franke, *On What Cannot Be Said*, 88.
54. Darrell L. Bock, *Purpose-Directed Theology: Getting Our Priorities Right in Evangelical Controversies* (Downers Grove, IL: IVP Academic, 2009), 13–36.

cates knowledge of intimacy univocally, it communicates this concerning God through the language of analogy. Thus our theology of this must be constructed upon Scriptures rightly interpreted.[55] This means we must also assess our own theological and cultural commitments and context concerning intimacy with God, as well as listen to and assess the breadth of the reflections of the entire Church throughout its history.

Biblical Theology

We must also be careful to examine intimacy with God within the context of biblical theology. The content of the themes related to intimacy with God have been revealed progressively. These themes are like lines of longitude on a globe.[56] Some themes are quite extensive and cut through large continents of the Bible, whereas some are much more limited to cutting through islands and peninsulas. We must take care not to strip our data of its place in God's progressive revelation. He gives increasing clarity and development from one end of the Bible to the other.

Another way of describing this biblical theology is to look at how intimacy with God fits into and is a part of the divine drama revealed in the Scriptures. There is the actual program of God taking place that began before the foundation of the world and will consummate in the eternal state. The biblical authors, directing their readers and being guided by the Holy Spirit, craft an epic script. Intimacy with the Author-Director is not only part of the narrative, but it demands us to embody the drama itself in our participation.[57] At the same time, the drama has propositional content. Vanhoozer argues that the directive nature of the drama of doctrine "often takes the form of a propositional project: something to be believed by me, done by me, hoped by me, sung by me."[58] It is within that context and calling that we find the Scripture's information on intimacy with God.

---

55. For this, I am indebted to the late Paul Feinberg's definition of theology from his unfinished systematic theology.
56. I am indebted to Kaiser and Hasel for this analogy. Walter C. Kaiser, Jr., *Toward an Old Testament Theology* (Grand Rapids: Zondervan, 1978), 69; and Gerhard Hasel, *Old Testament Theology: Basic Issues in the Current Debate*, 4th rev. and expanded ed. (Grand Rapids: Eerdmans, 1991), 114.
57. Kevin J. Vanhoozer, *The Drama of Doctrine: A Canonical-Linguistic Approach to Christian Theology* (Louisville: Westminster John Knox, 2005), 165.
58. Ibid., 104. He clarifies this "performative understanding" of Scripture by noting that it is "not a matter of replicating the author's situation (the world behind the text), or of repeating the author's words, but of unfolding what the author says (about the theodrama) into one's own situation (the world in front of the text). Vanhoozer, "A Drama-of-

THEOLOGICAL POSITIONING

Where does intimacy with God fit in relationship to systematic theology's broad themes and categories? For example, we can investigate any location on the earth by accessing Google Maps. And yet, there are categories of locations. Search for "Oregon" and we will get a view of the northwestern United States. If we search for "Salem, Oregon," we get a shaded map of that city outlined in red at the junction of Interstate 5 and Highway 22. Where is Corban University specifically located in Salem? It is on Deer Park Drive SE, between Aumsville Highway and Turner Road. In the same way, as we have discussed, everything has a theological context within the Bible's epic drama. However, where is intimacy with God located? What is its relative theological size and what gives it its broader theological significance? Intimacy with God has a certain place on theological maps of God and in His relationship to His people.

First, since intimacy with God is how He relates to us as His creatures it must be subsumed within the balance of the "twin biblical truths"[59] of His transcendence and immanence. We must be careful not to portray these as impersonal and personal respectively.[60] God relates personally to all of His creatures. His transcendence is His being above and beyond our world as the unlimited, self-sufficient, and heavenly Creator. He is separate from and independent from His created order and us as humans.[61] Carl Henry is more comprehensive when he says, "Biblical characterizations of divine transcendence are in no sense vague or conjectural, but clearly and concretely depict God's activity and relationships as creator, preserver and governor of the cosmos and man."[62] At the same time, God's immanence is His pervasive[63] presence with and in our world, that is, His being metaphysically and relationally close. Erickson is right in recognizing that God's immanence and transcendence are not to be viewed as His attributes. They actually "cut across" various attributes of God, nothing less than His greatness and goodness. All of God's attributes relate to

---

Redemption Model," in *Four Views on Moving beyond the Bible to Theology*, general ed. Gary T. Meadors (Grand Rapids: Zondervan, 2009), 167.

59. Stanley J. Grenz and Roger E. Olson, *20th Century Theology: God & the World in Transition* (Downers Grove, IL: IVP, 1992), 11.
60. John S. Feinberg, *No One Like Him: The Doctrine of God* (Wheaton, IL: Crossway, 2001), 59.
61. Ibid., 60.
62. Carl F. H. Henry, *God, Revelation and Authority, Vol. VI: God Who Stands and Stays, Part Two* (Wheaton, IL: Crossway, 1983, 1999), 36.
63. Ibid., 36

us and to this world in immanent and transcendent ways.[64] These concepts help us to regard intimacy with God as part of His overall relationship to us as His creations, so above and beyond and yet so near.

Second, intimacy with God also stems from who He is. It is a manifestation of His metaphysical and relational attributes. Metaphysically, God is omnipresent, which means the totality of His being is present everywhere.[65] He is "all in" everywhere. He is not physically present everywhere, since He is spirit. Since He is a spiritual being, His omnipresence is not merely spatial. We must not fall into a parody or caricature of viewing the universe as some sort of "spatial box with God either overflowing it or standing outside of it."[66] He is ontologically distinct from us. All this is to say every aspect of God's being is utterly immense and yet minutely close to us. The difficulty in grasping these concepts is why the Bible uses analogous language, which we will investigate in the next chapter.

God's omniscience is the metaphysical and epistemological essence of intimacy with Him. Oliphint notes that God's knowledge has two main aspects. First, He has a necessary knowledge that is an aspect of who He is. His necessity, aseity (self-existence), simplicity, and immutability all recognize the infinite knowledge of all things and of all possibilities He possesses at all times. Second, His knowledge is free. His knowledge is inextricably united with His will.[67] We are back to contingency again. What is not God is contingent upon Him. Thus He freely brings it into existence. Theologians have viewed this as God's determined or decreed will, coupled with His permissive will. Thus intimacy with God is nearly one-sided. His knowledge of us is so exhaustive and free. Our knowledge of Him is so miniscule and constrained. This is precisely why He must move toward us and also permits us to move toward Him.

This movement is known as God's condescension, which is the heart of intimacy with Him. However, divine condescension is not so much what God is but what He does and why He chooses to do so. It is the characteristics He takes on in order to interact with us.[68] God is not bound or subject to anything in His creation. His condescension is what He did not have to do but chooses

64. Millard J. Erickson, *Christian Theology*, unabridged one-volume ed. (Grand Rapids: Baker, 1985), 302.
65. Feinberg, *No One Like Him*, 249.
66. Hordern, *Speaking of God*, 121; and Henry, *God, Revelation and Authority, Vol. VI: God Who Stands and Stays Part Two*, 35.
67. K. Scott Oliphint, *God with Us: Divine Condescension and the Attributes of God* (Wheaton, IL: Crossway, 2011), 96.
68. Ibid., 12–13.

to do in order to make a relationship with His creatures possible. It began with His creation of humans as relational beings, is extended through His covenants, and yet it continues to arise out of what Anthony Esolen beautifully captures in the phrase, "omnipotent humility." In the incarnation, "He who had spoken the world into existence now came into that world as an infant, literally a being without speech—the Word made speechless."[69] Thus His condescension is about His bridging an infinite distance. His omnipresence demonstrates that this distance is not spatial, but relational. The knowledge of God is plain in His creation. However, Augustine recognized our need for His condescending revelation:

> And though He is everywhere present to the inner eye when it is sound and clear, He condescended to make Himself manifest to the outward eye of those whose inward sight is weak and dim. "For after that, in the wisdom of God, the world by wisdom knew not God, it pleased God by the foolishness of preaching to save them that believe" (1 Cor. 1:21).[70]

Again, that ultimate revelation is in His Son, whom He sent to serve all mankind. We must marvel as Thomas à Kempis did when he exclaimed to God, "You Yourself have condescended to serve man and have promised to give him Yourself."[71] And so, we must recognize His grace and mercy in reaching down to choose us to serve Him, and in so doing we draw near in delight.

AND SO . . .

After diving into the deep end of the philosophy and theology of intimacy with God, again it is a call for the body of Christ to identify our assumptions concerning an intimate relationship with God. A search on amazon.com for "intimacy with God" reveals how diverse we are in this area. For example, approaches like Matthew Robert Payne's have simple experiential/perspectival epistemological foundations influenced by Pentecostal-Charismatic theology and experiences.[72] He expresses his heartfelt claim for his book *Finding Intimacy with Jesus Made Simple: Key Truths to Draw You Closer* with these words:

---

69. Anthony Esolen, "Child Everlasting," *Touchstone: A Journal of Mere Christianity* 20, no. 10 (2007): 3.

70. St. Augustine, *On Christian Doctrine, in Four Books*, Chapter 12, Christian Classics Ethereal Library, http://www.ccel.org/ccel/augustine/doctrine.xii.html.

71. Thomas à Kempis, *The Imitation of Christ*, translated from Latin into Modern English (Milwaukee: Bruce Publishing Co., 1940), 104.

72. See also Mark Casto, *When Misfits Become Kings: Unlock Your Future through Intimacy with God* (Lake Mary, FL: Charisma House, 2015); Bill Johnson, *Face to Face With God: The*

> I have a very deep and close relationship with Jesus and much of this book was written by my knowledge, and yet much of the information about Jesus was revelation right out of Heaven via the Holy Spirit. It is this revelation that I listen to over and over again so that I can get it down into my spirit.[73]

In other words, the source for his view of a close relationship with God is personal experience. He even uses the term "personally" in the short book twenty-eight times and "personal" forty-seven times.[74] Thus his experience is often what he receives as direct and indirect revelation from God Himself. Therefore he assumes and has obtained a standard of intimacy he calls "deep":

> I know it is possible to have an intimate walk with Jesus, because I do. I also know I could go far deeper with Him because I personally know people who have a deeper walk with Him than I do. So don't look at my posts and my life and say to yourself, "that's ok for Matthew to say, but I couldn't ever be as close to Jesus as he is!" No, don't ever think that way.[75]

There are some principles supporting his view that many Christians share. We are able to draw near to God and experience intimacy with Him. God does reveal Himself to us through the Holy Spirit and we can deepen or develop our relationship with Him. And yet, there are other assumed principles that we need to question. Is God giving special revelation to individuals today? If He is, how do we know that He actually is in any given instance? Payne claims that he regularly has conversations not only with Jesus, but with each member of the Trinity, which provide him with a source of knowledge and intimacy. However, can we really distinguish the voices of the Father, Son, and Holy Spirit?[76] Is it legitimate to argue that just because "saints through history have heard Jesus speak to

---

Ultimate Quest to Experience His Presence (Lake Mary, FL: Charisma House, 2007). These Pentecostal experiential works approach intimacy with God with practical tips for prayer, spiritual plateaus, etc. See Muyenza, *Experience the Power of God's Presence*; and Meyer, *Knowing God Intimately*. Muyenza says that his book uses "Scripture and powerful real life examples," which demonstrates his Pentecostal approach that mainly emphasizes the baptism of the Holy Spirit and the sign gifts. David Taylor, *Face-to-face Appearances of Jesus: The Ultimate Intimacy* (Shippensburg, PA: Destiny Image, 2009). Taylor assumes that his own experience of appearances of Jesus to him and seeing him "face-to-face" are normative for believers today. This is supposed to bring prosperity and clear destiny.

73. Matthew Robert Payne, *Finding Intimacy with Jesus Made Simple* (Litchfield, IL: Revival Waves of Glory Books & Publishing, 2016), 196.

74. One can visit his website for a personal prophecy at http://personal-prophecy-today.com.

75. Payne, *Finding Intimacy with Jesus Made Simple*, 182.

76. Ibid., Kindle ed., loc. 548.

them" it is "not a major jump" to hear Jesus speaking to him and that He "longs to speak to you as well."[77] Does Jesus really share "some of His worries and pains" with us?[78] Does Jesus come down to visit us because He said, "And lo I am with you always"?[79] Are we really able to go to heaven and speak with Jesus?[80] Does Jesus bow down with us during a church service and worship His Father with us?[81] Does Jesus come down and ask us to do a waltz with Him down the aisle at church?[82] Do we have visions of visiting Jesus in heaven and have conversations with him in a couple of easy chairs with Him serving us drinks?[83]

Experience is only self-validating. We can't just say, "You didn't experience that," because they will only say, "Yes, I did." We can't just say, "Good for you, even if I don't or won't experience that." We must interpret the experience and question the assumptions behind it based upon sound theology and biblical interpretation. Where do the miraculous experiences of the divine recorded in the Scriptures fit within the totality of God's epic drama? Are they assumed to be normative for every believer for all time?[84] Where do current claims of voices, visitations, and visions fit into God's epic drama? What is the standard for whether an experience is actually from God or from other sources like the subconscious or evil spirits? What position of authority do these experiences have in the believer's life? To accept experiences without question is not wise but foolish and potentially idolatrous.

Another example of the church's need to examine its assumptions concerning intimacy with God, which is far from the previous one, comes from Thomas Keating, who has popularized the centering prayer movement. Keating's ideas are complex and broad, and so I will not be offering a full critique here. While his sincerity or spirituality cannot be questioned, his assumptions should be. He has not only sought to build upon the apophatic foundations of the Catholic mystics of St. John of the Cross and Teresa of Avila, but to wed Christian, secular psychology, and Buddhist philosophies. His epistemology assumes the need to empty oneself of as much sensible information through certain elements of meditation. He and others note that the difference between Buddhist meditation and centering prayer is one of intention. Zen attempts to purify the mind in

77. Payne, *Finding Intimacy with Jesus Made Simple*, loc. 652, 658.
78. Ibid., Loc. 989.
79. Ibid., Loc. 997.
80. Ibid., Loc. 999.
81. Ibid., Loc. 1003.
82. Ibid., Loc. 1012.
83. Ibid., Loc. 1380.
84. Is that the point of Joel 2:28–32 and Acts 2:16–22?

order to achieve enlightenment, whereas his view of prayer is supposedly not an attempt to achieve anything but an openness to God for Him to purify us and bring us into union with Him.[85]

Keating's metaphysical foundation appears at times to blur God's immanence and transcendence, and allows for a certain force or "divine energy" that is either Him or apart from Him. Through centering prayer we release the intuitive power of our human unconscious or higher consciousness "energy centers," similar to the Hindu *prana*. Supposedly we can move toward a pure consciousness. As a result, Keating claims that we need to identify our true self, as opposed to our false self that intrudes into our relationship with God.[86] It appears to Keating that when we search for God, He is already there within us. "We might conceive of God as at our deepest center and our True Self as a circle around it."[87] Yet this raises several questions.

What does he mean by an ensuing "transforming union"? Do we maintain our individuality or are we absorbed into the Divine? Is it truly Christian if, as one reviewer summarizes his approach, it is "a careful balance of both Christian and Buddhist philosophy"?[88] Are his assumptions the same as or different from transcendental meditation? Does our coming into contact with the Divine at the center of our consciousness reduce God to being merely the Immanent One whose transcendence is dissolving?[89] Does this approach have a biblical basis or simply a broader philosophical basis? Is Keating's foundation Scripture rightly interpreted or is it at the disposal of a medieval Catholic, mystical, and possibly gnostic system?

In sum, what should our main concern be with this summary thrust of our assumptions for our intimacy with God? At this point, as with my aerobatic plane ride, we should pause at the magnitude of God Himself and the issues involved with His interacting with us as humans. The gift of our existence and consciousness as His unique creations give us a jaw-dropping and overwhelming overview. There are horizons to our relationship with God we delightfully pursue as the good of this life. We gratefully acknowl-

---

85. John B. Shea, "Centering Prayer and Eastern Meditation," *Catholic Insight* 16, no. 5 (2008): 32.
86. Thomas Keating, *Open Mind, Open Heart* (New York: Continuum, 1986, 1992, 2002), 2.
87. Keating, *Intimacy with God*, 80.
88. "Intimacy with God: An Introduction to Centering Prayer," Book Depository, http://www.bookdepository.com/Intimacy-with-God-Father-Thomas-Keating/9780824525293.
89. Is his consistent emphasis upon uniting our self-consciousness with a God-consciousness the same as Buddhist envelopment into the One? See Murchdahd O'Madagain, *Centering Prayer and the Healing of the Unconscious* (New York: Lantern, 2011).

edge all understanding and the wisdom to navigate our relationship, which He reveals to us foundationally in His holy Scriptures. This can be different than the imbalances of secular individual subjectivity or practical atheism, Charismatic experientialism, and Catholic mysticism. And so we need to do our pre-, mid-, and post-flight study to make sure our bearing, approach, and communication with God are true, honorable, and wise. In our quest for intimacy with Him, we must revel in the scriptural balance of how He relates to us in His immanence and transcendence and how we must always reckon with who He is—the Omnipresent, Omniscient, Condescending One.

NOW WHAT?

1. What strikes you most when reflecting on your own assumptions about intimacy with God? Where do these assumptions come from?

2. What do you think about the fact that our very existence, consciousness, and delights are gifts from God?

3. Where does the theology of your experience of closeness to God come from?

4. What do you think a deep appreciation of God's transcendence, immanence, omniscience, omnipresence, and condescension does for your intimacy with God?

5. What are other positives, concerns, and errors with the assumptions behind the approaches of Payne and Keating?

CHAPTER 3

UNDERSTANDING THE FALL AND INTIMACY WITH GOD

People feel God is distant, far away, absent.

People run from God, are estranged and separated from Him.

People feel God is their enemy, that He hates them.

The challenge of intimacy with God is encapsulated for me in an infamous event in our family. During the course of our children's education, each of them was required to read famous American short stories. One of their least favorites was Sherwood Anderson's "Unlighted Lamps."[1] In it, Anderson depicts a small town in America c. 1908, and the relationship of a father—the town doctor—with his eighteen-year-old daughter. Late on a Sunday afternoon, the girl decided to go for a long walk, thinking about her father's recent comment that he was a victim of heart disease and might die at any moment. Anderson adds:

> With these words the Doctor had turned and walked out of his office, going down a wooden stairway to the street. He had wanted to put his arm about his daughter's shoulder as he talked to her, but never having shown

---

1. Sherwood Anderson, "Unlighted Lamps," in *Great American Short Stories*, eds. Wallace and Mary Stegner (New York: Dell, 1957), 287–308.

any feeling in his relations with her could not sufficiently release some tight thing in himself.[2]

During her walk she reflected on her lack of intimacy with her father. She had no real relationship with him, or with anyone in this small town for that matter. Her father not only buried himself in his work, but was also, obviously, a man closed off to intimate relationships with anyone, which appears to be why his wife had left him years earlier.

Before her return, the daughter and the father on their own determined to reach out to each other. The daughter "resolved that the night should not pass without an effort on her part to make the old dream come true"[3]—the dream of an intimate, loving relationship with her father. At the same time, her father, while on a house call, actually said out loud, "Tonight I'll do it. If it kills me I'll make myself talk to the girl."[4] This promise of resolution is palpable and mutually desirable. The story closes with him ascending to the top of the stairs to find his waiting daughter, but he suddenly then falls backward down the stairs, presumably the result of a heart attack, and dies.

No wonder my children found this story so distasteful. The father and daughter were both finally so close to getting close, yet Anderson leaves us without a happy restoration. Why would someone write such a depressing story?

Sherwood Anderson often contended that not only was small-town Americana extremely romanticized, but its citizens were as well. They were full of flaws and inabilities to cultivate intimate relationships, so flawed that he labeled them "grotesques."[5] And while there is truth in his assessment of early twentieth-century Americana, the Bible clearly declares that every human who has ever lived (and will live) is a grotesque. We sense this malady is evidenced not only in their relationships with each other, but also with God Himself. Ever since Adam and Eve's fateful choice to disobey God, human capacity for intimacy with their good Creator has been deeply

---

2. Ibid., 289.
3. Ibid., 298.
4. Ibid., 302.
5. Anderson develops this theme in his book of short stories *Winesburg, Ohio*, which begins with "The Book of the Grotesque." Sherwood Anderson, *Winesburg, Ohio* (Mineola, NY: Dover, 1995), 1–4. The issue may be pinpointed as, "What the grotesques really need is each other, but their estrangement is so extreme they cannot establish direct ties," https://americanliterature.com/author/sherwood-anderson/book/winesburg-ohio/introduction. See also Judith Arcana, "'Tandy': At the Core of Winesburg," *Studies in Short Fiction* (July 1, 1987): 66–67 for more on his Freudian perspective.

marred. What is the source of these flaws, this estrangement, these barriers? How can we understand them in order to draw near to God? Let's look at the backstory. [6]

Intimacy with God: The Way It Was Supposed to Be

The amazing capacity for intimacy with God begins with His creation. Unlike the father in Anderson's short story, God has always initiated intimacy with humans. In fact, it is a reflection of His very own nature as the Triune God. Creation is not only the act of the God, the Spirit, and His Word (Gen. 1:1–3; John 1:1–3; Col. 1:16–17) as individual members of the Godhead, but also the act of "Us" (Gen. 1:26).[7] This creative interaction has set the pattern for the active relationship God has with us.

God instilled the capacity for intimacy in humans themselves. He made man and woman in His image as the capstone of His creation. The Old Testament scholar Gerhard Von Rad rightly observes that when the text of Genesis 1:26 notes "the announcement of a divine resolution: 'Let us make man.' . . . God participates more intimately and intensively in this than in other works of creation."[8] The resemblance men and women have to God is found at minimum in the companionship and complementarity they have for each other. Hoekema aptly adds, "In this way human beings reflect God, who exists not as a solitary being but as a being in fellowship."[9] The active intention of this is when God shares His dominion over the rest of creation with them. We might wonder whether God and Adam and Eve were intimately discussing the management of His creation during their walks in the garden (Gen. 3:7).

Furthermore, built into the created order is the intimacy of humankind patterned after their Creator. Part of this dominion has been to fulfill the mandate to be fruitful and multiply (Gen. 1:28), an aspect of their one-flesh marriage union (Gen. 2:24). What follows is a simple summary description of their open and safe relationship, "And the man and his wife were both naked and were not ashamed" (Gen. 2:25). This is strategically placed in the narra-

---

6. Some of this chapter may be found in Tim Anderson, "Intimacy with God and the Fall," *Dedicated Journal* (October 2014), https://blogs.corban.edu/ministry/index.php/2014/10/intimacy-with-god-and-the-fall.
7. See Gordon J. Wenham, *Genesis 1–15* (Waco, TX: Word, 1987), for a good summary of the evidence that these first person plural pronouns in Genesis 1 and 3 refer to God as more than one person, as opposed to the "royal 'we,'" or God and angels views.
8. Gerhard Von Rad, *Genesis: A Commentary*, trans. John H. Marks (Philadelphia: Westminster, 1961), 55.
9. Anthony A. Hoekema, *Created in God's Image* (Grand Rapids: Eerdmans, 1986), 14.

tive at the end of their creation in chapter 2 and preceding the description of the fall in chapter 3. It describes the pattern of human intimacy and its subsequent distortion. Thus central to understanding the nature and relationship of God and His creation is the intimacy within the Godhead itself and the profound capacity for human intimacy with God and others.

Universal Estrangement: Not the Way It Was Supposed to Be

This designed capacity for intimacy with God was severed at one moment in history. The fall was the result of the serpent's test and a twist on a basic thesis: honest open sharing with God. The serpent deceived the woman into believing that God indeed had not been sharing everything with them. He was withholding intimate knowledge from them. Why hadn't He allowed them to experience the tree of the knowledge of good and evil? Had God really forbid them, and would He really punish them if they simply enjoyed some of it? It appears at that very moment that Eve was either to trust God because of the intimacy of their relationship up to that point, or go and make a trusting connection of intimacy with God. In other words, why not simply ask Him? But instead, they both rebelled and ate the forbidden fruit.

The consequence of this sin did not bring about "the promise of divine enlightenment." Rather, "mistrust and alienation replaced the security and intimacy they had enjoyed"[10] not only with each other, but also with God Himself. The self-conscious nakedness and inadequate attempt at self-protective covering underscore the destruction of their intimacy. Furthermore, the previous pattern of their walking with God in the garden in the cool of the day (Gen. 3:7) was interrupted forever. God calls for them, asking, "Where are you?" in order to draw them out of their hiding. Universal estrangement had begun.[11] Because they both did not trust in God's revealed law or will concerning the source of wisdom from "the tree of the knowledge of good and evil," the Lord God declared clearly that the consequence would be becoming in a most perverted way "like Us, knowing good and evil" (3:22). It appears, then, that the ban from the Garden (3:22–24), God's rejection of Cain's offering (Gen. 4:5–7), and the wandering of Cain (4:9–16) are some of the examples of this universal estrange-

---

10. Allen P. Ross, *Creation and Blessing: A Guide to the Study and Exposition of Genesis* (Grand Rapids: Baker, 1988), 137.
11. Adam was our representative in the garden, and thus sin, separation, and death came to all humans. See S. Lewis Johnson, "Romans 5:12—An Exercise in Exegesis and Theology," in *New Dimensions in New Testament Study*, eds. Richard N. Longenecker and Merrill C. Tenney (Grand Rapids: Zondervan, 1974), 298–316.

ment playing itself out. The Tower of Babel (Gen. 11:2–4), Jacob's wrestling with God (Gen. 32:24–32), Nadab and Abihu's "strange fire" (Lev. 10:1–3), and Saul's use of a medium (1 Sam. 28:6–7, 16) are just some of the examples strewn along the path of man's vain attempts to restore intimacy with God on their own terms (cf. Rom. 1:21–23).

The apostle Paul personalizes this universal estrangement by describing humanity as God's "enemies" (*echthroi*, Rom. 5:10). The human mind is set on the flesh and practices "enmity" (*echthra*) or open hostility toward God and His will (Rom. 8:7). What concept describes the recalcitrance and relational distance and discord more vividly than this? That is why it is so significant that Christ's atoning sacrifice provides forensic or legally imputed justification to the believing sinner (Rom. 3:24–26; 4:5; 5:1), as well as the complete removal of the boiling wrath with which God reciprocates our enmity. He even replaces it with reconciliation (*katallassō*) (Rom. 5:10–11)! Forensic justification is the foundation for this restored intimacy, because "having been justified by faith we have peace with God through our Lord Jesus Christ" (Rom. 5:1).

CONTINUING BARRIERS OF THE GROTESQUES

We must reckon with the grotesque effects of the fall by examining what the Scriptures reveal about continuing barriers into which humanity continues to run. In light of what we have seen from Adam and Eve, we can be deceived into cultivating illegitimate expectations for intimacy with God. This is reflected in an inability or refusal to take personal responsibility for our movement away from Him. Even feeling close to God may not be genuine, because of unawareness of problems that undermine our relationship with Him. Let's examine some continuing barriers.

Wickedness

Speaking broadly, one of the most heinous and overt detriments to intimacy with God is wickedness. The biblical authors rely on a handful of terms, such as evil (*ra* or *raah*), wrong/offence (*resha*), depravity (*ponēria*), and unrighteousness (*adikia*), to communicate this. Whatever these terms conjure up in our minds, the Bible is clear that these attitudes, actions, and people stand against righteousness. David, in self-defense, quoted this ancient proverb to Saul: "Out of the wicked (*rasha*) comes forth wickedness (*resha*)" (1 Sam. 24:13). God intimately knows human wickedness to the point where the psalmist asks Him to "seek out his wickedness until You find none" (Ps. 10:15).

God will not be close to the wicked and their attitudes and actions. David summarizes the basis of this in Psalm 5:4: "For You are not a God who takes pleasure in wickedness (*resha*), no evil (*ra*) dwells with You." The word for "dwell" (*gur*) indicates that God never entertains evil as a guest in His presence. We see this earlier when the wickedness of the pagan nations caused the Lord to drive them out from the Promised Land from before His people (Deut. 9:4–5; cf. Matt. 13:49). Later, because God's people wickedly trusted in the temple, He declared:

> "But go now to My place which was in Shiloh, where I made My name dwell at the first, and see what I did to it because of the wickedness of My people Israel. And now, because you have done all these things," declares the Lord, "and I spoke to you, rising up early and speaking, but you did not hear, and I called you but you did not answer, therefore, I will do to the house which is called by My name, in which you trust, and to the place which I gave you and your fathers, as I did to Shiloh. I will cast you out of My sight, as I have cast out all your brothers, all the offspring of Ephraim." (Jer. 7:12–15)

Notice His intimate communication and movement toward them, and yet dispersal of them away from His presence because of their wickedness (cf. Hos. 9:15). This is seen in Judas's betrayal of his intimacy with Christ as one of His close followers. His action that began with a false display of intimacy (*katephilēsen*, kiss earnestly) was described as "wickedness" (*adikia*, Acts 1:18), and he was ceremonially buried in a desolate place (1:20). The Lord's appearance will give intimate relief to the afflicted believers, but to those who "took pleasure in wickedness" He will give eternal destruction away from His presence (*adikia*, 2 Thess. 1:6–9; 2:12).

Sadly, God is not only moving away from the wicked, but they are consistently moving away from Him. Psalm 10:3–4 declares:

> For the wicked (*rasha*) boasts of his heart's desire,
> And the greedy man curses and spurns the Lord.
> The wicked, in the haughtiness of his countenance, does not seek Him.
> All his thoughts are, "There is no God."

Notice their spurning of and refusal to seek the Lord. Later the psalmist also states, "He says to himself, 'God has forgotten; He has hidden His face; He will never see it'" (Ps. 10:11).

As a result, wickedness causes people to experience being located in a place of relational distance from the Lord. Proverbs 15:29 declares, "The Lord is far from the wicked, but He hears the prayer of the righteous." These "wicked" are criminally evil (*rasha*).[12] God puts so much mileage between Him and the wicked that He will not hear their voices. The psalmist himself recognizes this simple truth: "If I regard wickedness in my heart, the Lord will not hear me" (Ps. 66:18). Generally, the wicked are unbelievers, since there were "believers" and "unbelievers" in the physical nation of Israel (Rom. 9:6). However, the Lord is not only near to the righteous, but He hears their prayers, and hears them close up, so to speak. Yet as believers, we must grapple with what this implies when we dream or plan evil in our hearts.

The cure for this devastating distance from God is our repudiation of wickedness and delightful movement toward Him. We see this in the psalmist's deep desire to spend one day in the Lord's courts rather than "a thousand outside" and to stand at the threshold of His house rather than to "dwell in the tents of wickedness" (Ps. 84:10). God blesses those who refuse to have intimate counsel with the wicked, but delight in acquiring an intimate knowledge of the Lord's instruction (Ps. 1:1–2). Similarly, Paul admonishes the Corinthians to cleanse the leaven of wickedness from their intimate fellowship with the Lord as their Passover sacrifice (*ponēria*, 1 Cor. 5:8). He also contrasts wicked false teachers with these foundational truths: "The Lord knows those who are His," but also, "Everyone who names the name of the Lord is to abstain from wickedness" (*adikia*, 2 Tim. 2:19). In other words, because of the Lord's intimate knowledge of His people, close identification with Him is inextricably united with abstaining from wickedness.

Worldliness and Satanic Opposition

Two other barriers to intimacy with God appear together in the context of James 4:8, one of the clearest passages exhorting believers to move close to God. James promises, "Draw near to God and He will draw near to you." This command[13] not only describes the privilege of drawing near to God, but our responsibility in it.[14] However, this ability to move toward intimacy with Him is hampered in the context by two roadblocks: worldliness and satanic

---

12. They are known for their evil plans vs. pleasant words (15:26) and their bribery (15:27).
13. *Eggisate*, aorist active imperative.
14. The only means for gaining intimacy with God in this age of salvation history is coming to God through His Son, Jesus Christ. There are several passages in Hebrews where Christ is the means to drawing near to God. Hebrews 4:16; 7:19, 25; and 10:22.

opposition. These Christians are being drawn away by powerful temptations that question their very allegiance to God.

James begins by admonishing them for the source of their worldliness and movement away from God. He says in 4:1–3:

> What is the source of quarrels and conflicts among you? Is not the source your pleasures that wage war in your members? You lust and do not have; so you commit murder. You are envious and cannot obtain; so you fight and quarrel. You do not have because you do not ask. You ask and do not receive, because you ask with wrong motives, so that you may spend it on your pleasures.

In other words, they are selfish, envious, and quarrelsome. Their selfishness causes them see their prayers to Him go unanswered and translates into a loyalty to the values of this present world system. They substitute drawing close in trust to the Creator and Redeemer who satisfies our deepest longings for an intimate friendship[15] with the world and its materialistic offerings.

Like a slap in the face, James sharply warns them that harboring this attitude makes them an unfaithful bride to God and His enemies. "You adulteresses, do you not know that friendship with the world is hostility toward God? Therefore whoever wishes to be a friend of the world makes himself an enemy of God" (4:4–5). Sounding like Jesus, there could be no more horrific and painful image James could use to describe this kind of sinful breach of intimacy with God (cf. Matt. 12:39; Mark 3:38). Peter Davids underscores the church context concerning this "drawing near": "This term normally indicates an activity of worship: All their church's worship is not a coming near, for their community disharmony rooted in preoccupation with worldly success makes it unacceptable."[16] Nevertheless, the cure for this first barrier is plainly given: draw near before God in humble repentance. Yet true repentance asks how the root of our worldliness, our lust for pleasure apart from God, reveals itself in our experience. How does it manifest itself in envy and fighting for what we want and how does that affect our sense of closeness to God? Thoennes summarizes this well: "Worldly lifestyles are antithetical to being God's people and

---

15. See Craig Keener, "Friendship," in *Dictionary of New Testament Backgrounds*, eds. Craig A. Evans and Stanley E. Porter (Downers Grove, IL: IVP, 200), 380–88.

16. Peter H. Davids, *James*, New International Biblical Commentary, 15 (Peabody, MA: Hendrickson, 1989), 102.

the options are not ambiguous."[17] Therefore, only in full disclosure can we draw near to our holy God of grace and mercy.

Yet as if our own worldly cravings are not enough of a challenge, Satan's opposition accompanies the lure of his world system. In verse 7, James exhorts believers to "resist the devil and he will flee from you." This is a forceful call to cease succumbing to Satan's temptations that will separate them from their nearness to God.[18] It is in the very next verse that he then exhorts them to move, to draw near to God. In other words, at the point of our humble repentance from our worldliness and our rejection of Satan's overtures through his earthly system, God will draw near to us. It is as if James was reflecting on Satan's role in the fall of humanity. This Evil One had caused Eve and Adam to doubt their close relationship with God, and uses this same strategy for all believers. We start looking around, thinking, "God must be holding out on me! I don't need to trust him with my desires and needs when I can find them elsewhere!" Voila, estrangement from God is cultivated and birthed! (cf. James 1:14–15). But God has an intimate knowledge of what is best for us in His design.

We cannot solicit the highest bidder for our affections. That is the grievous sin of duplicity or being "double-minded," literally "double-souled" (*dipsuchoi*, cf. James 1:8; 4:8b). We must refuse to listen to the Devil's lies about how to fulfill our desires. So James immediately exhorts the worldly in verses 8b–10:

> Cleanse your hands, you sinners; purify your hearts, you double-minded. Be miserable and mourn and weep; let your laughter be turned to mourning and your joy to gloom. Humble yourselves in the presence of the Lord, and He will exalt you.

Humble repentance assumes spiritual and emotional cleansing needs to take place. God is open to intimacy, but not as a sort of jovial Santa Claus. We must understand the seriousness of our sin and the damage it does to our relationship with God. We must seek to make things right with Him, rather than arrogantly assume He will benignly "forgive and forget" the hurt our unfaithfulness causes Him. Nevertheless, Moo aptly describes this whole

---

17. K. Erik Thoennes, *Godly Jealousy: A Theology of Intolerant Love* (Fearn: Christian Focus, 2005), 125.
18. Douglas J. Moo, *The Letter of James: An Introduction and Commentary*, Tyndale New Testament Commentaries (Grand Rapids: Eerdmans, 1985), 148.

image: "Those who sincerely repent and turn to God will find him, like the father of the prodigal son, eager to receive back his erring children."[19]

Arrogant Self-Sufficiency

A related sinful barrier is the effect arrogant self-sufficiency has on our intimacy with God. This is when His people distance themselves from Him by assuming they do not need His assistance in living a prosperous and safe life. In Psalm 73, Asaph's envy of the proudly wicked around him nearly caused his feet to stumble in His walk with God (v. 3). Yet when he drew close to God in His sanctuary, he saw God's displeasure with the arrogantly self-satisfied (v. 17), who He would ultimately destroy (vv. 17–20). After his transition into reveling in the Lord's presence that satisfies and protects him, Asaph concludes with an overwhelming sense of being in a marvelous place with God:

> Nevertheless I am continually with You;
> You have taken hold of my right hand.
> With Your counsel You will guide me,
> And afterward receive me to glory.
> Whom have I in heaven but You?
> And besides You, I desire nothing on earth.
> My flesh and my heart may fail,
> But God is the strength of my heart and my portion forever.
> For, behold, those who are far from You will perish;
> You have destroyed all those who are unfaithful to You.
> But as for me, the nearness of God is my good;
> I have made the Lord God my refuge,
> That I may tell of all Your works. (vv. 23–28)

He knows his place is "with" Him now and always. God touches his life with His guiding hand that will take him through this life and on to the glory of heaven! How could he arrogantly think that he could navigate paths by providing for his own needs! People who try this are unfaithful and far from God. The good things that sustain him now and forever are indivisibly united to God's nearness.

In Psalm 30, David also recognized his own self-deceived satisfaction that led to his feelings of estrangement from God. He had allowed himself to think

---

19.   Ibid.

he was fully responsible for his safe and prosperous lifestyle in Jerusalem. However, the Lord had allowed it all to be taken away by the insurrection of his own son, Absalom. It took this to bring to light his sin's connection to God's apparent absence.

> Now as for me, I said in my prosperity
> "I will never be moved,"
> O LORD, by Your favor You have made my mountain to stand strong;
> You hid your face, I was dismayed. (vv. 6–7)

He had made the illogical leap to surmise that his prosperity or ease of life (*shalu*) was a sure sign of his enduring and stable rule. The Hebrew term for stability here (*mot*) shows he assumed his lifestyle would not falter, give way, be shaken, or totter and fall. It is because of this faulty assumption that the Lord concealed or covered (*sathar*) His very warm, supportive, and intimate presence. This brought David to a point where he felt his life was in complete ruin and he would be forever separated from God's presence in the pit of death (v. 9). But he remembered that the Lord had touched his soul by loosening his mournful sackcloth and by girding him with gladness (v. 11).

David should have known about this barrier from Saul's life. The infamous sorceress of Endor incident in 1 Samuel 28 is a case when the Lord was deafeningly silent to Saul's self-sufficiency. When the Philistines seemed too great for Saul's armies, his fear and trembling heart initially caused him to seek the Lord's help by "dreams, or by Urim or by prophets" (v. 6). However, the Lord refused to be some sort of genie at his beck and call and refused to answer him (v. 6), so Saul secretly sought out a medium for help (v. 7). The conjured Samuel's incisive question speaks to the heart of Saul's relationship with the Lord: "Why then do you ask me, since the LORD has departed from you and has become your adversary" (v. 16). Arrogance causes us to do outlandish things. The broader context reveals that Saul's lack of closeness with the Lord was in stark contrast to David, "the man after God's own heart" (1 Sam. 13:14).

Through His message to the first-century church at Laodicea, Christ warns all churches concerning this very barrier. Not only were they "lukewarm" or indifferent to Him, they were so because of their arrogant self-sufficiency. "Because you say, 'I am rich, and have become wealthy, and have need of nothing,' and you do not know that you are wretched and miserable and poor and blind and naked" (Rev. 3:17). Christians seem to have a significant struggle with this self-deceptive barrier. For example, these people are very much like the Corinthians who also possessed an inflated sense of superiority and self-sufficiency. Paul, like Christ, confronted their arrogance (*phusioō*), though he did it through a series of very pointed questions: "For who regards you as superior? What do you have that you did not receive? And if you did receive it, why do you boast as if you had not received it?" (1 Cor. 4:7). Then, like Christ, he puts his finger on the problem, which was identical to that of the Laodiceans: "You are already filled, you have already become rich, you have become kings without us" (v. 8a).

Christ presses on to plot a wise course of action (*sumbouleuō*) for the Laodiceans. They must come to Him to purchase imperishable gold to buy their needed clothing and medicine (Rev. 3:18). If they refuse to come repentantly to Him for their needs, He will rebuke and discipline them lovingly (*phileō*, v. 19). Then in one of the most famous verses in the Bible, Christ describes Himself as standing at the intimate location of the portal or door (*thura*) to their church, knocking in order to be heard and to gain entrance into restored close fellowship with them. We need to picture in our minds Jesus Christ's stunning gesture: "Behold, I stand at the door and knock; if anyone hears My voice and opens the door, I will come in to him and will dine with him, and he with Me" (v. 20). It will be more than worth it for us to allow Him in. Out of His desire for intimacy He promises them that, if they overcome this temptation to arrogant self-sufficiency, He will grant them the place of honor and closeness with Him and His Father: "He who overcomes, I will grant to him to sit down with Me on My throne, as I also overcame and sat down with My Father on His throne" (v. 21). What an incredible reward to sit down with Christ on the very throne that was the very reward for His own perseverance toward and through the cross!

So we must remember that taking on an arrogant self-sufficient attitude is characteristic of the wicked (cf. Ps. 10:1, 6), seen even in Ahab and his quest for the white whale. We are assuming that we are ultimately responsible for any successes we have, or perhaps that we cannot be moved from our stable position in any aspect of life (cf. James 4:13–17). In so doing we move away from the Lord, Who takes this as a show of contempt, spurning Him and His gracious presence (Ps. 10:3). He then blocks not only our ability to see Him and to enjoy His gracious presence, but also withdraws His blessing of personal peace and stability.

Distraction

As heavy as these barriers are, it should not be surprising that often our own distraction is a cause as well. The familiar account of Mary, Martha, and

Jesus in Luke 10:38–42 is a poignant example. Martha welcomed Jesus into her home, but became distracted with her customary hostess preparations and became worried and bothered.[20] Mary was in the deeply humble and intimate position of sitting at Jesus's feet, as a disciple absorbing His teachings.[21] Yet Martha's distraction over a worthy activity caused her to miss a marvelous opportunity simply to be with the Lord. It actually drove her to resentment rather than reclining in the Lord's very presence. She even blamed Jesus for allowing such a situation to arise when she exclaimed, "Lord, don't you care that my sister has left me to do all the serving alone? Tell her to help me" (v. 40). Jesus is not drawn into Martha's distraction, but simply states, "Mary has chosen the good part." He affirms her choice to spend time with Him when she could have been drawn away from a time of closeness with Him.

Drowsiness can be a distraction from intimacy with the Lord. When He was going to empty His heart out to His Father about His impending assassination in the garden of Gethsemene (meaning "olive press"), He brought Peter, James, and John to a more intimate place nearby. However, they missed sharing in one of the most personal moments with Him three times, because they would not wake up and be watchful (*gregoreō*) even after He had chided them (Matt. 26:38; Mark 14:34). Similarly, Paul encourages the Colossians to devote themselves to prayer, "keeping alert (*gregoreō*) in it with an attitude of thanksgiving" (Col. 4:2). He exhorts the Thessalonians not to sleep— in other words, not to be distracted by the sinful nighttime activities of the world— but to "be alert and sober" (1 Thess. 5:6). Why? Because the Lord will come to them like a thief in the night (v. 2). He does add that because Christ died for us, "whether we are awake or asleep, we will live together with Him" (v. 10). Peter calls persecuted believers to "be on the alert," because the devil, like a roaring lion, wants to distract them from humbling themselves under the mighty hand of God that will exalt them at the time He deems proper (1 Peter 5:6–8). Christ arouses the church in Sardis (Rev. 3:2), whose people were so distracted from walking with Christ (v. 4), they were like the walking dead amidst their churchly activities (v. 1). Lenski illustrates their condition this way: "Sardis is like a leaking, sinking ship, in which captain and crew are

---

20. Charles Simeon had a good turn of phrase for this, "unseasonably anxious." *Horae Homileticae: Mark–Luke* (vol. 12; London: Holdsworth and Ball, 1832), 427.

21. "Mary's posture and eagerness to absorb Jesus's teaching at the expense of a more traditional womanly role (10:40) would have shocked most Jewish men" and maybe Martha as well. Craig S. Keener, *The IVP Bible Background Commentary: New Testament* (Downers Grove, IL: InterVarsity, 1993), Luke 10:39.

sunk in dull lethargy. They must wake up to the situation and thus must take measures to save the ship."[22] If they do wake up, Christ will return to them like a thief and will not blot out their name from the book of life (v. 5). They could lose their earthly reputation as a living church, which will bring regret to them in heaven (v. 5).[23]

Many of us get distracted by Christian activities and worldly enticements, and then ask, "Where's God?" Like being in an inner tube at the beach, the joy of floating in the water distracts us from our inability to swim against such a strong current and the wisdom of staying close to the shore. Relaxing in the sun and being lulled into a sleepy distraction finally brings drifting, and the shore is no longer visible. Like Martha and the people in these New Testament churches, we must not allow ourselves to become distracted and drift away from an intimate place at our Lord's feet, hearing His voice, and sharing all things personal with Him. We could find ourselves even amusing ourselves to death.[24]

Fear and Hiding

Fear is one of the most significant barriers to feeling close to God. It is true that we are to have a deep sense of fear of and respect for the Lord (Ps. 90:11; Prov. 1:7; 9:10; Eccl. 12:13; 2 Cor. 5:11; Eph. 5:21; 1 Peter 2:17; Rev. 14:7), and sinners must fear the danger of God's judgment (Ps. 119:120; Luke 12:5; Heb. 10:27, 31, 39). This does not mean we should have an unhealthy

---

22. R. C. H. Lenski, *The Interpretation of St. John's Revelation* (Columbus, OH: Lutheran Book Concern, 1935), 128.

23. It is inadequate to claim that Christ's promise to "not blot out his name from the book of life" as a loss of salvation (Rev. 3:5). Therefore, many take this as a *litotes* figure of speech, with Christ stating the negative to underscore asserting the positive. In other words, the overcomer will definitely have their name in the book of life. Fuller's loss of the reward of a good name/reputation upon entering heaven is a possible solution to a complex statement. To him,

> it is best understood not in soteriological terms but in the sense of promising the preservation of more than the faithful Christian's eternal existence: It promises a unique and honorable eternal identity. The unfaithful Christian, conversely, will find that even as he on earth was ashamed of Christ's *onoma*, Christ will in heaven be ashamed of his (Matt. 10:33; 2 Tim. 2:12). It is this promise and threat that makes endurance through the kinds of trials and temptations catalogued in Revelation 2–3 conceivable.

This is representative of the rewards theology from Dallas Seminary in the 1980s. J. William Fuller, "'I Will Not Erase His Name from the Book of Life' (Revelation 3:5)," *Journal of the Evangelical Theological Society* 26, no. 3 (1983): 306.

24. Neil Postman, *Amusing Ourselves to Death: Public Discourse in the Age of Show Business* (New York: Penguin, 1985).

anxiety born out of a fear of God's rejection or judgment. He provides something different.[25] Yet we all have had this emotional response to the possibility of the loss of acceptance, and the accompanying sense of unworthiness.

Fear can immobilize us. As close as the disciples were to Jesus, they had a fear of moving toward intimate knowledge with Him. After healing a man's demon-possessed son, and while everyone was amazed at God's greatness, Jesus pulled His men aside and said, "Let these words sink into your ears; for the Son of Man is going to be delivered into the hands of men" (Luke 9:44). Yet it is clear that they just did not comprehend, because Luke records, "But they did not understand this statement, and it was concealed from them so that they would not perceive it; and they were afraid to ask Him about this statement" (Luke 9:45; cf. Mark 9:32). They were fearful of pursuing the significance of this profound statement any further. Maybe they were afraid of sounding or looking foolish. Maybe they thought they should have known. Regardless, to ask Jesus was to risk losing acceptance and worthiness in His eyes, and possibly in the others' eyes. Nevertheless, even if it wasn't clear or revealed by the Holy Spirit at that time, asking for intimate knowledge from the Lord is not a sin. He may or may not choose to reveal personal information to His people. And yet, if we are impertinent and disrespectful in our requests, that kind of questioning doesn't deserve an answer.

Fear can come from interacting with a caricature of God rather than with who He really is. Jesus addressed this in the parable of the minas in Luke 19 and talents in Matthew 25. Because the Jews thought the kingdom of God

---

25. There is a striking and yet comforting pattern in the Scriptures where numerous times, the Lord has to tell people not to fear Him when they are in His presence. An immediate reaction to being confronted with the Creator God is overwhelming awe and worship. However, with this display, the Lord draws people back away from fear and into intimacy with Him. The Lord told Abraham not to fear when He came to promise Him a son (Gen. 15:l). When the Lord appeared to Isaac in order to confirm His blessing, He declared, "I am the God of your father Abraham; Do not fear, for I am with you" (Gen. 26:24). When the Israelites trembled at the Lord's revelation of Himself on Mount Sinai, Moses told them not to be afraid, because God had come to test them, and so that they remained fearful of Him (Exod. 20:20). When Gideon saw the angel of the Lord "face to face," the Lord Himself said, "Peace to you, do not fear; you shall not die" (Judg. 6:23). Jesus Himself had to instruct His disciples not to be afraid of Him. When He was walking on water, Jesus told His disciples, who thought He was a ghost, not to be afraid (Matt. 14:27; John 6:20). Jesus told Peter, James, and John not to be afraid after all they had just witnessed at His glorious transfiguration (Matt. 17:7). At His postresurrection appearance, Jesus told His disciples not to be afraid, since they had clung to His feet in worship (Matt. 28:10). Finally, when John had become like a dead man after a vision of the high priestly Jesus Christ, He intimately placed His right hand on him and said, "Do not be afraid" (Rev. 1:17).

would appear immediately (Luke 19:11), Jesus used these parables to encourage them to work faithfully until the kingdom comes. However, they behaved like the foolish slave and were burying the wealth the Master had entrusted to them. Why? Jesus indicates it was because they viewed God as a harsh Master. This slave's excuse for hiding the money in the ground (cf. Matt. 25:25) was simply, "I was afraid of you, because you are an exacting man; you take up what you did not lay down and reap what you did not sow" (19:21). There obviously is no intimacy here. Jesus simply indicated that the slave was afraid of his master. Was he afraid of failing his Master and His ensuing judgment? Was he unnecessarily intimidated by Him and by His stature? Yet the Master was encouraging ("Well done"), fair ("faithful in little, faithful in much"), and generous ("authority over ten cities"). Unlike Zaccheus in the previous verses who repaid his defrauding four times over (Luke 19:8), these fearfully paralyzed people hoarded rather than invested. Paul clearly delineates the drastic difference in Romans 8:15, "For you have not received a spirit of slavery leading to fear again, but you have received a spirit of adoption as sons by which we cry out, 'Abba! Father!'" (cf. Gal. 4:6). The spirit or mindset of a slave is to be afraid of their Master. However, salvation in Christ Jesus not only makes us right with God, but He adopts us as His own children! There is no fear here. Jesus would say to us, "I am sad when you do not believe that I have totally forgiven you or you feel uncomfortable approaching me."[26]

Blessedly, fear is banished by the reality of God's love. In one of the Bible's most significant passages concerning the Christian's confidence before God, John declares in 1 John 4:17–18 the black-and-white contrast between love and fear:

> By this, love is perfected with us, so that we may have confidence in the day of judgment; because as He is, so also are we in this world. There is no fear in love; but perfect love casts out fear, because fear involves punishment, and the one who fears is not perfected in love.

His contrast is meant to bring assurance to believers who were being tempted by false teachers to join their "true fellowship." So in verse 15 he reminds them that God abides in them and they abide in God. The term "abide," from the present tense of *menō*, may be unfamiliar to many today, but it simply means to stay, remain, live, or continue. *The Message* translation of verse

---

26. Brennan Manning, *The Ragamuffin Gospel: Embracing the Unconditional Love of God* (Sisters, OR: Multnomah, 1990), 154.

15 captures the continuous nature of this abiding: "Everyone who confesses that Jesus is God's Son participates continuously in an intimate relationship with God."[27] John inextricably unites this abiding to God's love in the next verse. True Christians know and trust the God who is love, and consciously remain in His love (v. 16). Our "confidence in the day of judgment" stems from this love being "perfected with us" (v. 17). "Perfected," from *teleioō*, means that it reaches its end or goal. When we experience God's love in this way, this love is brought into action toward Him and others (4:12, 19–21). John then declares that the antithesis of fear is love, as oil is for water. Phillips' translation draws out the nuances of this crippling fear: "Love contains no fear—indeed fully-developed love expels every particle of fear, for fear always contains some of the torture of feeling guilty. This means that the man who lives in fear has not yet had his love perfected." Here *phobos* or fear is a dread or angst,[28] which makes us servile and self-protective (cf. John 19:38; 20:19).[29] And yet abiding in God's love and living it out drives away (*exō ballei*) the gnawing fear of His rejection, disdain, and punishment for any and every sin that we know that He knows we commit. "His love ensures that we are saved, not punished."[30] We must revel in His love, forgiveness, and cleansing (1 John 1:9; 3:1). Though we may struggle with these illegitimate fearful feelings of God's damning rejection, we are still to come near to Him who loved us first and always.[31]

This barrier of fear is often associated with hiding from God. The fear we have been discussing causes withdrawal, evasion, and even flight from intimacy.[32] Christian psychologist John Townsend identifies two kinds of harm-

---

27. Also helpful is the *Good News Translation*, which renders verse 15, "If we declare that Jesus is the Son of God, we live in union with God and God lives in union with us." Andrew Murray lamented that many Christians, while trusting in their Savior and seeking to obey Him, "have hardly realized to what closeness of union, to what intimacy of fellowship, to what wondrous oneness of life and interest" the Lord Jesus has invited them. Andrew Murray, *Abide in Christ* (Springdale, PA: Whitaker House, 1979), 5.

28. *Phobos* here is similar to *deilia*. Daniel L. Akin, *1, 2, 3 John*, The New American Commentary, 38 (Nashville: Broadman & Holman, 2001), 186.

29. Stephen S. Smalley, *1, 2, 3 John*, Word Biblical Commentary, 51 (Waco: Word, 1984), 260.

30. Leon L. Morris, "1 John," in *New Bible Commentary: 21st Century Edition*, eds. D. A. Carson, et al., 4th ed. (Leicester/Downers Grove, IL: Inter-Varsity, 1994), 1407.

31. Even Moses told the people of Israel, "For I was afraid of the anger and hot displeasure with which the Lord was wrathful against you in order to destroy you, but the Lord listened to me that time also" (Deut. 9:19).

32. Plantinga argues that the sin of flight is the avoidance of our responsibility to God and others within the context of shalom, the peace, wholeness, and blessing that only comes from Him. Cornelius Plantinga Jr., *Not the Way It's Supposed to Be: A Breviary of Sin* (Grand Rapids: Eerdmans, 1995), 194–95.

ful hiding styles: internal and relational.[33] While he demonstrates how these manifest themselves in human relationships, we can easily see how they affect intimacy with God. On the one hand, internal hiding is avoiding painful internal feelings, thoughts, and memories concerning God and ourselves. We may hide from the reality of who we really are by idealizing ourselves, viewing ourselves in the best light possible. We may hide by projecting the bad parts of ourselves onto God or others, by being hostile toward Him, or by divorcing ourselves from closeness to Him. We may hide by devaluing intimacy with God by pretending He doesn't exist or is only for a special few. On the other hand, relational hiding is a pattern of relating to God by protecting ourselves from the perceived threat He may pose to us. We approach God by being defensive, superficial, or resentful. We may even avoid Him, retain a hostile distance from Him, alienate ourselves from Him, or substitute an activity or substance in place of Him. When the idea of intimacy with God comes to us, we can become like defensive porcupines or like the spouse who hides behind the newspaper or the television because of their fear of exposing something that could bring emotional discomfort or pain. Tragically, the fruit of this hiding is isolation.[34]

The Scriptures reveal a major motivation behind hiding in fear of facing the truth. Jesus described the world's judgment to Nicodemus not only as being a result of evil deeds and hatred of the Light, but he also states that this person "does not come to the Light for fear that his deeds will be exposed" (John 3:20). Even though the word "fear" is not used in the Greek text, the construction *mē* with the verb "exposed" (*elegchō*) denotes this person is fearful of the shame resulting from being convicted of a crime. Like roaches that flee when the light is turned on in the kitchen, humans hide from the Light that reveals God's truth and holiness and the contrasting evil. This is exactly what happened in the garden. Consider Genesis 3:8: "They heard the sound of the Lord God walking in the garden in the cool of the day, and the man and his wife hid themselves from the presence of the Lord God among the trees of the garden." When questioned about this, Adam's relational hiding revealed his internal hiding. "He [Adam] said, 'I heard the sound of You in the garden, and I was afraid because I was naked; so I hid myself'" (3:10). Isaiah expressed this movement away from God when he prophesied, "Woe to those who deeply hide their plans from the Lord, And whose deeds are done in a dark place, And they say, 'Who sees us?' or 'Who knows us?'" (Isa. 29:15). However, actual hiding is not possible. Jeremiah

---

33. John Townsend, *Hiding from Love* (Grand Rapids: Zondervan, 1991), 196–213.
34. Ibid., 149.

recorded the Lord saying, "Can a man hide himself in hiding places so I do not see him? . . . Do I not fill the heavens and the earth?" (Jer. 23:24; cf. 16:17). His judgment will soon follow those who try to hide from Him. The Lord said to Amos, "Though they hide on the summit of Carmel, I will search them out and take them from there; And though they conceal themselves from My sight on the floor of the sea, From there I will command the serpent and it will bite them" (Amos 9:3). One day, all hiders will be judged despite their refusal to repent: "and they said to the mountains and to the rocks, 'Fall on us and hide us from the presence of Him who sits on the throne, and from the wrath of the Lamb" (Rev. 6:16).

CONCLUSION

It should be clear that humans truly are grotesques—to harken back to Sherwood Anderson's literary theme. We are broken, and things are not as they should be. And yet we are fully culpable for cultivating our estrangement from God. It is as if the magnetic pull of our hearts and minds is reversed to God's polarity too often.

At the same time, reckoning with the radical effects of the fall of humanity does not legitimate expectations for easy, long-lasting and unassailable intimacy with God. One might wonder if ideas in our culture about storybook romances and an unrealistic fantasy of living happily ever after have helped, in part, to create an inability to take personal responsibility for human movement away from God. In his incisive study, Thomas Bergler describes an aspect of the typical middle-class American church as having worship services where

> the congregation sings top-forty-style songs addressed to God and heavily peppered with the words "I," "you," and "love." In the sermon, the pastor may talk about "falling in love with Jesus." With or without the romantic analogy, the preacher will spend a lot of time on the topic of God's love. Even in theologically conservative churches, you won't hear much about guilt, suffering or judgment.[35]

This can lead to fleeting feelings of a sort of intimacy with God that are not based in repentant obedient trust in the holy Creator and Redeemer, but in a form of adolescent idolatry and self-deception. We may one day find ourselves

---

35. Thomas E. Bergler, *The Juvenilization of American Christianity* (Grand Rapids: Eerdmans, 2012), 1.

looking at our "relationship" with God and discovering that He hasn't delivered what we expected, and allow Him just to exist but nothing more. Some may even "break up" with Him.

Nevertheless, we are not without hope. James's words continue to call us to "draw near to God" in humble repentance with the promise that He will draw near to us. Our calling from God is to trust and obey and to be loyal to Him as our Savior and Master. He is proven and trustworthy. In this damaged era preceding the return of Christ, He ever invites us to experience true intimacy with Him. It is part of our calling as His servants and children to respond. We can enjoy the closeness of His presence. We can experience communication with Him and hear His voice through His Word prompted by His Spirit. We can see His face and sense the lifting of His countenance as we recount His promises and celebrate His blessings. We can know His care as we feel His hand of blessing and deliverance. The fall can never fully separate us from God. May we draw near to Him with hearts like these prayers of our Puritan forefathers, who struggled with the same barriers we do:

> My soul is often a chariot without wheels,
> clogged and hindered in sin's miry clay;
> Mount it on eagle's wings and cause it to soar upward to thyself.[36]

> When I am tempted to think highly of myself,
> Grant me to see the wily power of my spiritual enemy;
> Help me to stand with a wary eye on the watch-tower of faith,
> And to cling with determined grasp to my humble Lord;
> If I fall let me hide myself in my redeemer's righteousness,
> And when I escape, may I ascribe all deliverance to thy grace.
> Keep me humble, meek, lowly.[37]

---

36. Arthur Bennett, ed., *The Valley of Vision: A Collection of Puritan Prayers and Devotions* (Carlisle, PA: The Banner of Truth Trust, 1975), 90.
37. Ibid., 88.

NOW WHAT?

1. How does your search for pleasure show itself in disloyalty to God?

2. How do your specific issues with selfishness, envy, and/or quarreling affect your sense of closeness to God?

3. Write out things you think God wants to hear from you, according to James 4:1–11.

4. What are the lies and temptations that Satan places before you that destroy your intimacy with God?

5. Write out some things that the humble repentance of James 4:8–10 would look and sound like toward God.

6. Where do you find yourself being most self-sufficient? How have you trusted in your own resources like Saul?

7. How do you think your self-sufficiency makes God feel?

8. What do you need to tell the Lord in order to restore your closeness to Him?

9. What is your major source(s) of distraction that draw(s) you away from closeness to God?

10. How can you turn those moments into opportunities for intimacy with God?

CHAPTER 4

INTERPRETING BIBLICAL SYMBOLS FOR GOD'S COMMUNICATION OF INTIMACY

Most of us have seen the most famous depictions of God in art, Michel-angelo's paintings in the Sistine Chapel (1508–1512). The preeminent work is his fresco or panel of the *Creation of Adam*. Here God, gray-haired and yet powerful, extends His bare mighty right arm and index finger to impart life to the naked Adam's passively extended left finger. Yet it is possible that Michelangelo did not only anthropomorphize God by giving Him a human-like body. Researchers into the *Creation of Adam*[1] and the *Separation of Light and Darkness*[2] are providing evidence that he concealed anatomical images of the human brain in and around God.[3] While the intent behind his enhancing the meaning of these images of God is not altogether clear,[4] they probably

---

1. F. L. Meshberger, "An Interpretation of Michelangelo's Creation of Adam based on Neuroanatomy," *Journal of the American Medical Association* 264, no. 14 (1990): 1837–41.
2. Ian Suk and Rafael J. Tamargo, "Concealed Neuroanatomy in Michelangelo's Separation of Light From Darkness in the Sistine Chapel," *Neurosurgery* 66, no. 5 (2010): 851–61.
3. This should not be too surprising, since Michelangelo was known to be a master of anatomy as well as art, due to his vast experience of dissecting cadavers.
4. For a couple of tentative suggestions, see Douglas R. Fields, "Michelangelo's Secret Message

"celebrate the glory of God and that of His most magnificent creation."[5] The more important issue is that when we allow ourselves to be drawn into these depictions of our Creator God, we experience more than words can effectively communicate. In this chapter we will explore the amazingly beautiful and sensory-rich arena of the figures of speech, that is, anthropomorphisms, used by the biblical writers to express intimacy with God. We will see and feel the symbols of God's face, eyes, hands, and ears, and how we are to interpret them. This will help us be able to experience how the Bible communicates God's intimate movement, knowledge, place, and touch with meaningful language outside of propositional statements.

We could jump right in to examining the depictions of God with human features, but that would be ill-advised. The long history of scholarly research that exists on the Bible's anthropomorphisms demands that we recognize our present interpretive assumptions and pursue a consistent and balanced and thus robust approach. In fact, there are at least four basic approaches that are born out of significant motivations and correctives. Understanding them will help us to better observe typologies and purposes in this figurative language of God and how it can communicate His closeness to us in ways unique to it.

First, some approach divine anthropomorphisms with extreme caution. Generally, they explain away or reject these images out of a reaction to a literalism and an underlying misunderstanding of God Himself. As a result there is almost a reluctance to accept this kind of language for God exists in the Bible. Some Christians today find it is often easier to skip over these images than to experience them. The early church set the pattern for approaching these metaphors with extreme caution.[6] In light of their culture, they were already critical of the highly anthropomorphic depictions of the gods in Greek mythology. As a result, they struggled with a literal reading of Scripture. Origen and those in his tradition did not want believers to fall into idolatry by attributing physical attributes to the transcendent One. Rather, Scripture should be interpreted theologically, that is, in a way "fitting to" or "worthy of" God. Christians should discover the meaning of difficult anthropomorphic or

---

in the Sistine Chapel: A Juxtaposition of God and the Human Brain," *Scientific American*, May 27 (2010), https://blogs.scientificamerican.com/guest-blog/michelangelos-secret-message-in-the-sistine-chapel-a-juxtaposition-of-god-and-the-human-brain.

5. Suk and Tamargo, "Concealed Neuroanatomy in Michelangelo's Separation of Light from Darkness in the Sistine Chapel," 859.

6. I am indebted to Sheridan's exposition of the patristic period's views on anthropomorphism. Mark Sheridan, *Language for God in Patristic Tradition: Wrestling with Biblical Anthropomorphism* (Downers Grove, IL: IVP, 2015), 18–20.

anthropopathic (human emotions) references in the Bible from other scriptural teachings. The pattern is set by the Bible itself in Numbers 23:19, which declares, "God is not like a man." Thus the metaphors do not reveal an exact reality about God,[7] only that He is accommodating Himself, like a Father talking to his young children. So, for example, these biblical scholars excluded most anthropomorphisms and problem texts that refer to God's anger, in light of their understanding of God's love, especially as it is revealed in Jesus Christ.

Those who follow the classic theistic view of Aquinas and others that God is immaterial and immutable, and thus cannot be embodied, argue that language about God necessarily communicates analogies.[8] At first glance, this seems justifiable. Yet Hamori argues that, as a result, this has led a great deal of biblical scholars to view anthropomorphisms in an all-or-nothing way. Either these biblical references do not contain anthropomorphic portrayals of God (but angels, men, or intentionally mysterious concepts), or they are anthropomorphic portrayals and are thus theologically unsophisticated and not worth the time or reflection. This view can simply be regarded as an unjustifiable naturalism or at least a tragic underestimation of these figures of speech.[9]

It is true that God's accommodation in communicating Himself to humans must not be taken too far. Poythress rightly argues that accommodation does *not* mean "God tolerated a process in which human writers of Scripture would include in their writings erroneous conceptions of their time, in order to serve a higher theological purpose."[10] In other words, God intended to use anthropomorphisms to communicate profound truths about Himself. Poythress is also correct in recognizing that when we infer that God communicates to us like a human father, this does not frustrate His ability to use anthropomorphisms to communicate exactly what He wants.[11] So if God's

---

7. Bultmann rejected biblical anthropomorphisms for his demythologization agenda. Rudolf Bultmann, *Jesus Christ and Mythology* (New York: Scribner, 1958), 18.

8. This thinking was established through Maimonides and on to Aquinas to the present. Cf. Esther J. Hamori, *"When Gods Were Men": The Embodied God in Biblical and Near Eastern Literature* (Berlin: W. de Gruyter, 2008), 39–41.

9. For more on the modern and recent history of the interpretation of divine anthropomorphisms, especially in the Pentateuch, see Anne K. Knafl, *Forming God: Divine Anthropomorphisms in the Pentateuch* (Winona Lake, IN: Eisenbrauns, 2014), 6–12.

10. Vern Poythress, "Rethinking Accommodation in Revelation," *Westminster Theological Journal* 76 (2014): 145.

11. "We infer that God is like a human father, and so he is hemmed in, against his will, by the circumstances and the limits of human capacities. But that is not correct. God is not limited like a human father, because he creates all the 'circumstances,' according to the doctrine of creation. Sin violates God's order, to be sure, but it is an intruder. In the original situation

intentionality lies behind these images, we must pursue hearing His voice and seeing Him in these unique ways.

Second, others view biblical anthropomorphisms as mere figures of speech that are quickly reduced to a descriptive statement. God's hand is simply His omnipotence, God's eyes are His omniscience, and so on. There is a certain practical benefit to this method in that we can summarize the truth being communicated. However, this view truncates the intent in and behind the choice of this literary device. Poythress is right that God or the scriptural writers could have expressed similar truths in other ways without the use of vivid metaphors. For example, as an alternative to God's striking His enemies with His mighty hand, we could say, "The Lord exercises his power to defeat the enemy utterly."[12] As helpful as this is, we cannot necessarily say that is the only or even the main concept that the anthropomorphism is intended to communicate. This approach doesn't tell us what the author wants the reader to experience as a result of using the figure of speech.

A third perspective of divine anthropomorphisms uses an open approach. It begins by assuming that if the biblical writers used these figures of speech, so can we. We can describe God with any figurative language that suits our purpose. Open Theism refuses to limit God to a static and emotionless Being supposedly found in classic Aquinas and Calvinism, even though this portrayal is more of an unfortunate caricature, like a political cartoon. Thus God changes His mind like the Bible says He does (Exod. 32:14; Judg. 2:18; 1 Sam. 15:11, 35; 2 Sam. 24:16; 1 Chron. 21:15; Jer. 15:6; 18:8–10; 26:3, 13, 19; 42:10; Joel 2:13–14; Amos 7:3, 6; Jon. 3:9–10). However, the term *nacham*— that is, to change one's mind, to relent, to be sorry, or to repent—is not a change in God's knowledge, plan, or nature, but simply His relational response to humans (Num. 23:19; 1 Sam. 15:29; Jer. 4:28).

William Young's *The Shack* is also a very popular example of an open approach to divine anthropomorphisms.[13] In this work of fiction, Young creatively has God revealing Himself as a Trinity to Mack, the protagonist. However, Young chooses to portray God the Father as a large black woman name Papa. In fact, he has Mack asking Jesus in shock and disbelief, "Am I

---

of creation, man as a creature cannot 'frustrate' God's desire to communicate, because God created man and is completely in charge." Poythress, "Rethinking Accommodation in Revelation," 148.

12. Ibid., 150.
13. Stoyan Zaimov, "'The Shack' Book Sales Soar, Tops Best-Seller Lists Despite Controversy," Christian Post, March 23, 2017, http://www.christianpost.com/news/the-shack-book-sales-soar-tops-best-seller-lists-despite-controversy-178435.

going crazy? Am I supposed to believe that God is a big black woman with a questionable sense of humor?"[14] The purpose behind this open approach to the figure of God as father is that Papa needed to be the father Mack never had.[15] Thus God is not and cannot be condemning. This may be helpful to some in their initial encounter with the God of the Bible. Nevertheless, we must be very careful not to ignore or replace God as Father as part of the Bible's overall teaching simply because it might be offensive. We must grasp this anthropomorphism's intent and biblical context to make sure such an important image of God is part of our understanding and experience of Him. Is God the Father only for us to know God's love and softness? What about His discipline? Furthermore, the Holy Spirit is depicted as a small distinctively Asian woman.[16] While we may appreciate Young's multiethnic Trinity that has feminine attributes, there is little, if any, precedent for this from a biblical perspective. There is a reason why the Holy Spirit is a person, and yet never anthropomorphized with a body in the Bible. The transcendent nature of God as Spirit is invisible, incomprehensible, and mysterious,[17] and so other metaphors are used (esp. wind and breath). At the same time, in Young's book Jesus is depicted as a relatable yet strapping Middle Eastern man[18] paralleled in the Gospels. "Papa" instructs Mack that, "The Bible doesn't teach you to follow rules. It is a picture of Jesus."[19] While true, this is reductionistic. The book of Acts, the Epistles and Revelation interact with Him as the exalted post-resurrection Jesus Christ the Lord who is worthy of our worship and submission (e.g., Acts 7:55–56; 9:1–20; 28:31; 1 Cor. 15:24–25; Eph. 1:20–23; Phil. 2:9–11; 2 Peter 1:16–18; 3:10; Rev. 1:12–17; 19:11–16). In short, this open approach to divine anthropomorphisms can be helpful,[20] yet minimalistic, distracting, and even idolatrous.

I advocate a fourth approach, which emphasizes the linguistic and existential elements of anthropomorphisms. This doesn't mean that we should

---

14. William P. Young, *The Shack* (Newbury Park, CA: Windblown Media, 2007), 88–89.
15. Ibid., 92.
16. Ibid., 84.
17. Graham Cole, *He Who Gives Life: The Doctrine of the Holy Spirit* (Wheaton, IL: Crossway, 2007), 46. For other implications of God as Spirit, see Feinberg, *No One Like Him*, 223–24.
18. Young, *The Shack*, 85–86.
19. Ibid., 197.
20. Young's open approach can have Jesus make claims that if untethered to a more substantial biblical theology, can lead to a sentimental standardless Christianity. For example, Jesus declares, "My ability to communicate is limitless, living and transforming, and it will always be tuned to Papa's goodness and love. And you will hear and see me in the Bible in fresh ways. Just don't look for rules and principles; look for relationship—a way of coming to be with us." Ibid., 198.

ignore the implications of the other approaches. We should be cautious about
how literally we interpret them, yet we may draw timeless theological truths
from them, and we may cautiously use contemporary metaphorical language
for God today. Understanding them linguistically and existentially refines
our approach and helps us to avoid viewing them with a naïve literalism or
as dispensable metaphors which we can simply substitute with other words
or phrases to arrive at the same meaning.[21] Therefore, first, we must assume
these images are indispensable to our understanding and experiencing of
God's actions and attitudes.[22] Because He is transcendent, holy, beautiful,
and awe-inspiring, experiencing what is beyond our words to express does
not come to us as finite creatures without some sort of translation or media-
tion. God and the biblical writers intentionally communicate with figurative
language.[23] This is like that (but not completely). This is as if it is that (but not
completely). More specifically, the human body, senses, and personality are
the objects with which we have the most direct, firsthand acquaintance. Thus,
the principle of proceeding from the known to the unknown makes it natural
for us as human beings to see the rest of the world in light of that experience,
and so the Bible uses these analogies because they are vivid and powerful
paths to our imagination,[24] because they have a "familiar feel."[25] Like gestures
or art, they often make comparisons to what we as humans perceive, sense,
feel, or value, and to activities and their results.[26] They often do this by getting
us to identify something tangible in our world, in this case the human body,
with God Himself.[27]

Second, these anthropomorphisms commit us to certain attitudes and
actions toward God. When He and the biblical authors communicate with

---

21. D. Michael Cox, "Neither Literal nor Metaphorical: Divine Body Traditions, Indispensible
    Pictures, and Wittgensteinian 'Secondary Sense'," *Modern Theology* 31, no. 3 (2015): 467.
22. G. B. Caird, *The Language and Imagery of the Bible* (London: Duckworth, 1980), 176.
23. Cox argues for the intentionality of God and the writers incisively. "To the believer, then,
    the emergence of this mystical language owes not simply to the unaided genius of the
    poetic imagination, but to the divine initiative (cf. 2 Peter 1:21), first through the prophets
    and climactically through his Son (cf. Heb. 1:1). That is, God has given secondary senses
    to our language through revelation, which we might picture as God's gifting us with the
    forms of a language we do not yet fully understand." In a Wittgensteinian sense, we need
    to ask what the language games of the author's day are, so that we can have "ears to hear
    and eyes to see" and "get it" in order to experience God in unique ways through them.
    Cox, "Neither Literal nor Metaphorical," 464.
24. Caird, *The Language and Imagery of the Bible*, 173–74.
25. Cox, "Neither Literal nor Metaphorical," 461–62.
26. Caird, *The Language and Imagery of the Bible*, 145–47.
27. Ibid., 149–53.

us on this nuanced and poetic level, they are opening up the possibility of increased intimacy.[28] These connections enable us to draw closer to Him beyond merely the rational. Schoville says it well: "These become the frame-work by which God who is beyond our comprehension becomes a person—one whom we can trust and love."[29] In other words, these images make God more tangible and relatable. They don't contradict the rest of what Scripture reveals to us about our relationship with God, but enhance and fill it out. And of course, the reality of these images leads us to partake in the intimate expression in God becoming a man in Jesus Christ.[30] All this to say, divine anthropomorphisms aid us as humans in understanding and experiencing a close personal relationship with the Triune God.

A final introductory note needs to be made concerning how God reveals His body parts. Mark Smith demonstrates that there may be three descriptions of God's "body" in the Bible.[31] First, God appears to reveal Himself in a "natural" human-scale body on earth. This seems to be unique to Genesis. In 2:7 when God breathed the breath of life into Adam, one may picture a human-sized theophany of God similar to when Adam and Eve "heard the sound of the Lord God walking in the garden" (3:8), when one of the three "men" approached Abraham, or when the "man" wrestled with Jacob (32:25, 30). Second, God appears to reveal Himself in a superhuman-sized "liturgical" body on earth that is not physical like a human body. It belongs to the group of themes associated with the temple or palace of God located on the holy mountain.[32] When the Lord ratified His covenant in the presence of Moses and the seventy elders, Exodus 24:10 says, "and they saw the God of Israel; and under His feet there appeared to be a pavement of sapphire, as clear as the sky itself." This may be a vision of the glory of God like in Exodus 16:10–11. There also may be a broader cosmic context in light of the blue of the sapphire signifying the heavens.[33] Similarly, when God revealed His glory to Moses in Exodus 33:23, He told him that He will take His hand away and reveal His back. Then He descended and "stood there with him as he called upon the

---

28. Cox, "Neither Literal nor Metaphorical," 461.
29. Keith N. Schoville, "Anthropomorphism," in *Baker Theological Dictionary of the Bible*, ed. Walter Elwell (Grand Rapids: Baker, 1984), 27.
30. Ibid.
31. Mark Smith, "The Three Bodies of God in the Hebrew Bible," *Journal of Biblical Literature* 134, no. 3 (2015): 471–88.
32. Ibid., 478.
33. Umberto Cassuto, *A Commentary on the Book of Exodus*, 3rd Edition (Winona Lake, IN: Eisenbrauns, 1967), 314.

name of the LORD" (Exod. 34:5). Then, as He promised, "The LORD passed by in front of Him" (34:6). Isaiah's vision of the Lord in the temple seems to fit this category as well (Isa. 6:1). Finally, God appears to reveal Himself with a cosmic "mystical" body in the heavens. God declares His immensity in Isaiah 66:1: "Heaven is My throne and the earth is My footstool. Where then is a house you could build for Me? And where is a place that I may rest?" And again in 40:12: "Who has measured the waters in the hollow of His hand, And marked off the heavens by the span (of His hand)." The Lord revealed His glory to Ezekiel in the expanse above Him in the "appearance as a man" and Ezekiel noticed His fire-like loins (1:26–28). This is similar to Daniel's vision of the Ancient of Days (Dan. 7:9).

The point of these distinctions is, then, to help us not only nuance our understanding of theophanies, but remember His anthropomorphisms are also parts of the whole of His revealed nature. It also underscores that He is not merely human-like but much larger. He is not like the ancient gods with their limitations and failings. He is the holy One, yet the one with Whom humans can intimately relate. Thus God's revelation of Himself is figurative in a way that we can understand, and yet something in which we can always participate existentially. Now let us look at how God communicates intimacy with Him through His "body parts."

GOD'S FACE

In the Bible, the concept of the face is the main visual characteristic of a person.[34] At minimum, it emphasizes their personal presence. As a result, we humans have built-in facial recognition software that reads the unique and particular faces of others. In fact, in the ancient Near East, the phrase "my face" or "your face" is the same as using the personal pronouns "I," "me," "you," etc.[35] At the same time, the face communicates, and thus is not just a body part, the front of someone's head.[36] Irwin is indeed correct: "Looking upon and communicating with others, bringing us into relation with them, face and body constitute the best picture of our soul—that is, of that which

---

34. Martin H. Manser, *Dictionary of Bible Themes: The Accessible and Comprehensive Tool for Topical Studies* (London: Martin Manser, 2009).
35. Luering says it is often a "mere oriental circumlocution for the personal pronoun." H. L. E. Luering, "Face," in *The International Standard Bible Encyclopaedia*, eds. James Orr, et al. (Chicago: The Howard-Severance Company, 1915), 1085.
36. Darlene R. Gautsch, "Face," in *Holman Illustrated Bible Dictionary*, eds. Chad Brand, et al. (Nashville: Holman Bible Publishers, 2003), 546.

we essentially are."[37] And so the face communicates intimate and personal thoughts, emotions, moods, and attitudes.[38] Keil and Delitzsch aptly described God's face as "the personality of God as turned towards man."[39] Thus it is an amazing and well-suited vehicle to communicate intimacy with His person.

One of the most significant biblical themes regarding the intimacy of God's face[40] can be seen in the words of Numbers 6:24–26, which recur elsewhere (see Pss. 4:6; 31:16; 44:3; 67:1–2; 80:3, 7, 19).

> The LORD bless you, and keep you;
> The LORD make His face shine on you,
> And be gracious to you;
> The LORD lift up His countenance on you,
> And give you peace.

The simplicity and yet richness of its poetic structure cannot be missed. The Lord (YHWH) is repeated three times. While grammatically redundant and unnecessary, it is He who is the source of their intimate blessing. In addition, the structure of the poetic pacing of each line expands: verse 24 is three words and twelve syllables, verse 25 is five words and fourteen syllables, and verse 26 is seven words and sixteen syllables. Read the verses again with this crescendo in mind, then notice how it culminates in His solemn promise, "and I then will bless them" in verse 27. Furthermore, the first clause of each line indicates God's movement toward His people, while the second clause expresses His activity on their behalf.[41]

His face shining (*'or panim*) is a figurative expression of God literally demonstrating His pleasure, favor, and partiality when He faces His people (cf. Prov. 16:15). Miller captures this in saying that it is a sign of His friendly and well-wishing nearness.[42] It is possible that it is generally known as God's

---

37. Alec Irwin, "Face of Mystery, Mystery of a Face: An Anthropological Trajectory in Wittgenstein, Cavell, and Kaufman's Biohistorical Theology," *Harvard Theological Review* 88, no. 3 (1995): 393.

38. Manser, *Dictionary of Bible Themes*.

39. Carl Friedrich Keil and Franz Delitzsch, eds., *Commentary on the Old Testament*, vol. 1 (Peabody, MA: Hendrickson, 1996), 676–77.

40. For a specific biblical theology of instances of when humans met God face to face, see David H. Wenkel, *Shining Like the Sun: A Biblical Theology of Meeting God Face to Face* (Wooster, OH: Weaver, 2016).

41. Patrick D. Miller, Jr., "The Blessing of God: An Interpretation of Numbers 6:22–27," *Interpretation* 29, no. 3 (1975): 243.

42. Ibid., 245.

gracious joy (Job 29:24). It is the opposite of God's seeming absence amidst dark cold days of oppression and need. When He lifts up His countenance (*nasa panim*), it may be functionally equivalent to His smile.[43] Even though He is invisible as Spirit, this is a "facial" gesture God gives His people to experience Him and His grace. This is all due to the Lord tying His face to His name in verse 27: "So they shall invoke My name on the sons of Israel, and I then will bless them." All of the person and reputation of God is expressed in His face and thus in His blessing.

Aaron and his sons' prescribed gesture of blessing upon the people of Israel has shone a long and warm light over all of God's people since.[44] God had blessed the people with freedom from bondage in Egypt and was providing direction, physical sustenance, offspring, protection, and most importantly, Himself as their God. Yet this blessing was to be instituted for the settled hope of perpetual care of God for future generations. Psalm 67 uses the same language of this blessing to express God's worldwide mission of providing hope and grace through His people:

> God be gracious to us and bless us,
> And cause His face to shine upon us—Selah.
> That Your way may be known on the earth,
> Your salvation among all nations. (vv. 1–2)

In fact, in 1979 Israeli archaeologist Gabi Barkai unearthed inscriptions of this blessing on burial amulets or pendants in the Hinnom Valley adjacent to the Old City of Jerusalem that date back to the sixth or seventh century B.C.[45] As His people, we need to look to God's very face. He will raise it like the sunrise to look us in the face with an unmistakable and full expression of compassion, grace, and peace. When it is used as a formal benediction in many church services, it should send the people of God out into the world

---

43. Gruber argues for this phrase being functionally equivalent to God's smile, but not lexically equivalent. Mayer I. Gruber, "The Many Faces of the Hebrew *nasa panim* 'lift up the face,'" *Zeitschrift für die alttestamentliche Wissenschaft* 95, no. 2 (1983): 253.

44. "An important factor in this passage must not be overlooked. Aaron and his sons are not to pray or call this blessing down upon the people. As anointed and ordained priests they stand in the place of God and speak authoritatively in his name. They put the name of God upon the people. Here we have a clear statement of the function of those specifically ordained to represent God in the assembly of the Lord." Gerard Van Groningen, "Numbers," in *Evangelical Commentary on the Bible*, 3:390.

45. R. Dennis Cole, *Numbers*, The New American Commentary, 3B (Nashville: Broadman & Holman, 2000), 128.

with an enduring existential sense of the intimate and gracious presence of the Lord.

Despite the beauty of this benediction, God's face may not always be "visible." David entreated the Lord with these words in Psalm 27:9:

> Do not hide Your face from me,
> Do not turn Your servant away in anger;
> You have been my help;
> Do not abandon me nor forsake me,
> O God of my salvation!

Amidst suffering, God may seem to hide or turn away His face from His people. This may leave them feeling abandoned or forsaken in their hour of need. This absence of God is so important to understanding intimacy with Him that we will look at what the Bible says about it in a later chapter. Nevertheless, we are called to commit to moving toward the intimacy of God's face. According to the preceding verse (27:8), David demonstrates his obedient posture in this:

> When You said, "Seek My face," my heart said to You,
> "Your face, O LORD, I shall seek."

He trusts in the fact that because the Lord is righteous and loves righteousness, "the upright will behold His face" (Ps. 11:7). Thus Psalm 105:4 calls God's people to "Seek the LORD and His strength; seek His face continually." According to verse 3, this is to be done with one's joyful heart: "Let the heart of those who seek the LORD be glad." According to verse 5, this is to be accomplished by remembering "His wonders" and "His marvels and the judgments uttered by His mouth." In other words, we seek experiencing the face of God by wholeheartedly ruminating on memories of His previous gestures of blessing to His people.

The unique aspect of seeing God's face for Christians is that we are able to experience God's glory in the face of Christ. Paul declares in 2 Corinthians 4:6:

> For God, who said, "Light shall shine out of darkness," is the One who has shone in our hearts to give the Light of the knowledge of the glory of God in the face of Christ.

Satan has blinded unbelievers so that they cannot see "the light of the gospel of the glory of Christ, who is the image of God" (4:4). Pause and slowly read each phrase of this verse again. "The light" is opposed to the darkness of walking in lies and shame (4:2). "The gospel" is the mercy of God in Christ (4:1) described in the Word of God (4:2), which reveals "the glory of Christ" who is the risen Lord (4:5, 14). We see the face of God in Christ when the veil, a hardened mind and heart, is removed by Christ. This occurs whenever a person turns to Him for freedom from shame.[46] Then, and only then, can we see the bright light of the truth and power of God's glory in Christ's facial gesture of His transforming mercy and power. This is the good news of the gospel! We can experience the very face of God in Christ and we can be transformed by it![47] Yet there is more to God's facial expression because He has eyes.

GOD'S EYES

The deeply personal intertwining of God's body parts is evident in how the Bible reveals that God, whose face turns to or away from us, sees us intimately through His eyes. On the one hand, it is common for the wicked to deny God's ability to see their deeds because they don't experience Him stepping in to stop them (Ps. 94:2–7). However, the psalmist chides the people, call-

---

46. This has been happening since Adam and Eve failed and hid themselves from the face of God (Gen. 3:8).

47. The experience transformed Peter, James, and John when they saw Jesus's face shine like the sun at His transfiguration (Matt. 17:2). Peter later argued:

> For we did not follow cleverly devised tales when we made known to you the power and coming of our Lord Jesus Christ, but we were eyewitnesses of His majesty. [17] For when He received honor and glory from God the Father, such an utterance as this was made to Him by the Majestic Glory, "This is My beloved Son with whom I am well-pleased"— [18] and we ourselves heard this utterance made from heaven when we were with Him on the holy mountain. [19] So we have the prophetic word made more sure, to which you do well to pay attention as to a lamp shining in a dark place, until the day dawns and the morning star arises in your hearts. (2 Peter 1:16–19)

Kuyper's reflection on walking in the light of the Lord's countenance provides us with an enduring view and direction of life:

> We can not look at God in the light of his countenance without having the gloom of our faces give place to higher relaxation. For in the light of God's countenance we know Him. When it shines out, his spirit draws near to make us see, observe and feel what God is to us. Not in a doctrinal way, not in a point of creed, but in utterances of the spirit of unnamable grace and mercy, of overwhelming love and tenderness, and of Divine compassion, which enters every wound of the soul at once and anoints it with holy balm.

Abraham Kuyper, *Near to the Heart of God*, trans. J. H. de Vries (Grand Rapids: Eerdmans-Sevensma, 1918), 104.

ing them senseless and stupid for accepting such an arrogant claim because it should be self-evident that "He who formed the eye, does He not see?" (Ps. 94:8–9). On the other hand, it is common for people to ascribe a divine eye to objects other than God. Examples abound, from the all-seeing eye of Sauron that searches Middle Earth for the ring in Tolkien's *Lord of the Rings*, to the all-seeing "Eye of Providence" on top of the triangle of the seal of the US $1 bill,[48] to Yahoo's popular ASE video-game-server browser. Yet the Bible uses this figure to communicate God's intimacy with His people and not just His omniscience. Howell is right: "It is not that God cannot see, because that is a human thing to do, but rather that He sees in a more profound way—and one in which he can enable humans to do as well."[49] God's sight is ontologically different than our own since He is omniscient and omnipresent. But His sight gives us ours as His creations in His image. Thus God sees us intimately, and we can see Him that way as well (cf. Rev. 22:4).

There are numerous examples of God's intimate look with His eyes. A significant instance is in Genesis 6:8 when Moses wrote, "But Noah found favor in the eyes of the Lord." The phrase "if I have found favor in Your eyes/sight . . ." became a standard request for many of the Lord's leaders: Abraham (Gen. 18:3), Moses (Exod. 33:13; 34:9; Num. 11:15), Gideon (Judg. 6:17), and David (2 Sam. 15:25; cf. Acts 7:46). In other words, God is never obligated to bestow His favor, and yet does so out of His relationship with them. So on the one hand, many view God's awareness of Noah's righteousness, blamelessness, and walk with God in 6:9 as the reason for His favor. Genesis 6:8 is at the end of the *toledot* (i.e., "These are the generations of . . .) of Adam and is the contrast of humans at that time with Noah. On the other hand, does the favor of the Lord have to be something that God was obligated to reward Noah, that is, was it a merited or earned righteousness? Biblical scholars are increasingly leaning toward an emphasis on God's favor, not the righteousness of Noah.[50] God's favor is bestowed on the basis of His grace and kindness, not because of some obligation or merit. They view the favor Noah received as undeserved. The NEB takes the merit of Noah's life too far in its rendering, "Noah won the favor of the Lord."

---

48. See also the magical relic, All-Seeing Eye or Triangle of Light, in the 2001 *Lara Croft: Tomb Raider* movie.

49. Brian C. Howell, *In the Eyes of God: A Metaphorical Approach to Biblical Anthropomorphic Language* (Cambridge: James C. Clarke, 2013), 86.

50. See esp. Carol M. Kaminski, *Was Noah Good? Finding Favour in the Flood Narrative*, Library of the Hebrew Bible/Old Testament Studies, 563 (London: Bloomsbury T&T Clark, 2014).

But does favor in God's eyes have to be about being deserving or undeserving? It could be seen a relational sense, like The Living Bible's "But Noah was a pleasure to the Lord."[51] Noah was shown to be righteous in contrast to others and this pleased the Lord, but not in the sense that he earned righteousness for justification.[52] This is a righteousness that caused God not to be sorry He had made Noah (6:6). Hence there seems to be a tension. God's favor in choosing this one man is not based on his righteousness, but his righteousness appears to flow from his faith. Thus the Orthodox Jewish Bible translates 6:8 with, "But Noach found *chen* (grace, unmerited favor) in the eyes of Hashem."

Can you sense the Lord's eyes on us from this passage from Genesis? As with Noah and the others, God is like a beloved parent who watches from the kitchen window the interaction of His children with the unsaved neighborhood youth. He sees in great detail the evil around us and is attentive to our response. We must then "work out" our salvation knowing that He is working in us for His good pleasure (Phil. 2:12–13). We must "prove" ourselves "to be blameless and innocent, children of God above reproach in the midst of a crooked and perverse generation, among whom" we will "appear as lights in the world" (Phil. 2:15). We must anticipate and feel His favor in His eyes, because our Father in heaven even sees our private monetary offerings, prayers, and fasting and will reward us in His way and time (Matt. 6:4, 6, 18). When we as citizens or widows live a life of quiet godliness, this is good and acceptable in the sight of the Lord (1 Tim. 2:3; 5:4, cf. 1 John 3:22). This is because God's equipping us to do His will as He works in us is "pleasing in His sight" (Heb. 13:21).

God's eyes also express His intimate knowledge and movement from a certain place or vantage point. David interweaves His understanding and location in Psalm 34:15–18 when he was reflecting on having resorted to faking "madness" before Abimelech:

---

51. Maybe even *The Message*'s "But Noah was different. God liked what he saw in Noah."
52. Mathews provides a helpful thoughtful reflection on this:

> This does not mean that Noah's character automatically secures divine favor, for God is under no obligation to bestow his favor. It presupposes a relationship. The proper emphasis in our passage is God's gracious favor, just as we see his preservation of the human family in chaps. 1–11 despite human sin. For the apostle Paul the promissory favor is realized by faith, hence a gift (grace) that results in righteousness (Rom. 4:13–16). Genesis's "grace" and "righteousness" (6:8–9) joined by Noah's "faith" is brought together in the theological reflection of the writer to the Hebrews. He interpreted Noah's obedient "fear" as "faith" that resulted in a saving "righteousness" (Heb. 11:7).

K. A. Mathews, *Genesis 1–11:26*, The New American Commentary, 1A (Nashville: Broadman & Holman, 1996), 346.

> The eyes of the LORD are toward the righteous
> And His ears are *open* to their cry.
> The face of the LORD is against evildoers,
> To cut off the memory of them from the earth.
> The righteous cry, and the LORD hears
> And delivers them out of all their troubles.
> The LORD is near to the brokenhearted
> And saves those who are crushed in spirit.

The Lord is moving His eyes in the direction of where the righteous are in the midst of troublesome evildoers.[53] The Hebrew preposition *el* primarily indicates motion toward someone or thing,[54] in this case in the context of the physical direction or location of the righteous and His being "near to the brokenhearted." Similarly, this preposition is used when the Lord is turning to His people to bless them when they are in the midst of a threatening conflict (Lev. 26:9). Later Isaiah called for God to "Look down from heaven and see from Your holy and glorious habitation" that the "stirrings" of His compassionate heart was seemingly restrained "toward" him (63:15). In other words, when God's eyes move toward His people,[55] it is assumed that His heart does as well. We see this same look in the eyes of the Lord Jesus when He "was going through all the cities and villages" (Matt. 9:35). Matthew describes His reaction as He drew near to them: "Seeing the people, He felt compassion for them, because they were distressed and dispirited like sheep without a shepherd" (Matt. 9:36; cf. Mark 6:34).

On a final note, God has had an intimate place in His heart for His people described by the famous reference to "the apple of His eye." The precedent for this image is from the Song of Moses in Deuteronomy 32 when God guarded Israel "as the pupil of His eye" (32:10). Moses called out the Israelites because of their fickle tendencies, to "do that which is evil in the sight of the LORD" (31:29). So in his song, he recounted the old family story of their unfaithfulness despite the Lord's mercy and grace. The Lord had set apart His people as His portion of His inheritance when He found them in the desert and encir-

---

53. Peter cites this text and God's watchfulness to underscore the believer's responsibility for blameless conduct amidst trials (1 Peter 3:12).

54. Jack B. Scott, "91 אֵל," in *Theological Workbook of the Old Testament*, eds. R. Laird Harris, Gleason L. Archer Jr., and Bruce K. Waltke (Chicago: Moody, 1999), 41.

55. The Lord was said to have His eyes on the land (Deut. 11:12) and on the temple (1 Kings 8:29; 2 Chron. 7:15–16).

cled them (32:8–10). He cared for them and guarded them as the *ishon eno,* or literally "the darkness of His eye."

The NIV and ESV translate *ishon* as "apple (of the eye)," as does the ESV and NASB in Psalm 17:8 and Zechariah 2:8. They do this not because it is a reference to fruit, but because of the English idiom of something precious and cherished.[56] The picture here is of the dark part[57] of the eye, the pupil, which is surrounded by the white iris. It is the center of the eye that is vulnerable and thus highly protected. We automatically wince and blink at the thought of an irritant, let alone an enemy's finger, even getting close to our pupil. Thus Moses described God's watchful guarding (*natzar*) of His people with this image and united it to an eagle caring for her young (32:11). In Psalm 17:8, David appropriately used this image when praying, "Keep me as the apple of the eye; hide me in the shadow of Your wings." Why? Because his wicked deadly enemies who surround him have stripped him of anything of value (v. 9). The culmination of this figure is in the Lord's graphic promise in Zechariah 2:8. "For thus says the LORD of hosts, 'After glory He has sent me against the nations which plunder you, for he who touches you, touches the apple of His eye.'" When the nations abused and debilitated the Lord's people, they were in reality touching and wounding Him in His dearest and most sensitive part.[58]

We should be feeling the painful wounding of the apple of God's eye. He willingly allowed His most sensitive and precious Son to be wounded so that we can be His dear children. Paul put this idea into a series of questions with unmistakable answers:

> If God is for us, who is against us? He who did not spare His own Son, but delivered Him over for us all, how will He not freely give us all things? Who will bring a charge against God's elect? God is the one who justifies; who is the one who condemns? Christ Jesus is He who died, yes, rather was raised who is at the right hand of God who also intercedes for us. Who will separate us from the love of Christ? (Rom. 8:31b–35a)

---

56. James Swanson, *Dictionary of Biblical Languages with Semantic Domains: Hebrew (Old Testament)* (Oak Harbor, WA: Logos Research Systems, Inc., 1997). See Martin B. Ogle, "The Apple of the Eye," *Transactions of the American Philosophical Society* 73 (1942): 181–91.
57. *Ishon* is translated as darkness in Proverbs 7:9 and 20:20.
58. Mark J. Boda, "Haggai, Zechariah," in *The NIV Application Commentary* (Grand Rapids: Zondervan, 2004), 236; Eugene H. Merrill, *An Exegetical Commentary: Haggai, Zechariah, Malachi* (Chicago: Moody, 1994), 123.

No one can be against us. No one can bring a painful charge of shameful condemnation against us. Why? Christ Jesus, the apple of God's eye, died an agonizing death so that we can know His intimate protection and love.

GOD'S HANDS AND ARMS

The literary and existential impact of God's hands and arms[59] can be terrifying, as Jonathan Edwards described in his famous 1741 Great Awakening sermon, "Sinners in the Hands of an Angry God."[60] Biblically, they are described as strong and mighty in His deliverance of His people and the destruction of their enemies.[61] The Lord even grants exaltation at His right hand (Pss. 110:1, 5; 118:15–16). Yet His hands and arms can be experienced as tender and helpful.

Notice how Jesus, as God in human flesh, used His hands in intimate situations. Mark 10:13–16 describes their tenderness. We see that Jesus must have been somewhat approachable, since the people bring their children simply that He might touch them. In fact, He was indignant at His disciples for shooing them away. He wanted them to permit and not hinder the children from coming to Him. These little ones understood with simple humility that the intimate touch of Jesus meant blessing and even healing. So in a tender expression, Jesus "took them in His arms and began blessing them, laying His hands on them" (10:16). Another of the greatest examples of Jesus's intimate use of His hands was at the Last Supper in John 13. He got up, put on a servant's towel, and washed His disciples' feet and wiped them with that very towel (13:4–5). Why did He stoop to performing manual labor? John says that, prompted by His knowledge that He would "depart out of this world to the Father" and because His "having loved His own who were in the world, He loved them to the end" (13:1).

Thus God's hands and arms guide and uphold His people. In Deuteronomy 33:27, just before his death, Moses culminates his blessing of Israel by describing where God's arms were in relation to their enemies in the land promised to them:

---

59. The mention of Diego Maradona's "hand of God" goal for Argentina vs. England in the quarterfinals of the 1986 World Cup still engenders an existential response to die-hard soccer fans worldwide.

60. Jonathan Edwards, "Sinners in the Hands of an Angry God: A Sermon Preached at Enfield, July 8th, 1741," ed. Reiner Smolinski, *Electronic Texts in American Studies* 54, http://digitalcommons.unl.edu/cgi/viewcontent.cgi?article=1053&context=etas.

61. Exod. 13:3, 9, 14, 16; 15:6; Deut. 3:24; 4:34; 5:15; 6:21; 7:8, 19; 9:26; 26:8; Josh. 4:24; Isa. 23:11; etc.

> The eternal God is a dwelling place,
> And underneath are the everlasting arms;
> And He drove out the enemy from before you,
> And said, "Destroy!"

He pictured God's intimate location and touch even when He is the one "Who rides the heavens to your help; and through the skies in His majesty" (33:26). In Isaiah 42:6 the Lord promised His Servant not only to "hold You by the hand" but to "watch over You" as He appointed Him "as a covenant to the people, as a light to the nations." And so, in our most desperate of circumstances, like David, the Lord Jesus, and Stephen we must place our very lives in God's hands. They all declared, "Into your hand I commit my spirit" (Ps. 31:5; Luke 23:46; Acts 7:59). We can literally trust Him to keep us from falling and hurling headlong, "because the LORD is the One who holds" our hand (Ps. 37:24). We must picture God when we utter these words to Him, "If I should say, 'My foot has slipped,' Your lovingkindness, O LORD, will hold me up" (Ps. 94:18).

GOD'S EARS

A final divine body part to experience in this chapter is God's ears. In some sense, that God has ears is commonly understood. People utter the wish "from your lips to God's ears," hoping what someone just said will be heard by God and He then would make it so. Some utter this in sarcastic skepticism as if saying, "Good luck with that coming true."[62] However, the biblical authors sense and trust in the reality of God's ears.

Humble confidence in God caused believers to speak directly into God's ear. In fact, human requests to God often begged for His attention without being presumptuous.[63] The psalmist called to the Lord "out of the depths" that He would hear his voice and "Let your ears be attentive to the voice of my supplication" (Ps. 130:1–2). Consider how the psalmist in Psalm 10:17 visualized God's ear:

> O LORD, You have heard the desire of the humble;
> You will strengthen their heart, You will incline Your ear.

---

62. "From your lips to God's ear," Urban Dictionary, http://www.urbandictionary.com/define. php?term=From%20your%20lips%20to%20God%27s%20ears.
63. Leonard J. Coppes, "2084 קָשַׁב," in Harris, Archer, and Waltke, eds., *Theological Wordbook of the Old Testament*, 817.

He is confident that the Lord will *qashab ozen*, that is, bend or turn His ear toward him to pay close attention to his pleas and make careful note of them.[64] Similarly, in Psalm 5 David not only called for the Lord to "heed the sound of my cry for help" (v. 2), but "Give ear to my words" (v. 1; cf. Pss. 54:2; 80:1). The word for "give ear" (*azan*) is from the idea of broadening out the ear with the hand in order to listen. So Daniel, who was in captivity far from the Promised Land, asked:

> O my God, incline Your ear and hear! Open Your eyes and see our desolations and the city which is called by Your name; for we are not presenting our supplications before You on account of any merits of our own, but on account of Your great compassion. (Dan. 9:18)

His appeal was for God to lean in closer from His position as Lord of heaven and grant his request. Isaiah combined his dependency on the Lord's hand with His ear in Isaiah 59:1:

> Behold, the LORD's hand is not so short
> That it cannot save;
> Nor is His ear so dull
> That it cannot hear.

And so in his first letter, John wrote to those who believed in the name of the Son of God, in order to bring them confidence that they possess not only eternal life:

> This is the confidence which we have before Him, that, if we ask anything according to His will, He hears us. And if we know that He hears us in whatever we ask, we know that we have the requests which we have asked from Him. (1 John 5:14–15)

Even though Christ the Son of God is in heaven, whatever prayers we ask according to His plans and purposes He hears and answers them. Even though He is preparing for His return to judge the earth and set up His kingdom He

---

64. Ernst Jenni and Claus Westermann, *Theological Lexicon of the Old Testament* (Peabody, MA: Hendrickson, 1997), 1174. The hiphil imperfect shows the psalmist's trust in the continuing kind of action of the Lord in the future.

hears and answers our prayers. Even while He is preparing a place for us, He hears and answers our prayers.[65]

This image of the ears of God is so simple and so vivid, it cannot help but bring us a profound confidence. Even when a little girl was asked if she knew what prayer was, she confidently answered, "That's easy! It is when God puts His big ear next to my think."

CONCLUSION

God's body parts in the Scriptures cause us to be drawn into profound experiences of Him. We can sense Him turning His face toward us in mercy and grace, looking at us with His eyes of favor, guiding and upholding us with His hands, and leaning His ears toward us in loving attention. These images are not merely figures of speech. They aid us in gaining a composite image of God we can experience. This is with His literary permission, so to speak. In other words, He not only allows the writers to describe Him with body parts, but invites the readers to use their imagination and senses to participate with them and move toward our God who has these qualities.

God is calling us to commit to an existential reading of these scriptural figures within their literary structure and context. We must turn our faces toward Him, attentively look at Him, reach out to experience His touch, and confidently speak our hearts into His waiting ears. Michelangelo's anthropo-morphisms in the Sistine Chapel do celebrate the glory of God and that of His most magnificent creation by capturing an awe-inspiring transcendence. Yet the connection of all of Who God is relationally and affectively tied to the human mind and heart. Therefore, we can and must reach out to our Creator with much more confidence and facility than Michelangelo's Adam. No longer mere passive receivers of God's touch of life at creation, we can reach across the gap between the human and divine because the Divine has reached out first. We must continually look into the face of Christ and be transformed by His gospel.

---

65. Our confidence in our prayers to Him is because we count on our right standing before God because of Him and we abide in Him (Heb. 4:16; 10:19; 1 John 2:28; 3:21).

NOW WHAT?

1. What do you think the Lord is calling you to commit yourself to, in light of these intimate metaphors used for Him?

2. What do you feel you need to tell God in light of the "parts" of His body in the Bible discussed in this chapter?

3. How can you use your face, eyes, hands, arms, and ears more like the way God uses His?

CHAPTER 5

INTERPRETING THE BIBLICAL IMAGE OF GOD OUR FATHER AS A SCRIPT OF INTIMACY FOR THE SHAMED[1]

Audrey Meisner had an affair that caused her to be pregnant. Shame nearly destroyed everything in their lives. Audrey shares her memories of walking out of the doctor's office that first time with Bob.

> I was buckling. I couldn't walk. And I was hanging onto his arm. And I remember feeling this strength from Bob. And I was going where is this coming from? Like don't you know my mom and dad started the first Christian TV show in Canada? Like, we are well known. Everyone knows our family in this nation. And I am—I am a disgrace.

---

1. This chapter is adapted from my articles, "God Our Father as a Script of Intimacy for Those Suffering Shame," *Journal of Spiritual Formation & Soul Care* 9, no. 2 (2016): 247–69; and "God Our Father as a Script of Intimacy for the Shamed," *Dedicated Journal*, February 18, 2016, https://blogs.corban.edu/ministry/index.php/2016/02/god-our-father-as-a-script-of-intimacy-for-the-shamed.

I am a disgrace. Do you get it? Do you understand the message I'm sending to everybody? That this is the worst. And that desperation—I was alone in my kitchen. Nobody was home. And I made a phone call to the abortion clinic. And it's not political. It's not because of my belief system. I did not believe in abortion. But I was desperate.

Bob recounts his struggles, "And the challenge, you know, in our journey to wholeness, the biggest challenge that I had as a dad was will I be able to love this baby as my own? Or will he forever be a reminder of the betrayal and the rejection?"[2] Disgrace and shame lead to despair.

Everyone can lament their suffering of shame. Its misery is not merely because it is a deep psychological and spiritual or soul pain. Shame arises out of its relational context and thus the shamed may feel condemnation, rejection, abandonment, betrayal, humiliation, etc. Thus past sins and current attractions (e.g. adultery, homosexuality, alcoholism) cause many to struggle to approach intimacy with God and Christianity out of the shame they continually suffer. However, the church, and especially pastors and ministry leaders, can help those under the weight of unnecessary shame to give themselves over to new and much healthier ways of understanding God and the church. Current psychological research shows those who wrestle with negative memories and immoral impulses/habits need new "scripts" (like a play or movie), alternative ways of thinking/feeling about foundational issues. Obviously one negative script is the shame narrative, and in one sense, feelings of shame are normal when experiencing guilt from sin. We call those without this moral compass sociopaths. However, the church may give "sinners" a script that God is merely an angry judge who hates what they have done and detests them for the urges they may still feel. But people cannot find relational intimacy with God in this state. In his work with homosexuals and the church, Dr. Mark Yarhouse, for example, has suggested Christian leaders need to provide other biblical scripts beyond the very limited concept of shame. In particular, people need to know God as a good Father, which—as a script—undercuts simplistic notions of God only as an angry or disappointed judge.[3]

---

2. "Overcoming the Obstacles of Infidelity (Part 2 of 2)," Focus on the Family Broadcast transcript, http://www.focusonthefamily.com/media/daily-broadcast/overcoming-the-obstacles-of-infidelity-pt2.

3. Yarhouse gave this charge when addressing pastors and ministry leaders in Salem, Oregon, in October of 2013. See also Mark A. Yarhouse, *Homosexuality and the Christian: A Guide for Parents, Pastors and Friends* (Grand Rapids: Zondervan, 2010).

This chapter will develop the script of God as our good and intimate Father, which should influence our perceptions and pursuits of intimacy with Him. This script is an invitation to an attentive, patient, kind, firm, close relationship with God. However, we need to understand "script theory" and the two major concepts of shame at the root of the "shame script" so many follow today. All of this should provide a substantive measure of relief to the sufferers of unnecessary shame.

SCRIPT THEORY AND ITS APPLICATIONS

The concept of the "script" has emerged out of behaviorist studies into motivation, memory, personality patterns, and attachment theory. Primarily, human responses to stimuli are biological/emotional, followed by our cognitive awareness of the initial action. Tomkins posits that a "scene" or a sequence of events linked together by the affects or biological/emotional responses to them have patterns, and so he has described them as a person's overall "script."[4] These scripts go on to influence behavior by maximizing positive effects and by minimizing negative ones. Thus we find ourselves living out storylines that are deeply emotional, even physiological.

The Function of Scripts

We must distinguish between a secular and a theological sense of how scripts function. While secular script theory has been useful in establishing key terms and contexts, they have looked past or ignored God and a biblical worldview. For example, the social constructionist work of Gagnon and Simon on Sexual Script Theory (SST) has had a big impact on sexual self-definition.[5] One's subjective understanding about their own sexuality is a significant determiner of their sexual actions and their subsequent qualitative assessments/boundaries of those actions. However, Jones and Hostler theologically delineate a Christian sexual script, and show that while scripts are subjectively and pragmatically formed, they do not create what is objectively true or right.[6] This is why a true script from the Creator of all humans must direct all scripts.

---

4. Silvan Tomkins, "Script Theory," in *The Emergence of Personality*, eds. Joel Arnoff, et al. (New York: Springer, 1987), 147–216.
5. John H. Gagnon and William Simon, *Sexual Conduct: The Social Sources of Human Sexuality* (Chicago: Aldine, 1973).
6. Stanton L. Jones and Heather R. Hostler, "Sexual Script Theory: An Integrative Exploration of the Possibilities and Limits of Sexual Self-definition," *Journal of Psychology and Theology* 30 (2002): 120–30.

"Life script" studies reveal how intensely relational scripts are because they demonstrate personal and culturally shared expectations. Personally, life scripts are shaped by memories of past events—in part—out of emotionally charged biographical memories from childhood,[7] as well as certain phenomena, events, and experiences.[8] Often these memories are idealized and determine the prototypical timing and "order of life events" (e.g., "A man should become a father by the time he is . . . ," "My relationship with my father consists of . . . ," etc.). These then become shared "cultural life scripts" (CLS),[9] shaped both by emotionally positive and negative experiences, "life moments."[10] The key is that they often produce interpretations of a person's current and future events. Therefore, taking time to understand how these personal and cultural scripts function is a step to being able to change or transform false, immoral, inadequate, and harmful scripts like shame.[11]

The Intimate Significance of Father Scripts

Understanding God as our intimate and good Father is linked to "father scripts." Attachment theory has shown that this script (either referring to one as a father or to a son about their father) is a significant affectional bond. Bowlby's seminal research on the child's tie to their mother delineates elements of attraction one has for another.[12] This bond includes the desire for individuals to be near to their attachments, their return to them as safe havens, and their view of them as secure bases of operation for venturing

7. Steve M. J. Janssen, "Is There a Cultural Life Script for Public Events?" *Applied Cognitive Psychology* 29, no. 1 (2015): 61–68; Shamsul Haque and Penelope A. Hasking, "Life Scripts for Emotionally Charged Autobiographical Memories: A Cultural Explanation of the Reminiscence Bump," *Memory* 18, no. 7 (2010): 712–29.
8. Jonathan Koppel and Dorthe Berntsen, "The Cultural Life Script as Cognitive Schema: How the Life Script Shapes Memory for Fictional Life Stories," *Memory* 22, no. 8 (2014): 949–71; Richard G. Erskine, *Life Scripts: A Transactional Analysis of Unconscious Relational Patterns* (London: Karnac, 2010).
9. Steve M. J. Janssen, Ai Uemiya and Makiko Naka, "Age and Gender Effects on the Cultural Life Script of Japanese Adults," *Journal of Cognitive Psychology* 26, no. 3 (2014): 307–21; Christina Lundsgaard Ottsen and Dorthe Berntsen, "The Cultural Life Script of Qatar and across Cultures: Effects of Gender and Religion," *Memory* 22, no. 4 (2014): 390–407.
10. Justin T. Coleman, "Examining the Life Script of African-Americans: A Test of the Cultural Life Script," *Applied Cognitive Psychology* 28, no. 3 (2014): 419–26.
11. Sarah Wilson, "The Meaning of Life Scripts," *The Guardian*, http://www.theguardian.com/lifeandstyle/2009/mar/08/life-scripts; Azriel Grysman, et al., "Self-enhancement and the Life Script in Future Thinking across the Lifespan," *Memory* 23, no. 5 (2015): 774–85.
12. John Bowlby, "The Nature of a Child's Tie to His Mother," *International Journal of Psychoanalysis* 39 (1958): 350–73; *A Secure Base: Parent-Child Attachment and Healthy Human Development* (London: Routledge, 1988), 99–157.

out into the world. Absence of or separation from their attachment creates anxiety and even distress.[13] Thus affectional bond and attachment is a powerful aspect of the relationship between children and their parents, and for our purposes, children with their fathers and believers with their God.

From a Christian standpoint, Limke and Mayfield effectively show that attachment to fathers predicts attachment to God.[14] In their study, they use the Experiences in Close Relationships scale (ECR) to measure levels of attachment-related anxiety and avoidance with romantic relationship partners. To assess levels of attachment-related anxiety about abandonment by God and avoidance of intimacy with God, they use the Attachment to God Inventory (AGI). At the same time, to assess religious and existential well-being, they used the Spiritual Well-Being Scale (SWS). They found strong support that attachment to God is similar to (vs. opposite from) attachment to fathers.[15] In fact, attachment to fathers and not to mothers predicts attachment to God. They recognize that this is supported by the Christian view that God is a "heavenly father," and that their study also furthers the recent research in attachment studies which emphasizes the important role fathers have on the development of attachment relationships.[16]

Many will question the relevancy and even appropriateness of perpetuating the fatherhood of God script in light of bad fathers.[17] Rather than welcoming intimacy with an ideal good Father, memories of their absent and abusing father prompt anger, fear, pain, and avoidance.[18] An emotionally gripping example of a negative father script is Pierre M. Balthazar's reflection on the

---

13. Bowlby, *A Secure Base*, 99–157.
14. Alicia Limke and Patrick B. Mayfield, "Attachment to God: Differentiating the Contributions of Fathers and Mothers Using the Experiences in Parental Relationships Scale," *Journal of Psychology and Theology* 39, no. 2 (2011): 122–29.
15. Ibid., 126–28.
16. Ibid., 127.
17. There was a relative neglect of the father in psychological and sociological research from the 1940s on. Most studies were matricentric and focused on the child-rearing assumptions of Western industrialized society. See John Nash, "The Father in Contemporary Culture and Current Psychological Literature," *Child Development* 36, no. 1 (1965): 261–97.
18. William Carroll, "God as Unloving Father," *The Christian Century* 108, no. 8 (1991): 255–56. Carroll, a homosexual and an ordained minister, has viewed God as an unloving Father. He states, "Some of the greatest pain gays experience is rejection by immediate family members. Ironically, this happens even though many gay people were considered wonderful children. . . . This makes the rejecting father even harder to understand" (255). Gay and lesbian people have come to think of God as the unloving, rejecting father "for our perception of God is shaped by an unloving church" (255). "I am beginning to recognize that my image of God as unloving father is the distortion of an unloving church that claims to speak for God" (255).

Lord's Prayer "our Father" through the experience of a neglected child.[19] This father does not live up to his responsibilities, but ignores the mother, regularly comes home late at night, and abuses both mother and child physically, sexually, and emotionally. Only when the child has some success in life does the father call them his own. To find comfort, the child adopts other people as fathers in order to attain any affective expressions to resolve their feelings of uncertainty. However, even with access to surrogate "fathers," children may be on a quest to know their biological father because fathers represent freedom, excitement, and individuation.[20] Given all this, is it even possible to enter into intimacy with a divine Father?

Reintroducing intimacy and relatedness is a means of redirecting the bad father script. Balthazar reminds us that even our initial interpersonal knowledge is imperfect; it is inevitably a mixture of isolation, loneliness, fear, awe, love, and intimacy. Nevertheless, certain steps forward must be taken or there will be destructive consequences. Refusing to enter or reenter into intimacy is detrimental to our health. Cultivating prejudicial attitudes toward unfamiliar intimacy may lead us into a life of distant isolation. However, intimacy can lead us beyond our barriers and can destroy our exclusiveness. It can help us understand others and bring us closer to them. This pursuit of intimacy does not mean avoiding or forgetting the anger toward the bad father. It also does not mean there cannot be any sense of differentiating oneself from the bad father and the subsequent script. It does entail several steps. It means a willingness to approach the pain of separation and identify the sources of memories that trigger mistrust, confusion, neglect, alienation, and/or despair. We must grapple with moving past psychological and spiritual stagnation to forgiveness in order to find freedom. We must be willing to explore the idea that God can be identified as father, and enter into some sort of relatedness, moving toward intimacy with Him.[21]

In sum, scripts are important personal and cultural motivators that integrate memory and personality. They presuppose what life is supposed to look like, how one should feel about it, and how one should respond to life's circumstances. They influence relational attachment and affection. So at this point we can seek to unfold shame, one of the most significant and powerful

---

19. Pierre M. Balthazar, "How Anger toward Absentee Fathers May Make It Difficult to Call God 'Father,'" *Pastoral Psychology* 55 (2007): 543–49.
20. Ibid., 546.
21. Ibid., 549.

cultural scripts. It needs to be clearly understood so it can be transformed by the biblical script of God as a good and intimate Father.

SHAME

What exactly is shame, and how is it a script? While it is impossible to do adequate justice to defining or summarizing the research (past and/or current) on shame, some general concepts can be delineated. First, shame is something that everyone experiences as a subset of universal social emotions, alongside others like humiliation and embarrassment.[22] Second, psychological and sociological perspectives of shame agree that it is a negative state and feeling that arises out of one's realization of a failure to live up to someone's expectations or ideals, whether one's self-image or a social image.[23] As a result, shame functions both as a concrete personal and cultural script as well as a script about the failure to live up to aspects of such scripts. In other words, one's very acceptance of the notion that failure to conform to a script results in shame, that is, the loss of one's honor, purity, strength, and rightness, demonstrates that shame in itself is a script. Third, shame is part of what shapes our identity. It is an element of the "spiral of reciprocal perspectives" that help form the very image we have of ourselves ("my image of you, my image of your image of me, my image of your image of my image of you," and so on, in sequence).[24] Fourth, the world in which the Bible was written had a thoroughgoing understanding of shame and its relationship to honor/dishonor. God is honorable as Creator and Covenant-maker, whereas sin is at minimum a failure to honor God. It results in the shame and dishonor that Christ took upon Himself to satisfy God and to remove our shame.[25]

---

22. Carlos Guillermo Bigliani, Carlos E. Sluzki and Rodolfo Moguillansky, *Shame and Humiliation: A Dialogue Between Psychoanalytic and Systemic Approaches* (London: Karnac, 2013), 66.

23. Nicolay Gausel, "What Does 'I Feel Ashamed' Mean? Avoiding the Pitfall of Definition by Understanding Subjective Emotion Language," in *Psychology of Shame: New Research*, ed. Kevin G. Lockhart (New York: Nova, 2014), 159–60. See also G. Davies, "Shame," in *New Dictionary of Christian Ethics & Pastoral Theology*, eds. David J. Atkinson, et al. (Downers Grove, IL: InterVarsity, 1995), 785.

24. Bigliani, Sluzki, and Moguillansky, *Shame and Humiliation*, 66.

25. A wealth of material is available on honor and shame in the biblical text and world. See for example Bradford A. Mullen, "Shame," in *Baker Theological Dictionary of the Bible*, ed. Walter A. Elwell (Grand Rapids: Baker, 1996 [2000]), 735; Jayson Georges. "From Shame to Honor: A Theological Reading of Romans for Honor-Shame Contexts," *Missiology: An International Review* 38, no. 3 (2010): 295–307; G. B. Funderburk, "Shame," in *The Zondervan Pictorial Encyclopedia of the Bible*, Vol. 5, general ed. Merrill C. Tenney, (Grand Rapids: Zondervan, 1976), 372–73; Sam Hamstra, Jr., "Honor," in Elwell, ed.,

In general, Western cultures tend to have stronger elements of a guilt-oriented culture whereas Eastern cultures (at least those of the 10/40 window[26] and the Far East[27]) tend to have stronger elements of a shame-orientation. Shame-based cultures stress group identity and there are external social pressures behind shame, which undergird "honor-based violence" and "honor killings." Such acts are attempts to rectify the shame brought upon a family by an individual's (usually a young woman) violation of a law or tradition related to marriage or purity.[28] It tends to predominate in Muslim and Hindu societies where individual rights are restricted by communal unities, where the patriarch is the ultimate authority, and religious norms cannot be transgressed. These structures control marriage and reproduction as a sign of the socioeconomic status of families and tribes. Thus female behavior is especially regulated since it is crucial to perceptions of honor and shame.[29] More broadly, however, shame is often so internalized that the external group need not even be present. Thus there are no known cultures that are exclusively shame-based or guilt-based.[30]

Guilt is often associated with shame. Guilt is both objective and subjective. Objective guilt is the state of having broken a law or a failure to live up to a certain standard. Subjective guilt is the painful negative feeling of being in the wrong, an "internal sense of moral failure."[31] Thus Andy Crouch summarizes shame and guilt cultures well: "In a shame culture, you know you are good or bad by what your community says about you. By contrast, in a guilt culture, you know you are good or bad by how you feel about your behavior and choices."[32]

Baker Theological Dictionary of the Bible, 355; Jerome H. Neyrey, *Honor and Shame in the Gospel of Matthew* (Louisville: Westminster, 1998).

26. Roland Muller, *Honor and Shame: Unlocking the Door* (Birmingham, UK: Xlibris, 2000), 18. The 10/40 window is a term used in missions to refer to the parts of the world between 10 and 40 degrees above the equator.

27. Timothy D. Boyle, "Communicating the Gospel in Terms of Shame," *Japan Christian Quarterly* 50, no. 1 (1984): 41–46.

28. Recep Dogan, "The Dynamics of Honor Killings and the Perpetrators' Experiences," *Homicide Studies* 20, no. 1 (2016): 53–79; Phyllis Chesler, "Worldwide Trends in Honor Killings," *Middle East Quarterly* 17, no. 2 (2010): 3–11.

29. Phyllis Chesler and Nathan Bloom, "Hindu vs. Muslim Honor Killings," *Middle East Quarterly* 19, no. 3 (2012): 43.

30. Timothy C. Tennent, *Theology in the Context of World Christianity: How the Global Church Is Influencing the Way We Think about and Discuss Theology* (Grand Rapids: Zondervan, 2007), 79.

31. Ibid., 79. His book has a very good section on the theology of shame in the Bible, 83–91. See also David J. Atkinson, "Guilt," in Atkinson, et al., eds., *New Dictionary of Christian Ethics & Pastoral Theology*, 425.

32. Andy Crouch, "The Return of Shame," *Christianity Today* (March 2015): 37.

From a Christian perspective, shame and guilt are the natural emotions that arise out of the conscience or heart, indicating that God's objective standards and personal desires have been violated. These violations are often connected to other individuals and the community as a whole. The Great Commandments to "love the LORD your God" and to "love your neighbor as yourself" profoundly and simply encapsulate God's design of relationships (Deut. 6:5; Lev. 19:18; Matt. 22:34–40; Mark 12:28–34). Therefore, one's relationship to God and neighbor are strained at best, and intimacy is severed. In other words, shame and guilt are produced. However, when these become the script in human hands for "shaming" the sinner, like the Pharisees' bullying of the woman caught in adultery (John 8:3–5), unnecessary, and often hopeless paths back into favor with God and community are created. An equally biblical script to shame and guilt is the path back. For these suffering sinners, our good Father provides intimacy with Him and with His people.

GOD OUR FATHER: INTIMACY FOR THE SHAMED

The script of God as our good and intimate Father is so central to Christianity that it may be deemed a Christian control belief. It is a broad and significant biblical topic that is not simply an analogy for God, but an essential part of His personhood.[33] For this study we will need to focus on its intimate elements without ignoring its redemptive foundation.[34] At the same time, Western culture's traditional family roles influence our views of intimacy with God as Father.[35] However, again this script is significant for those

---

33. H. Wayne House effectively argues, "The use of Father, in contrast to other terms such as Rock or King, is an essential part of his person-hood rather than merely a description of how he acts or even relates to us. He is the eternal Father, even as the Son is the eternal Son. In the relationship of Father and Son, the Son, as is characteristic of a son, is subordinate to the authority of the Father; and the Father, in some sense, is the eternal producer, begetter, of the eternal Son." "'God, Gender and Biblical Metaphor' (Ch 17) by Judy L. Brown," *Journal for Biblical Manhood and Womanhood* 10, no. 1 (2005): 69.

34. Numerous authors have written on the Christian's relationship to God as father. Cf. Floyd McClung, Jr., *The Father Heart of God: Experiencing the Depths of His Love for You* (Eugene, OR: Harvest House, 2004); Lisa Cline, *To Know God as Father* (Mobile, AL: Axiom Press, 2011); Michael R. Phillips' allegory, *A God to Call Father: Discovering Intimacy with God* (Carol Stream, IL: Tyndale, 1994), etc.

35. David Guretzki, "Does Abba mean Daddy?" *Faith Today* 27, no. 36 (2009); and Gregory C. Cochrane, "Remembering the Father in Fatherhood: Biblical Foundations and Practical Implications of the Doctrine of the Fatherhood of God," *Journal of Discipleship and Family Ministry* 1, no. 2 (2011): 14–24. Cf. also, Ken Canfield, "The Modern Fatherhood Movement and Ministry to Fathers in the Faith Community," *Journal of Discipleship and Family Ministry* 1, no. 2 (2011): 26–33; Betty Stafford, "Motherliness Should Be Included in the Godhead," *National Catholic Reporter* (February 6, 2009): 21; Jack Frost, *Experiencing*

who struggle with certain Christian identity scripts that heap shame on those who do not conform and do not provide an alternative except for being "that kind" of Christian. People will find a positive identity in what they feel is safe, secure, and good. The Bible presents just such an identity for the believing sinner. In short, while the Bible never excuses sin, it presents intimacy with God as our good Father, the one who intimately meets the needs of His children. He demonstrates this by adopting us and meeting our basic life needs, all the while revealing His motivations of love and compassion.

Adoption: We Need Him to Be Our Father

The Bible's script of God as our Father begins with the reality of our human existence as a fatherless people gladly parented by Satan, the father of lies (John 8:44). However, out of all the peoples of the world, God adopted Israel as His chosen children as an act of redeeming them out of slavery (Exod. 4:22–23; Rom. 9:4–5).[36] Thus Israel is the prototype of what all humanity needs because of their slavery to sin.

A closer look into the background of the New Testament adoption script is important at this point. The Greek term for adoption is only used by the apostle Paul (Rom. 8:15, 23; 9:4; Gal. 4:5; Eph. 1:5). Since the term *huiothesia* is not found in the LXX or in the literature of Second Temple Judaism, Paul was more than likely drawing on the commonly known Greco-Roman practice. The particular features of their laws of adoption enlighten Paul's script:

> (1) that an adopted son was taken out of his previous situation and placed in an entirely new relationship to his new adopting father, who became his new *paterfamilias*; (2) that an adopted son started a new life as part of his new family, with all of his old relationships and obligations cancelled; (3) that an adopted son was considered no less important than any other biologically born son in his adopting fathers family; and, (4) that an adopted son expe-

---

Father's Embrace (Shippensburg, PA: Destiny Image, 2002); John Eldredge, Fathered by God: Learning What Your Dad Could Never Teach You (Nashville: Thomas Nelson, 2009).

36. A sampling of this topic may be found in Svetlana Knobnya, "God the Father in the Old Testament," European Journal of Theology 20, no. 2 (2011): 139–48; Gottfried Quell, "The Father Concept in the Old Testament," in Theological Dictionary of the New Testament, ed. Gerhard Kittel, trans. Geoffrey Bromiley (Grand Rapids: Eerdmans, 1967), 5:959–74; in the same volume Gottlob Schenk, "pater," 5:975–1022; C. L. Crouch, "Genesis 1:26–27 as a Statement of Humanities Divine Parentage," Journal of Theological Studies, NS 61, no. 1 (2010): 1–15; Scott Hahn, A Father Who Keeps His Promises: God's Covenant Love in Scripture (Cincinnati: Servant Books, 1998); Christopher J. H. Wright, Knowing God the Father through the Old Testament (Downers Grove, IL: IVP Academic, 2007).

rienced a changed status, with his old name set aside and a new name given him by his adopting father.[37]

Because the Jews and Greeks would connect with Paul's adoption reference, they would also grasp how it applies to their relationship with God through Christ. This new but familiar concept is a game-changer. An examination of Paul's three major references to adoption will fill out this important aspect of God as an intimate Father script.

The adoption script references of Paul share the common essence of God's adopting believing sinners as His children. Each reference has a nuance that when added together provide a fuller view of this relationship. Each reveals the depths God goes to in order to alleviate our suffering of the effects of sin.

In Ephesians 1:3–6, Paul positions the believer's adoption within the grand scheme of God's salvation of the church. He has blessed us with every available spiritual blessing, and in love "He predestined us to adoption as sons through Jesus Christ to Himself, according to the kind intention of His will, to the praise of the glory of His grace, which He freely bestowed on us in the Beloved." We were desperate, and so He chose us to be His children out of love, grace and kindness. In 2:1–3, he describes our need for adoption and it is morally revolting. We follow "the prince of the power of the air" and are "sons of disobedience" and "children of wrath." Like rebellious, filthy, psychologically damaged, thieving, violent street children who serve a gang leader, or like self-satisfied and self-righteous kings, God adopted us out of our desperate need and state. He did all this so we could be a part of His close-knit family. In His Son, He has blessed us with everything He could have by choosing us out of His great love, kind desire, and unmerited grace to be pure and blameless in His presence. We are now truly clean and healed children, loved, accepted, and cared for by a good Father. Grasping this is a necessary first step in replacing one's shame script.

In Galatians 4:1–11, Paul positions our adoption within the context of freedom from slavery to legalism. In verses 3–7 he explains:

> So also we, while we were children, were held in bondage under the elemental things of the world. But when the fullness of the time came, God sent forth His Son, born of a woman, born under the Law, so that He might

---

37. Richard N. Longenecker, "The Metaphor of Adoption in Paul's Letters," *The Covenant Quarterly* 72, no. 3–4 (2014): 72.

redeem those who were under the Law, that we might receive the adoption as sons. Because you are sons, God has sent forth the Spirit of His Son into our hearts, crying, "Abba! Father!" Therefore you are no longer a slave, but a son; and if a son, then an heir through God.

When the Galatians were slavishly serving Old Testament Law or the laws of other gods, God the Father purchased them out of slavery by paying for it with the death of His very own Son and adopting them as His very own children. This is a call to every Christian to draw near to Him in love rather than serving Him out of legalism. He intimately knows us and now we know Him (4:8–9). So we must not revert to a slave/master mentality in order to earn His favor (4:10–11).

In Romans 8:12–17, Paul explains our adoption within the context of the new life generated by justification by faith and the leading of the Holy Spirit toward godly living. The flesh is a harsh taskmaster:

> So then, brethren, we are under obligation, not to the flesh, to live according to the flesh—for if you are living according to the flesh, you must die; but if by the Spirit you are putting to death the deeds of the body, you will live. For all who are being led by the Spirit of God, these are sons of God. For you have not received a spirit of slavery leading to fear again, but you have received a spirit [or "the Spirit"] of adoption as sons by which we cry out, "Abba! Father!" The Spirit Himself testifies with our spirit that we are children of God, and if children, heirs also, heirs of God and fellow heirs with Christ, if indeed we suffer with Him so that we may also be glorified with Him.

While we live in a sinful world of temptations and suffering, we have hope because we have been adopted as God our Father's children. Being adopted as God's children is about our position or status and not our performance. In other words, our relationship is not based on the righteous or perfect moral performance we can *never* achieve. This will produce the nagging fear of rejection and shame. Yet God our Father's adoption of us is intended to produce a new mindset that we should consciously remember our position as His children granted by Him and remember our dependence on Him in love and gratitude.

Adoption is truly intimate. We can call Him, "Abba, Father." This Aramaic term is one of endearment and intimacy, as well as respect and loyalty. Here, the needy and humble believer cries out "Abba, Father" in prayer. In Mark 14:36 Jesus used it beseech His own Father. While it is true that the word "Abba" is a familiar term used by small children, excessive familiarity not bounded by a healthy respect does not apply to its usage here. Before we transfer our "Papa" or "Daddy" to this term, we should note that in biblical times the head of the family was a somewhat imposing and dignified figure. "The Roman *paterfamilias* still had the right to put members of his household to death, even if the right was used rarely; cf. Gen. 38:24."[38] God is at the center of this family affectional bond. The Spirit of God confirms with our spirit that we are His children, but as Morris incisively observes, "The Spirit does not cause us to cry 'I am God's son', but 'God is my Father.' The believer looks at God rather than contemplating himself."[39]

In sum, our adoption as believers represents our permanent legal standing as God our Father's children. This new relationship results in intimate peace, security, and privilege that only children can enjoy. And yet there is even more to this reality and script.

Family Fellowship: Our Family Privilege

It must be added at this point that the relationship that comes with God's adoption provides open access to Him. The apostle John says in 1 John 1:3 that the gospel itself declares this. We have deep and abiding fellowship with God our Father, with His Son, and with each other: "What we have seen and heard we proclaim to you also, so that you too may have fellowship with us; and indeed our fellowship is with the Father, and with His Son Jesus Christ." The fellowship is *koinonia*, having things in common or partnership. This is so radically different than a script of shame. All believers have mutuality with God our Father and His other children.

In Matthew 6:6, Jesus claims that being one of God's children assumes the ability to have intimate fellowship with Him: "But you, when you pray, go into your inner room, close your door and pray to your Father who is in secret, and your Father who sees *what is done* in secret will reward you." We can and should have private conversations with Him. Those who base their relationship with God upon their performance have to put on a show of right standing with Him before the world. Insecure and legalistic, they do not have true intimacy. They have to pretend. They arrogantly shame sinners who have not performed like they have. Yet Jesus argues that God the Father will have none of this. His Father invites His children to draw near and communicate in secret.

---

38. Leon Morris, *The Epistle to the Romans* (Downers Grove, IL: IVP, 1988), 316.
39. Ibid.

Life Needs: We Need Him to Provide Our Basics

There is much more to the intimacy of the God Our Father script than a new relationship status. We are not to think of this as simply changing the option from "rebellious orphan" to "child of God" on our Facebook page. This script is lived out in the real world of our basic needs. We have a real Father in God, a real Father who intimately takes care of us.

Our Provisions

As needy children, God our Father has intimate knowledge of our needs. Jesus knew this well, and recognized that badgering religious prayers by those who do not think of God as their Father devolve into something more along the lines of a business transaction.

> And when you are praying, do not use meaningless repetition as the Gentiles do, for they suppose that they will be heard for their many words. So do not be like them; for your Father knows what you need before you ask Him. (Matt. 6:7–8)

Jesus follows this teaching by giving His disciples the Lord's Prayer, a pattern of communication with God as their Father in heaven. He is the kind of God who, like a good Father, knows exactly what our daily bread should be, what sins we need forgiven, and what the Evil One is trying to get us to do at any given moment. This aspect of the script is His cure for our worry.

> For this reason I say to you, do not be worried about your life, *as to* what you will eat or what you will drink; nor for your body, *as to* what you will put on. Is not life more than food, and the body more than clothing? Look at the birds of the air, that they do not sow, nor reap nor gather into barns, and *yet* your heavenly Father feeds them. Are you not worth much more than they? (Matt. 6:25–26)

Orphans anxiously wonder if they will have enough food to fill their growling stomachs on a daily basis. They shiver in the cold because of worn and inadequate clothing. However, God the Father is trustworthy in providing His children with their basic needs because they are more valuable to Him than the other creations He obviously provides for. A deep-seated peace should come to the shamed with this aspect of the script, but even more so with further understanding of what God the Father furnishes for His children.

George Mueller consistently experienced this. After one specific answer to prayer for his beloved orphans in Bristol, he wrote:

> Truly, it is worth being poor and greatly tried in faith, for the sake of having day by day such precious proofs of the loving interest which our kind Father takes in everything that concerns us. And how should our Father do otherwise? He that has given us the greatest possible proof of His love which He could have done, in giving us His own Son, surely He will with Him also freely give us all things.[40]

Our further understanding must come through our eyes, hands, and feet of faith in Him who intimately knows and meets our needs.

Our Direction

God the Father provides intimate involvement in the direction of our lives. He has done this throughout history. He acted as a loving Father to His rebellious people in their wilderness wanderings and rebellion. In Deuteronomy 1:31, Moses tenderly reminded them to remember all the times "in the wilderness where you saw how the Lord your God carried you, just as a man carries his son, in all the way which you have walked until you came to this place.'" He carried them in His arms to where He wanted them to go and protected them from their enemies. This truth has been memorialized in the famous poem "Footprints in the Sand," in which someone is walking life's journey on a beach with God, leaving two sets of footprints in the sand behind them. At the person's saddest and most hopeless times, the two sets become one. While the person believes the Lord has abandoned them at those times, God simply explained, "My precious, precious child. I love you, and I would never, never leave you during your times of trial and suffering. When you saw only one set of footprints, it was then that I carried you." Indeed, we as believers have experienced the Lord's intimate direction and leading when He had to carry us to our ultimate destination, which was His all along.

God our Father also directs believers in His ministry paths for them. According to 1 Thessalonians 3:11, Paul prayerfully entrusts himself to God His Father for clarity and protection to get to the persecuted Thessalonians: "Now may our God and Father Himself and Jesus our Lord direct our way to

---

40. George Mueller, *Answers to Prayer from George Müller's Narratives*, Compiled by A. E. C. Brooks (Chicago: Moody, 1895), Loc. 248.

you." His way was obstructed by the Jews of the city, who bullied and mobbed these believers (Acts 17:1–14; 1 Thess. 3:1–5; 2 Thess. 1:4). Paul couldn't stand it one minute longer, sending Timothy on ahead knowing the Thessalonians needed significant encouragement. The longing for this deep fellowship was mutual (3:6). In fact, Paul admits this:

> For what thanks can we render to God for you in return for all the joy with which we rejoice before our God on your account, as we night and day keep praying most earnestly that we may see your face, and may complete what is lacking in your faith? (1 Thess. 3:9–10)

So in keeping with this motivation, Paul prays for "our God and Father Himself and Jesus our Lord" to direct Silvanus' (Silas) and his way to them. Martin is right that "Spiritual power is required to remove a spiritual hindrance. Therefore it only makes sense to ask in prayer that God might 'clear the way.'"[41]

However, like Paul, we must remember we can and should entrust ourselves to God's intimate involvement in our ministry paths in order that we may provide assistance to those who are tempted to lose faith in God. As sovereign God, He shapes the very direction of our lives to get us where He wants us to go with the least amount of resistance. Solomon states in Proverbs 3:6 that God "will make your paths straight." He will do this even in the midst of the frustration of our being shamed or bullied, even giving us love for our tormentors (1 Thess. 3:12).

Our Comfort

God our Father also provides comfort, something that Paul also communicated to the persecuted Thessalonians: "Now may our Lord Jesus Christ Himself and God our Father, who has loved us and given us eternal comfort and good hope by grace, comfort and strengthen your hearts in every good work and word" (2 Thess. 2:16–17). The Father has already given us eternal comfort as His children. Because the two participles "loved" and "given" share a common article, they are the same reality.[42] Yet the Lord Jesus Christ is their basis. The great love of the Father has caused Him to give us Christ as this glorious comfort and hope. His comfort (*paraklēsin*), consolation, or encouragement is our settled assurance of His love and support forever! Nothing and no one can undo our being

---

41. D. Michael Martin, *1, 2 Thessalonians*, The New American Commentary, 33 (Nashville: Broadman & Holman, 1995), 111–12.

42. Ibid., 258.

His children. It is a confidence the world cannot have because it has rejected the truth and will be judged ultimately at the Day of the Lord (2 Thess. 2:12).

In light of his own experience, Paul reminds the Thessalonians of God the Father's comfort because persecutors attempt bring or restore honor to themselves. They heap shame upon believers in order to bring them under their control. However, God's children live by His grace. Amidst all persecution, false teaching, and oppression, our Father will give us comfort, hope, and strength to continue on with what He has called us to do and be until His Son returns for us. Hearts weakened by these pressures may give out, and the person no longer moves forward. However, the Father's comfort and strength touch our fragile hearts, the center of our being, and intimately provide just what we need to continue being people that honor Him and minister to others in and outside His family. We should bless

> the God and Father of our Lord Jesus Christ, the Father of mercies and God of all comfort, who comforts us in all our affliction so that we will be able to comfort those who are in any affliction with the comfort with which we ourselves are comforted by God. For just as the sufferings of Christ are ours in abundance, so also our comfort is abundant through Christ. (2 Cor. 1:3–5)

Our Father intimately knows how to comfort us in our most difficult of times.

Our Discipline

God our Father also provides discipline. He is not only intimate and good, but holy and righteous. The writer of Hebrews reminds believers of the discipline process in Hebrews 12:3–11:

> For consider Him who has endured such hostility by sinners against Himself, so that you will not grow weary and lose heart.
> You have not yet resisted to the point of shedding blood in your striving against sin; and you have forgotten the exhortation which is addressed to you as sons,
> "MY SON, DO NOT REGARD LIGHTLY THE DISCIPLINE OF THE LORD,
> NOR FAINT WHEN YOU ARE REPROVED BY HIM;
> FOR THOSE WHOM THE LORD LOVES HE DISCIPLINES,
> AND HE SCOURGES EVERY SON WHOM HE RECEIVES." [from Prov. 3:12]
> It is for discipline that you endure; God deals with you as with sons; for what son is there whom *his* father does not discipline? But if you are without disci-

pline, of which all have become partakers, then you are illegitimate children and not sons. Furthermore, we had earthly fathers to discipline us, and we respected them; shall we not much rather be subject to the Father of spirits, and live? For they disciplined us for a short time as seemed best to them, but He disciplines us for our good, so that we may share His holiness. All discipline for the moment seems not to be joyful, but sorrowful; yet to those who have been trained by it, afterwards it yields the peaceful fruit of righteousness.

How can a father's discipline be intimate? God disciplines us as his own beloved children. We are far from being illegitimate children born outside of marriage without any legal status. His discipline here (*paideia, paideuō*), which is from the same word as child (*paidion*), is for us as His legitimate sons and daughters. The verb for discipline "denotes the upbringing and handling of the child which is growing up to maturity and which thus needs direction, teaching, instruction and a certain measure of compulsion in the form of discipline or even chastisement." The noun emphasizes "both the way of education and cultivation which has to be traversed and also the goal which is to be attained."[43] Concerning intimacy, the process of restoring closeness is through the training of a child's character through negative consequences. Human parents may employ time-outs, spanking, grounding, withholding of certain privileges, and/or extra responsibilities to achieve this desired result. The writer of Hebrews argues that God our Father will discipline us for sins like bitterness and immorality (12:14–17). He lovingly does this for our good so that we may be like Him, holy and pure (12:10–11), and so that we are not separated from Him because of bad attitudes and behavior.

Without moral consequences, we often do not draw near to Him. Undisciplined sons and daughters do not ultimately feel close to their parents, but resent them for not caring enough about them to take time to discipline their rebellious and selfish attitudes and behavior. Their consciences want resolution to their guilt and shame. Consequences of disobedience, while unpleasant, produce "the peaceful fruit of righteousness" which allows for restored intimacy with the parents.[44] God is not a permissive parent, who allows His

---

43. Georg Bertram, "Παιδεύω, Παιδεία, Παιδευτής, Ἀπαίδευτος, Παιδαγωγός," in *Theological Dictionary of the New Testament*, eds. Gerhard Kittel, Geoffrey W. Bromiley, and Gerhard Friedrich (Grand Rapids: Eerdmans, 1964–), 5:596.

44. Donald F. Walke and Heather Lewis Quagliana, "Integrating Scripture with Parent Training in Behavioral Interventions," *Journal of Psychology & Christianity* 20, no. 2 (2007): 122–31.

children to dishonor and mock Him by their attitudes and behavior like Eli's sons, Hophni and Phinehas (1 Sam. 2:29–30). God provides discipline for His own children in order to resolve their problems and draw them in. Children respect and respond to that.[45]

His Motivations: We Need His Love and Compassion

The shamed may be asking at this point in the delineation of this intimacy with God as our Father script, "Why would He meet my needs? Does He simply do it out of duty? Is some higher court requiring Him to pay child-support?" As we have seen, shame scripts are not replaced easily. Besides providing reminders of God's choice of us when He adopted us, His motivations as our Father are foundational to this script.

1. God Our Father's Intimate Love for Us

Love is clearly the motivation behind God becoming our Father and acting as our Father. John is nearly overwhelmed by this fact and calls all Christians who read his letter to "See ['Behold; Look in amazement'] how great a love the Father has bestowed on us, that we would be called children of God; and *such* we are" (1 John 3:1). It is exclusive for God's own children. This is why "the world does not know us, because it did not know Him." It sets us apart from everyone else on our planet. We are God's children. He is our Father.

Jude makes it clear that being God's loved children is simply who we are: "Jude, a bond-servant of Jesus Christ, and brother of James, To those who are the called, beloved in God the Father, and kept for Jesus Christ" (Jude 1). He called us to salvation and provides for us on earth for Christ's return. Jude includes this truth as what should be an accepted script for churches, which are being infiltrated by pretenders who creep in to steal away believers to follow them into immoral behavior. He not only greets them with the truth of God's love for them as their Father, but later calls them to save others from these cancerous fakes with this truth:

> But you, beloved, building yourselves up on your most holy faith, praying in the Holy Spirit, keep yourselves in the love of God, waiting anxiously for the

---

45. See Wade R. Johnston, "Spare the Rod, Hate the Child: Augustine and Luther on Discipline and Corporal Punishment," *Logia* 20, no. 4 (2011): 11–16. Both men experienced excessive corporal punishment as children but also knew their parents meant the best for them. Therefore, they argued for discipline in love.

mercy of our Lord Jesus Christ to eternal life. And have mercy on some, who are doubting; save others, snatching them out of the fire; and on some have mercy with fear, hating even the garment polluted by the flesh. (Jude 20–23)

Is God's Fatherly love only found in what He does for us or merely in the fact that He condescends to communicate with us? Does He feel anything for us? Theologians and philosophers of the past have argued that God is without emotion, impassive. If He had emotion, He would be susceptible to change when He interacts with others outside Himself. Can God's Fatherly love be emotionally sidelined by calling it a mere anthropopathism? It is true that Psalm 103:13, "As a father pities his children, so the LORD pities those who fear Him" (NKJV), uses "as" and is a figure of speech. However, God still has pity, which is prompted by His will to move to meet the need of another out of His care and love. It also does not help to draw upon flawed word studies to claim that God's love is different than ours because His love is *agapaō*, a self-sacrificing choice not based on emotion, as opposed to *phileō*, a brotherly fond affection.[46] He loves and cares for His children with great feeling as much as He judges His enemies with His wrath.

2. God Our Father's Intimate Compassion on Us

Compassion is another clear motivation of God's relationship to us as our Father. There is perhaps no clearer illustration of this than in Luke 15:11–32 and the deeply profound parable of the Prodigal Son . . . the Lost Son. A full-scale exposition of this parable is not necessary in order to grasp how significant this window into God's intimate compassion for His children is for replacing shame and guilt. However, it deserves some substantive reflection on the context, elements, and implications of the Father's compassion.

Shame and Relational Distance

Shame and guilt are woven into the gritty context of this parable. Like many who function out of a shame script, the Pharisees and scribes claim Jesus should be ashamed of Himself. He has become too relationally close to sinners (*hamartoloi*, 15:1–2). When Jesus was asked this question in Matthew 9, He framed His response with a focus on compassion for the sick: "It is not those who are healthy who need a physician, but those who are sick" (9:12). He frames His

---

46. D. A. Carson, *The Difficult Doctrine of the Love of God* (Wheaton, IL: Crossway, 2000), 29, 45–64.

answer in Luke around lostness (*apollumi*), separation, and distance (the parables of the Lost Sheep, Lost Coin, and then Lost Son). From a wide-angle lens to a microscope, Jesus leads them to intimacy with God the Father.

The narrative of the parable stresses the physical and relational distance created by the prodigal son. His selfish choice was to go "on a journey to a distant country" (Luke 15:13). This is picked up again when his return home is described as "but while he was still a long way off" (15:20). He was truly lost and distant. He burned his bridges by not only bringing shame upon himself, but upon his family, and especially his Father. His father had to liquidate a large portion of his assets—he did not just go to the bank to withdraw cash. He went round to all those who could buy his assets. He had to sell off a portion of their land, livestock, etc. The dishonor he demonstrated to his Father was indeed shameful. The son would later realize this for himself: "Father, I have sinned against heaven . . . and in your sight" (15:18, 21), underscoring that this is a key to Jesus's thrust. The turning point is in the prodigal son's return. His plan is an attempt to save face:[47] "So he got up and came to his father" (15:20). The relational distance is about to be narrowed, but in an unexpected way.

The shame-oriented cultural script demanded restoration of honor to the Father. If the son returned, appropriate demonstrations of shame were to be heaped on him and accepted. At the village or city gates, the elders of the city would remind the son of his selfish shaming of his father and family. The son would then approach his father's home, only to have to wait outside until his father allowed him to take audience with him. His father would eventually grant it only to receive his son's apology. One possible avenue of "reconciliation" would be that the son would then be expected to move to a neighboring village in order to take an apprenticeship to support himself and rarely if ever return to his father's home again.

Shame's Reversal in Restored Intimacy

The radical reversal in the son's restored intimacy comes in the culturally unexpected display of the Father's motivation . . . compassion, not shaming justice. Jesus carefully draws out the Father's increasing levels of intimacy/closeness. The Father had been looking for His prodigal, "but while he was still a long way off his father saw him" (15:20). Then his true motivation is

---

47. Kenneth E. Bailey, *The Cross and the Prodigal: Luke 15 through the Eyes of Middle Eastern Peasants* (Downers Grove, IL: IVP, 2005), 49–62.

revealed: "and felt compassion for him" (*splaychnizomai*, 15:20). This term is associated in part with a visceral reaction of deep sympathy, care, kindness, mercy, and love. There is no indifference, bitterness, disgust, or humiliation. Nouwen is insightful here:

> I am beginning now to see how radically the character of my spiritual journey will change when I no longer think of God as hiding out and making it as difficult as possible for me to find him, but, instead, as the one who is looking for me while I am doing the hiding. When I look through God's eyes at my lost self and discover God's joy at my coming home, then my life may become less anguished and more trusting.[48]

Thus this Father is clearly God, the one Who has consistently shown this kind of compassion to prodigals in biblical history.[49] Luke has already recorded Jesus's counter-cultural example of the compassion of the "good" Samaritan that would also shock His hearers who thought of them as a shameful people (Luke 10:30–37).

The Father's compassion prompted Him to respond in more ways that would contradict the shame-oriented script of his culture. Jesus communicates this masterfully in three simple phrases: "and ran," "and embraced him," "and kissed him" (15:20). Running for an aged Eastern man was not only unusual but undignified, even when he was in a hurry.[50] The embrace is literally "fell on his neck" (*epipiptō*). This action coupled with kissing is for overwhelmingly emotional celebrations of unions and reunions.[51] This was not merely a hug, but the embrace of the part of the body closest to the center of the countenance (vs. feet, hands, head, etc.) and gives the Father the ability to kiss (*kataphileō*) his long-lost son. He was lost and now is not only found, but returned to the intimacy that fathers and sons are supposed to have.

---

48. Henri J. M. Nouwen, *The Return of the Prodigal Son: A Story of Homecoming* (New York: Image, 1992), 106–7.

49. His response to adulterous Israel, like Hosea's response to his adulterous wife, Gomer, is one of the most counterintuitive examples of all time: "I will sow her for Myself in the land. I will also have compassion on her who had not obtained compassion, And I will say to those who were not My people, 'You are My people!' And they will say, 'You are my God!'" (Hos. 2:23; cf. also 11:28).

50. Roger David Aus, "Luke 15:11–32 and R. Eliezer ben Hyrcanus' Rise to Fame," *Journal of Biblical Literature* 104, no. 3 (1985): 457.

51. This is reminiscent of Laban's running to embrace Jacob after his gracious assistance to Rachel at the well (Gen. 29:13), of Esau's reunion with Jacob (Gen. 33:4), and Jacob/Israel's blessing of the sons of his long-lost son, Joseph (Gen. 48:10).

"The Elder Son" and the Shame Script

However, the script of shame and dishonor rears its grotesque head. The elder son's attitude toward his shameful prodigal brother is palpable. He represents the cultural script imbedded in and propagated by the shepherds of the community, the Pharisees and scribes. Religious watchdogs for religious/cultural purity and precision of adherence to God's "expressed" prescriptions for righteousness serve an important purpose for any community. But when they arrogantly and hypocritically institutionalize their spiritual roles and segregate "sinners" (past or present) from "the holy" with their power of shame, they create a parallel and yet counterfeit Christianity.

The older son's reaction is a "missing climax."[52] His personal and cultural script of shame processes the Father's mercy differently, to say the least. While the prodigal experiences restoration to intimacy with his Father, his elder brother has been out working, being the only responsible child in the family. After a full day of labor in the field, he approaches his house only to hear something strange. One of the family servants provides an apt summary of intimacy restored: "Your brother has come . . . because he has received him back safe and sound" (15:27). Again, the missing climax. He became enraged (*orgizō*), which stopped him in his tracks. His deep-seated shame-scripted anger flowed emotionally, volitionally, and physiologically, and barred him from even going in to see his shamefully irresponsible brother, let alone feel happiness or join in any celebration. It is Thanksgiving dinner, and the first thing that comes to mind is, "Why is he here?" Bailey is indeed correct in his assessment of this situation: "For certain types of people, grace is not only amazing but infuriating."[53] This shows that this brother's shame script defines his relationship with his Father as one of a servant to his Master.[54] He underscores that he has been "serving you," and that he has "never neglected a command of yours" (15:29). However, this cannot produce any real closeness, any genuine love. He claimed that, despite the favor he should have earned, "yet you never let me celebrate with my friends" (15:29). In this claim, the little phrase "with you" appears to be conspicuously absent. Thus the worst aspect of the shame-oriented script is that the Father would not be invited to the elder son's party.

---

52. Bailey, *The Cross and the Prodigal*, 81.
53. Ibid., 82.
54. Timothy Keller, "Basis of Prayer: 'Our Father,'" YouTube video, 35:40, August 10, 2015, https://www.youtube.com/watch?v=vqxXABgRhVo.

God the Father and a Compassionate Script

Depicting His own Father, Jesus passionately seeks to provide a substitute and more accurate personal and cultural script for His audience. Again He reveals His Father's compassion even for the shamers with the element, "His father came out and began pleading with him" (15:28). With the few if only tender words Jesus utters to the Pharisees and scribes,[55] the Father reiterates intimacy: "Son, you have always been with me, and all I have is yours" (15:31). So it is beyond logical that "we had to celebrate and rejoice," because intimacy has been miraculously restored like a resurrection from the dead.

Hopefully, by this point the basics of the script of God as our intimate Father have come into clearer focus. This biblical theology depicts God our Father as the Ultimate One who intimately meets the needs of His children. He does this by adopting us as His children with all the privileges that come with it. He can be trusted to meet our basic life needs of provision, comfort, direction, and even discipline. There is nothing that we need that He does not know about before we even ask Him, and nothing that He will not supply. All of His providing is clearly motivated by His deep love and merciful and kind compassion. Internalizing and practicing this real script should inspire the Christian to be full of profound gratitude for this family privilege and to have a strong desire to draw near to God our Father in vulnerable trust and peaceful security. Even more, Christians have work to do with counteracting other unhealthy and counterfeit scripts like the shame-oriented one.

IMPLICATIONS OF THE
GOD-AS-INTIMATE-FATHER SCRIPT AND SHAME

Mary Magdalene and Zaccheus could have suffered painful projections of the shame script as they sought to follow Jesus. Due to their past sins and potential and/or current temptations and attractions, they may have felt unworthy of God's continued acceptance because of the script that personally and culturally motivated them. It was deeply integrated into their memory and personality. Their relational attachment and affection to God and others could have been placed in jeopardy by "well-meaning" believers whose place in the Christian community was to be watch dogs for religious and cultural purity and precise adherence to God's "expressed" prescriptions for righteousness. They could have been held suspect and not really accepted as truly God's

---

55. John Piper, "A Tender Word for Pharisees," YouTube video, 39:43, February 18, 2014, https://www.youtube.com/watch?v=wuREA32ktIU (accessed April 25, 2019).

children. They could have spent their Christian lives in soulful lament of their own community's implicit condemnation and rejection of them as unworthy and deficient people. However, who in the history of Christianity would ever fail to celebrate the full forgiveness and life change of these two sinful people by the power of God in Jesus Christ? Yet many struggle with incorporating people just like these two, who have sinful pasts and may continue to struggle. What are some steps we can take to deal with this?

Personal and Community Assessment

Like addressing a painful cancer, we first need assessment. We need to ask a series of probing questions both of ourselves and of those around us. What script is being lived out? Is there a struggle with shame on some level? Is God thought to be constantly disapproving of them and they can never measure up?[56] Do they continually think He is distant and indifferent to them?

Script theory has shown that our "father script" is pivotal to our view of God. We need to have tools by which we can assess what the view of their own father is. Many have inadequate or even abusive fathers. While terrible and inexcusable, the Bible is replete with fatherly failures: Abraham, Lot, Jacob, Jephthah, Eli, David, Solomon, etc. Yet biblical revelation does not retract from establishing and proclaiming God's nature and character as Father. Thus in sharp contrast stands God our Father. He alone is the one good Father who is always patient, kind, firm, close, attentive.[57] He has adopted us. He is the one who is trustworthy to intimately meet our foundational needs out of love and compassion for us.

We must push on to determine where we find our intimacy. With whom do we pursue the close, safe sharing of ourselves? As one of God's creatures and children, our closest vulnerable attraction should be to God our Father first. This profoundly real script should be a part of a truly biblical theology of God, every believer's life, and the church's proclamation, discipleship, and pastoral counseling. We must hold as a deep conviction that it is more than a mental script passed on merely by rote. It should be a part of the evangelical church's culture, psychology, and even physiology.

---

56. When one of my colleagues, Dr. Ryan Stark, read a bit of this chapter, he readily agreed, "The idea of the good Father is obviously right, but it is also a useful reminder that things like shame, etc., can get blown way out of proportion if we do not see God as a good father but rather as an angry volcano god who requires virgin sacrifices every year."

57. "Father, Fatherhood," in *Dictionary of Biblical Imagery*, gen. eds. Leland Ryken, James C. Wilhoit, and Tremper Longman III (Downers Grove, IL: IVP, 1998), 274.

Relational Acceptance and Assimilation

This biblical theology of God as our good and intimate Father carries with it not just the reality of intimacy for His children, but certain relational and ethical responsibilities as well. Mawhinney is indeed correct in his analysis of adoption and its popular version. His revision in light of the data is helpful:

> Adoption as sons means both encouragement and obligation. In fact both of these flow from the single notion of intimacy. Paul's thought moves easily from ethical obligation to sonship to absence of fear to the fatherly presence of God through the Spirit. It can do so because this intimacy with Paul's God is both a demanding and encouraging relationship. Such intimacy is not limited to the cradle. The believer does not live his life as a perpetual infant. Intimacy grows as the son matures and comes to know his Father ever more closely, as the son's heart becomes more in tune with the Father's, as the son comes to appreciate his Father more and more, and as the son comes to think and act more like his Father. Sonship means blessings and responsibilities.[58]

His children should go on to reflect the Father's compassion and love as it flows from a thoroughly internalized script—seeking to meet needs, not just welcoming but incorporating "sinners" into the very bosom of the church.

This loving assimilation is especially needed by all of the lamenting divorced, addicted, abused, damaged people who come to the church hoping for some relief from the personally and culturally shared script that holds them captive to shame. We must assess how the God-as-Father script is affecting our attachments or affections with "sinners." How are we really doing with sinners? Is our personal and corporate psychology governed by compassion or judgmentalism? This compassion does not excuse sin. All sin should be disgusting to us because God is white hot and blinding in His holiness. However, can we see past that sin to the sinner, who is made in God's own image and a trophy of His grace to be celebrated every time we see or think of them? Those who have yet to come to the God who reaches out to mournful sinners need to experience His adoption, provision, and compassion.

More research needs to be done in applying this script. Churches have been venturing into this realm. Tim Wright, in his *The Prodigal Hugging Church*, has recognized the value of acceptance of prodigals into the Christian community.

---

58. Allen Mawhinney, "God as Father: Two Popular Theories Reconsidered," *Journal of the Evangelical Theological Society* 31, no. 2 (1988): 189.

However, his approach is focused more on relating to the culture of the prodigal than it is on God as their Father. Still, he does ask some insightful questions in regards to evaluating the risks of this approach. For example, he states:

> Interacting with culture the way Jesus did is filled with risks and dangers. The first risk is alienating, angering and scandalizing faithful church members. As you move forward as a Prodigal Hugging Church, how will you care for and love the "older siblings"?[59]

His assumptions about faithful church members need evaluation. Is it helpful to cast such a wide stereotypical net over "faithful church members" that in Luke 15 are recalcitrant shaming legalists? He goes on to add another risk assessment that is actually quite insightful:

> The other risk is subtler. In our attempts to embrace, welcome, celebrate, affirm, engage, use and serve culture, we risk losing ourselves by condoning culture, being absorbed by it, or being tainted by its values.[60]

This is a critical process to navigate. Churches may view the sins of sinners in a variety of unbiblical ways from sin as disease, as only personal faults, as addictions, as unforgivable, as morally relative, etc. These views need careful theological scrutiny without which the sinners are either encouraged to move past their sin as quickly as possible without ever grappling with what it actually is before God and others, or are encouraged to remain in the guilt and shame of their sin until due penance has been achieved. Neither of these options is biblically acceptable.[61]

It is imperative that Christians in shame- or guilt-based cultures and situations fully internalize the real script that God is our intimate Father who in adopting us releases us from languishing in shame to participate in His love and compassion in our secret places as well as the public ones. Then God the Father intervenes and transforms. This is what He has done with the shame

---

59. Tim Wright, *The Prodigal Hugging Church: A Scandalous Approach to Mission for the 21st Century* (Minneapolis: Augsburg Fortress, 2001), 52.
60. Ibid.
61. In addition, other biblical scripts can be used to aid the acceptance and assimilation of "sinners" into the Christian community. Theological analysis should begin with the Bible's transparent and more obvious longitudinal themes: Creator/creature relationship, God's kingship and humans made in His image, the Lamb of God and substitution, reconciliation of enemies, loving loyalty to the only true God amidst tribal and ancestral spirits, and others.

that threated to destroy Audrey and Bob Meisner and their family.[62] Audrey recounts a significant conversation with her own father:

> Dad, I just don't know. I just don't know how I can do this. There's actually a baby in me. And I don't know. And my dad just put his head—hand on my shoulder. And he just said one thing, the power of a father's words. He said, Audrey, that's what you did. But that is not who you are.

Bob expresses his own struggles as a father of this child and their journey to wholeness. With Audrey four months pregnant they had to tell their children and deal with the shame:,

> One evening, they came. And we sat as a family on the floor. But before I ever spoke a word, I pulled a large blanket from the bed and with Audrey there on the floor, I took that blanket and I covered her from head to foot. And I wrapped my arms around her. And I look deep into my children's eyes. And I said, kids, this is what God does when we make a mistake. He comes to us. And he covers us. And he wraps his arms around us. And he says, I will never leave you. I will never forsake you.

Yet it was a still a journey for Bob. He had to answer what he was to do about this baby. He describes one morning, begging his pastor to tell him what to do. His answer was crucial to Bob's next steps and ultimate journey as a father and husband. "Bob, there's a baby on your doorstep. What do you do? Will you participate with this fatherless generation? Or will you become a father to the fatherless? Bob, you've got to grow up." So in the hospital room when the child was born, Bob chose his words very carefully:

> I gave him my name Robert because I don't want him to ever question one day in his life whose boy he is. He's my son. His middle name is Theodore. It means divine gift. He's not an accident. He's not a mistake. He's not the result of a sexual affair. Just like my other three children, he's born out of the heart of God and entrusted to us.

---

62. "Overcoming the Obstacles of Infidelity (Part 2 of 2)."

How can Bob do this? How can Audrey overcome her shame? How can their son and his siblings live freely? They refuse to adopt a script of shame and remain rooted in one of God as their good and intimate Father.

May we see God our Father like Billy, age four, who when asked what love is, responded that it is "when someone loves you, the way they say your name is different. You just know that your name is safe in their mouth." This quote is found in numerous locations on the Internet. There is no way to know whether it is a real statement of a child named Billy—but ultimately, it doesn't really matter.[63]

NOW WHAT?

1. What is the script that you are living out?

    A. Do you struggle with shame?

    B. Do you think God constantly disapproves of you and you can never measure up?

    C. Do you think He is distant and is indifferent to you?

2. What difference would it make if you were confident that God is your Father?

3. If you had a less than good father, whom did you seek out to meet your intimate needs?

4. What does it mean to you to know that if you have trusted in Christ's sacrifice for you that you have been adopted by God and He is your Father now?

5. How have you seen God your Father meet your needs?

---

63. "Quotes: Love, as Perceived by Some Children 4 to 8 Years-of-Age," Religious Tolerance, http://www.religioustolerance.org/love_is.htm.

6. Where do you find your intimacy? Close safe sharing of yourself. Let it be with God your Father first.

7. How are you doing with your attitude toward sinners? Do you feel compassion or anger?

8. Listen to the lyrics of "Good Good Father" by Chris Tomlin, and reflect on God as our good intimate Father.[64]

---

64. Pat Barrett and Anthony Brown, "Good, Good Father," released September 9, 2014, track 7 on the album *Housefires II,* Housefires, compact disk. Chris Tomlin's cover of this song won the GMA Dove Song of the Year for 2016. Tomlin interviews Pat Barrett about the origin of the song. See "Chris Tomlin—'Good Good Father' (Story Behind the Song)," The 95.5 Fish, http://955thefish.com/content/music/chris-tomlin-good-good-father-story-behind-the-song. See their children's book based upon this song: Chris Tomlin and Pat Barrett, *Good, Good Father,* illustrated by Lorna Hussey (Nashville: Tommy Nelson/Thomas Nelson, 2016). Not everyone appreciates every lyric in the song, however; see John Aigner, "Chris Tomlin's 'Good Good Father' Wins GMA Song of the Year," Ponder Anew, http://www.patheos.com/blogs/ponderanew/2016/10/19/chris-tomlins-good-good-father-wins-gma-song-of-the-year.

CHAPTER 6

INTERPRETING BIBLICAL IMAGES OF MARRIAGE AND CHRIST

Nothing in the Bible appears to communicate a closer intimacy with God than its images of marriage. In the Old Testament, God is Israel's bridegroom and husband. In the New, Christ is the bridegroom and husband of the Church, His bride and wife. Nevertheless, the church has struggled interpreting and applying these images. We seem to be pulled away from sound biblical theology and legitimate logical implications. A couple of examples from the edges of mainstream Christianity can help orient the struggle and the need for this chapter.

Roman Catholicism: Recently, Jessica Hayes, a thirty-eight-year-old Indiana high school theology teacher, married Jesus Christ.[1] She wore a white wedding dress to her ceremony, in which she took her solemn vows to become a "consecrated virgin." She swore never to have carnal intercourse and received

---

1. Sara Wagner, "Fort Wayne Woman Marries God," August 15, 2015, updated August 19, 2015, http://wane.com/2015/08/15/fort-wayne-woman-marries-god/; Kiri Blakeley, "'I am married to Jesus's: Consecrated Virgin, 38, Marries God in Wedding Ceremony That Attracts Hundreds," *Daily Mail*, http://www.dailymail.co.uk/news/article-3202430/I-married-Jesus-Religion-teacher-38-marries-God-wedding-ceremony-attracts-hundreds.html.

a wedding ring as a sign of their union. This relatively rare Roman Catholic practice[2] is part of a broader theology of "marriage to Christ." Hayes elaborates,

> I think that in some sense, we're all called to be married. It's just a matter of discerning how. So, my marriage is to Christ and someone else's marriage is to their spouse. A priest's marriage is to the church. That's a good desire that's planted in us by God. The real question is how, how is this lived most joyfully in me.

Love is her motivation. She elaborates,

> As Catholics and as Christians, we're all called to that loving relationship with our God. So, I'm called to live it out in this way. Married couples are called to live that out in their married vocation and their love of their family. It's a way of life that really anticipates what all of us will live in heaven, that union with ourselves and Christ and a real knowing and loving of him. My path is choosing that closer following now because that's where my greatest joys lie.[3]

Pope John Paul II called for consecrated virgins to model their lives after the perpetual Virgin Mary. They should be "virgins in heart and body, brides with a total and exclusive attachment to the love of Christ."[4] While this is born out of deep desire to serve Christ wholeheartedly, it shows a misguided understanding of the biblical metaphors of Christ and His church.

Charismatics: Mike Bickle, the head of IHOP, the International House of Prayer, has organized a significant amount of their ministry around romantic imagery of Christ and the Church. Bickle has been teaching on Song of Solomon to his people for more than twenty-five years because God audibly told him to.[5] In 1988, he was reading a wedding card inscribed with a verse from the Song of Solomon. He began to pray and weep, "Jesus, seal my heart with your

---

2. Hayes is one of 230 "consecrated virgins" in the United States and one of 3,500 worldwide. The practice supposedly dates back to the times of the apostles, but died out during the Middle Ages. It was revived by Pope Paul VI in 1970. Blakeley, "'I Am Married to Jesus's'"; Cindy Larson, "Dwenger Teacher Finds Her Calling as Consecrated Virgin," *The News-Sentinel*, Fort Wayne, IN, August 14, 2015.

3. Wagner, "Fort Wayne Woman Marries God."

4. Cindy Wooden, "Pre-Vatican II Rite of Consecrated Virgins Lauded," *National Catholic Reporter*, 31, no. 32 (1995): 7.

5. Clair Dubois receives love-letter prophecies from Jesus and has recorded them in her *Love Letters to My Bride: Recent Prophecies from Jesus to the Bride of Christ* (CreateSpace Independent Publishing Platform, 2015).

seal of love." At that moment, another prophet had heard the Lord's audible voice calling Bickle to make the Song of Solomon a focus of his ministry.[6] Bickle began to understand that true believers must view Jesus "through the eyes of a bride with loyal, devoted love" and must "feel loved and in love" with Christ. Without this intimacy in worship, Christ would not return to Earth.[7] With communication cues from Song of Solomon, Bickle has taught that Christians are to pray "bridal intercession."[8] As we will see, this common reasoning among evangelicals provides justification for using the Bible's marriage imagery with emotional romantic themes related to Christ and His Church.

On the other hand, I grew up within conservative evangelicalism with what may be a pendulum knee-jerk in the opposite direction of the examples above. Through church and seminary, I adopted a rather sanitized eschatological view. True, believers are the bride of Christ. However, the main point of this image is the rapture or Second Coming when we will be able to be with Him in heaven. With a steady diet of pretribulationalism, the emphasis concerning the Christ-and-His-church marriage image in my view was not about what it would mean for us in our day, but more do to with the time that it would occur.

In this chapter, I will display the Bible's story of the divine Bridegroom and bride, Husband and wife. We will dig deep into the presentations of these

---

6. Mike Bickle, "The Bridal Seal of Mature Love," May 19, 2014, https://mikebickle.org/watch/?guid=2014_05_09_2000_MB_FCF. "I did not like the Song of Solomon when I first read it. It was like 'Ugh!' I mean really, I did not get anything! I just said, 'Lord, are You sure that You are really want me to do this, to study this book?' Well, some years later I am really glad because I began to see the heart of Jesus in a new and a powerful way." Mike Bickle, "The Bridal Cry: Surprised by Desire," transcript, Novermber 5, 2013, http://www.mikebickle.org.edgesuite.net/MikeBickleVOD/2003/20031105-T-The_Bridal_Cry.pdf. As a result he has claimed that when people really receive the Holy Spirit, "It will wreck your life and your plans. It's true and you know it. The Bible calls it lovesickness (Song 2:5). The bride said, 'I'm lost in love, I'm lost in love.'" Thus "the emotional makeup of the Body of Christ will be transformed." They will be completely changed by this imagery. "Then the lovesick bride, even in her weakness, feels confident. She feels clean. She feels fearless; when you're lovesick you feel fearless. It's alive inside; you're lost in love. . . . You won't be able to buy off His bride. You won't be able to train her into domestication. You won't be able to make her polite, in that political sense. She's going to be reckless. She's going to be careless, in a holy, godly way."

7. Jeff Tietz, "Love and Death In the House of Prayer," *Rolling Stone* (January 21, 2014), http://www.rollingstone.com/culture/news/love-and-death-in-the-house-of-prayer-20140121#ixzz2r3bc5dsZ.

8. Ibid. "'[Jesus] is not coming until the people of God are crying out globally in intercession with a bridal identity,' Bickle has preached. If the Second Coming depends upon 'romantic communion' with Christ, and the alternative is satanic hegemony, then any error in worship should be made on the side of erotic intimacy—to lust and repent is surely better than abandoning Jesus in his hour of need."

images in the Old and New Testaments to allow them to wonderfully enrich our conception of and quest for an intimate relationship with Christ Himself. In doing this, they will also provide freedom from misconceptions and perhaps idolatrous errors. This freedom comes from accurately answering the following questions and others like them. Do the metaphors for Christ's wedding and marriage to His people correspond to a variety of allegorizations and contemporary Western concepts? Are we to be pursuing some sort of divine romance? Is sexual intercourse a metaphor for an intimate union with Him? In short, how do these metaphors illumine intimacy with Christ?

THE BIBLE'S DIVINE BRIDEGROOM-AND-BRIDE STORY

How does this movement toward intimacy in marriage work? Since metaphors are founded upon a logical equivalent in real life,[9] what does the biblical analogy of the bridegroom/bride (*chathan/kallah*) correspond to? In ancient Israel, entering into marriage was entering into a covenant relationship (Prov. 2:17; Mal. 2:14).[10] It had several well-known elements. The process began with a choice, two fathers' arrangement of a marriage, or a man's choice of an eligible woman. Often the groom's father approached the bride's father to work out a contractual agreement or covenant (*ketubah*), establishing the betrothal agreement and period of preparation for their union (*kiddushin*). The groom would pay the dowry or bride price (*mohar*) to the bride's family and he would go to prepare their own home. The ceremony itself may have included symbols of the groom's choice of, covenant with, and care for her.[11] He covered her with his garment, which would signify their new relationship and his commitment to care for her needs.[12] He may have sworn an oath of faithfulness to her. He may have raised his hand to heaven, calling upon God as his witness to this covenant. He then may have made a verbal declaration to the effect, "She is my wife and I am husband from this day and forever."[13] The joyful wedding feast followed and

---

9. For a good summary of metaphor theory, see Colin Hamer, *Marital Imagery in the Bible: An Exploration of Genesis 2:24 and Its Significance for the Understanding of New Testament Divorce and Remarriage Teaching* (London: Apostolos, 2015), 26–33.
10. Daniel I. Block, "Marriage and the Family in Ancient Israel," in *Marriage and the Family in the Biblical World*, ed. Ken M. Campbell (Downers Grove, IL: IVP, 2003), 44–45.
11. See Ezek. 16:8–13.
12. See Deut. 22:30; 27:20; Ruth 3:9; Ezek. 16:8; Mal. 2:16.
13. See Block's reference to the source of this in "Marriage and the Family in Ancient Israel," 45 n.48, and his *The Book of Ezekiel 1–24*, New International Commentary on the Old Testament (Grand Rapids: Eerdmans, 1997), 483.

was celebrated by invited guests only. The bride would wait and prepare herself for the groom's arrival. The groom then would then come for his bride to take her to his own home where they would consummate their relationship and establish their own family.

Because marriage exists in a fallen world, it should be noted that the husband and wife each had the right to the other's sexual purity.[14] Even fornication and rape were two sides of this same coin, robbing them both of what was to be theirs. In Deuteronomy 22:13–21, it appears that after they consummated their marriage with sexual intercourse, the evidence of her virginity on a stained sheet was kept by her parents. In case her purity was ever questioned, this could be brought out as evidence in her defense.[15] Her virginity, including her need to cry out in the midst of rape, was viewed as her responsibility (Deut. 22:23–27).[16] Edenburg rightly claims the sexual consummation of marriage "created bonds of exclusive intimacy" that stemmed from "the analogy between the marital bond and the political alliance as applied to Yhwh's relations with his people."[17] Thus, the couple owed each other the same highest degree of faithfulness they owed to the Lord Himself.[18] So with these structures of betrothal and marriage in mind, let's examine how the Bible uses these real-life elements and applies them metaphorically to other target concepts. This is the necessary foundation to understanding the intimate nature of the relationship between Christ and the Church.

---

14. E.g., "My beloved is mine, and I am his" (Song 2:16; cf. also 6:3; 7:1).
15. This is the traditional view of what the actual evidence of her virginity would be. Block, "Marriage and the Family in Ancient Israel," 46. For support for the two basic views on this evidence, see for the traditional view Eugene H. Merrill, *Deuteronomy*, New American Commentary (Nashville: Broadman & Holman, 1994), 302–3; and for the menstruation view Gordan J. Wenham, "*Betûlah*—A Girl of Marriageable Age," *Vetus Testamentum* 22 (1972): 330–36. For an extensive treatment of the interpretive issues and options on the charges and penalties, see Bruce Wells, "Sex, Lies, and Virginal Rape: The Slandered Bride and False Accusation in Deuteronomy," *Journal of Biblical Literature* 124, no. 1 (2005): 41–72.
16. Edenburg argues that these laws concerning the betrothed virgin were a departure from ancient Near Eastern legal tradition and indicated "a unique outlook in which she bears unconditional responsibility for protecting her virginity from the time her husband pays her bride-price to the time he takes full possession of her." Cynthia Edenburg, "Ideology and Social Context of the Deuteronomic Women's Sex Laws (Deuteronomy 22:13–29)," *Journal of Biblical Literature* 128, no. 1 (2009): 54.
17. Ibid., 60.
18. Note the parallels in Deuteronomy 22:13–29 with the sexual overtones of idolatry in Deuteronomy 13:1–18.

The Old Testament

The bridegroom/bride imagery is only used for God's people a few times in the Old Testament. Nevertheless, it is an explicit illustration of God's movement toward intimacy with His chosen people as they anticipate and prepare during betrothal.[19] In Isaiah 61:10, Zion[20] personifying God's people will rejoice in His provision of salvation and righteousness after their exile as He joyfully adorns them both as a bridegroom with a priest's turban and as a bride with jewels (cf. Isa. 49:18). This is in preparation for the presentation of the couple to each other at the wedding ceremony.[21] Then they will be ready for marriage. Furthermore, after their exile God will actually well up with joy and delight at the prospect of their reunion in Isaiah 62:4–5 (ESV):

> You shall no more be termed Forsaken,
>> and your land shall no more be termed Desolate,
> but you shall be called My Delight Is in Her,
>> and your land Married;
> for the Lord delights in you,
>> and your land shall be married.
> For as a young man marries a young woman,
>> so shall your sons marry you,
> and as the bridegroom rejoices over the bride,
>> so shall your God rejoice over you.

Their marriage covenant is established, and they can share their home on their Promised Land property together.

The choice and preparation themes are strong in Ezekiel 16:8 (ESV), where the Lord married Jerusalem.

---

19. Song of Solomon will be addressed later in this chapter. In other figurative instances, bridegroom and bride are not used for God and His people directly. In Psalm 19:5 the bridegroom is compared to the daily expectancy of the rising of the sun. The prophets describe the Lord's banishing all joy that the bridegroom and bride naturally experience in anticipation of their wedding. He replaces it with judgment and desolation because of the impurity of the nation of Israel (Jer. 7:34; 16:9; 25:10; 33:11; Joel 1:8; 2:16; cf. Rev. 18:23).
20. It is interesting to note how classic covenant theology continuity scholars like Edward J. Young seem to automatically assume that the speaker here is "the Church of God, the elect, the true Israel." *The Book of Isaiah* (Grand Rapids: Eerdmans, 1972), 3:465.
21. Young assumes that this is "how God envelops the Church in salvation." Ibid., 3:466.

> When I passed by you again and saw you, behold, you were at the age for love, and I spread the corner of my garment over you and covered your nakedness; I made my vow to you and entered into a covenant with you, declares the Lord God, and you became mine.

Here He sees Jerusalem as a filthy orphaned child bloody from birth. Yet when she "came of age" (puberty), He entered into a marriage relationship with her. After choosing her, the marriage process is threefold. He first covers her shameful nakedness. Like Boaz and Ruth (Ruth 3:9), the Lord covers Jerusalem with his protective garment or skirt. He then enters betrothal by making His solemn covenant vow. The peak is His aiding her in preparing for their marriage. He not only cleanses the birth blood from her, but adorns her with all the splendorous clothing and jewelry of royalty (Ezek. 16:9–14). However, the thrust of this analogy is her adulterous response to all of His overtures of faithful love.

So intimacy in this image represents the movement of God toward the place He has for His people. He chooses them to be His "bride" even with His intimate knowledge of their unworthiness from their moral filthiness. Out of His great loyal love for them and the covenant between them, He gets His hands dirty by washing them. He gives them gifts and does more to prepare them for a wonderful life together in their own land than they could imagine. The sickening tragedy of this is the bride's breaking of their oath (16:59), turning away to join herself to others in wanton adultery. She chases after other lovers despite God's faithful love and generosity. Yet it appears that nothing could give God more delight than when one day He would chase away their enemies and joyously restore them to their own intimate place, the Promised Land.

The New Testament

The New Testament brings these vivid teachings from the Old Testament and unites it with Jesus Christ. Explicitly the bridegroom is Christ. In His teachings, the metaphor underscores His movement as Messiah toward intimacy with His people, and their joyful anticipation and preparation for Him and His kingdom. Therefore as the forerunner (Isa. 40:3; Matt. 3:3, etc.), John the Baptist refers to Jesus as the bridegroom (*numphios*), and to himself as the best man or friend of the bridegroom (*paranumphos*) (John 3:29). John's anticipation and preparation is rewarded and he is full of joy as he finally hears the bridegroom's voice. Jesus underscores this joy at His arrival when He is asked why John's disciples and the Pharisees fast and His disciples do not. He simply identifies

Himself as the bridegroom[22] and declares that His presence in Israel should be celebrated like a wedding feast and not with ceremonial fasting. In short, being one of His disciples is to be like participating in a wedding feast.

Nevertheless, Jesus would not always be with them. There would be separation from the intimacy intended for their union. He longs to gather them to Himself for intimacy and protection like a hen gathers her chicks (Matt. 23:37–30). But He "came to His own, and those who were His own did not receive Him" (John 1:11), because they love power and money (Matt. 23:1–36) more than Him. So Jesus changes the time frame of the bridegroom/bride imagery to call His people, His disciples, to anticipate and prepare for His arrival after His imminent absence from them. He uses the parable of the ten virgins, His only other reference to the bridegroom concept, to compare the delaying of His coming as the Son of Man with that of a bridegroom's delay (Matt. 25:1–13). Five awaiting virgins are foolishly unprepared for Him and five were prudently prepared (25:2–9). The foolish ones are not on intimate terms with the bridegroom. He claims, "Truly I say to you, I do not know you" when they want to be let in late to the wedding feast (25:10–12). And so Jesus concludes with the succinct warning about their anticipation and preparation. "Be on the alert then, for you do not know the day nor the hour" of the Bridegroom's, that is, His return (25:13).[23]

This same movement of Christ toward being intimately united with His bride and our anticipation and need for preparation is described in the marriage supper of the Lamb and the descending of the New Jerusalem in the book of Revelation. The focal point of the celebration of the marriage supper is joy and gladness (Isa. 62:4–5) because the time for the feast has come and "His bride has made herself ready." The demonstration of her readiness is in the clothing given to her, "fine linen, bright and clean," which symbolizes "the righteous acts of the saints" (Rev. 19:7–8). Then at the consummation of the marriage, the New Jerusalem, specifically ascribed as a "holy city," is itself "made ready as a bride adorned for her husband" (Rev. 21:2). After the wedding John is shown "the bride, the wife of the Lamb," "the holy city, Jerusalem, coming down out of heaven from God" (Rev. 21:9–10). The anticipated culmination of the marriage covenant occurs. A new kinship unit has been formed and they now are able to live together forever. It is not surprising,

---

22. This emphasis on this imagery is significant, since all of the Synoptic Gospels include it in their account of this discussion (Matt. 9:14–15; Mark 2:18–20; Luke 5:33–35).

23. For Jesus's expectation of the appropriate response to God's invitation to be a part of His kingdom, see His parable of the wedding feast of the king's son in Matthew 22:1–14.

then, that the final reference of this image underscores not only preparation/ anticipation emphasis, but also the longing for the Bridegroom to make His way to His bride. "The Spirit and the bride say, 'Come'" (Rev. 22:17a).[24]

THE BIBLE'S DIVINE HUSBAND-AND-WIFE STORY

The husband/wife metaphor is one of the most compelling pictures for God's people in the Bible. It can cause us to stagger and drop us to our knees as well as enliven and motivate us to be extraordinarily sacrificial for others. It has two central aspects: one from the marriage relationship itself, and the other from the roles within that relationship. The marriage image itself stresses faithful love, whereas the husband's role initiates love and sacrifice for his wife and the wife's role is responsive to the husband in trust, respect, and submission. At the same time, these two aspects overlap to stress the unique union of marriage itself.

The Old Testament

Intimacy through faithfulness (vs. infidelity) is the focus of the marriage image for God and His people in the Old Testament, especially in the prophetic literature. The Lord only describes His relationship to Israel as a marriage to demonstrate the destructive alienation their idolatrous spiritual adultery causes. Hosea's marriage to the prostitute Gomer is the heartbreaking real-life metaphor for this. Yet He promised exiled Israel He would cause them to forget their shame because "your husband is your Maker, whose name is the Lord of hosts" (Isa. 54:5). He would call them from exile "like a wife forsaken and grieved in spirit, even like a wife of one's youth when she is rejected" (Isa. 54:6). This rejection was symbolized by His divorcing them. In Jeremiah 3:8, He gave the northern kingdom a certificate of divorce (*etsepher kerituteha*).

---

24. It is interesting to note that these same marriage themes find theological parallels elsewhere. One striking example is in Ephesians 1:4–8 and 5:25–32. Out of love God the Father began the process toward gaining a new people by choosing us before the foundation of the world (1:4). He prepares us as His people to be "holy and blameless" (1:4; 5:25). As in adoption, God enacts a legal covenant to make us part of His new family unit (1:5; 5:30–32). The Father has paid the ultimate (dowry) price for us by providing the death of His own Son as our Kinsman Redeemer (1:7; 5:25). He has done this to forgive us of our many trespasses and cleanse us of our impurity (1:7; 5:26). The Father freely and graciously lavishes us with the gift of this new relationship out of His good pleasure and for His praise (1:5–6; 5:29). As this kind of bride, this kind of adopted child, this member of Christ's body, the Church, we cannot help but entrust ourselves to this Lord Jesus Christ, to powerfully love His people, and to hope in His calling for the age to come (1:15–23; 5:22–33). We must long to be united with our Savior and Lord. We must prepare ourselves daily as we anticipate His imminent return.

Later He left Judah (Isa. 54:6–7). This divorce appears to be warranted from Israel's breaking off of their relationship with Him.[25]

This infidelity of God's wife is graphically depicted not only as adultery but adultery of a gross kind: harlotry or prostitution. One of the rawest descriptions of this "whoredom"[26] is in Ezekiel 23. Here the Lord recounts the activities of two women, Oholoah and Ohlibah, who represent Samaria and Jerusalem, the capital cities of the northern and southern kingdoms. He uses a variety of terms and phrases to convey attitudes and behaviors that caused Him to be "disgusted with her" (23:18). They played the harlot/whore (23:2, 5, 30), and "bestowed her harlotries" or "gave herself as a prostitute" (NIV, 23:7), on foreign men who represent foreign gods. These "harlotries" increase to a staggering amount (23:11, 14). But most importantly, He also classifies it as committing acts of "adultery" (*naaph*, 23:37) against Him as their husband to whom they were to be completely faithful.

Their motivation was the opposite of real love, even though she pursued her "lovers" (23:5, 9), and they came to her "bed of love" (23:17). She would "lust after" Assyrians and Babylonians, etc. (23:7). This was idolatry with all their gods. It caused her to defile herself (23:7, 13, 17, 30, 38) by her "lewdness" or corrupt, destructive acts (*chabal*, 23:21, 27, 29, 35, 48, 49).

What makes this account so disturbing is the sexually intimate language the Lord uses. Israel had "played the harlot" in Egypt when "their breasts were fondled and their virgin bosoms caressed" (23:3, NIV). There "in her youth

---

25. Amazingly, after what the Lord considers a short exile, He reunited with His adulterous wife:

> "For a brief moment I deserted you,
>   but with great compassion I will gather you.
> In overflowing anger for a moment
>   I hid my face from you,
> but with everlasting love I will have compassion on you,"
>   says the LORD, your Redeemer. (Isa. 54:7–8)

Thus it may be that this divorce imagery could actually be considered a period of separation in light of God's "great compassion" and unconditional covenant with His people. The Lord made the claim in Ezekiel 16:60–63 that He would "remember My covenant with you in the days of your youth, and I will establish an everlasting covenant with you." This was to bring about repentance through their shame and humiliation. And yet He closes this admonishment with "so that you may remember and be ashamed and never open your mouth anymore because of you humiliation, when I have forgiven you for all that you have done."

26. *Zanah* is the most common term signifying Israel's whoredom/harlotry/prostitution (*zenuth* and *taznuth*) in the Old Testament. *Naaph*, which emphasizes the act of committing adultery, is also used (Jer. 3:8, 9; 13:27; Ezek. 16:38; 23:37; Hos. 4:13–14). The New Testament uses *moichalis* (Matt. 12:29; 16:4; Mark 8:38; James 4:4) and *moicheuō* (Rev. 2:22).

men had lain with her and handled her virgin bosom and poured out their whoring lust upon her" (23:8, ESV; cf. 23:21). She uncovered her nakedness, and the unsavory men "went in to her" (23:44). Yet this wanton sexual activity turned violent. Her "lovers" abused her by stripping her naked, slaughtering her children, leaving her publicly disgraced (23:9–10, 25–26).

The Lord has been deeply affected by the spiritual adultery of His people throughout their history.[27] The loving intimacy they should have joyously shared is thrown away too often. It is discarded for replicas of supposed powerful beings that promise to satisfy their needs and longings. Patterson's summary of these images is indeed correct: "Thus throughout not only God's undying love for and faithfulness to his own are underscored, but as well his standards of holiness and justice. What was needed was a corresponding love and devotion on the part of God's people."[28]

The New Testament

Jesus Christ continues the Old Testament trajectory claiming that the present state of Israel is one of spiritual unfaithfulness to God. They have not only drifted far from God even amidst their fastidious religiosity, but refuse to openly and warmly accept His own Son. When some of the scribes and Pharisees demand a miraculous sign from Him to prove His identity, He responds incisively, "An evil and adulterous generation craves for a sign" (Matt. 12:38–39).[29] In Mark 8:38, Jesus unites refusing to follow Him and His teachings with this same concept: "For whoever is ashamed of Me and My words in this adulterous and sinful generation, the Son of Man will also be ashamed of him when He comes in the glory of His Father with the holy angels." The anticipated intimacy of their relationship can never materialize because the Messiah's people are unprepared.

---

27. Throughout Israel's history the Lord is provoked to jealousy, as can be seen in numerous passages in the Pentateuch (e.g., Exod. 34:11–16; Lev. 17:7; 20:4–6; Num. 15:38–40; Deut. 31:16), historical books (e.g., Judg. 2:16–17; 8:27, 33), as well as the prophets (e.g., Isa. 1:21–23; 57:3; Jer. 2:20, 23–25; 3:1–6; 13:20–27; Ezek. 16:15–43a; 23:1–49; Hos. 1–3; Mic. 1:7) and the New Testament (e.g., Matt. 12:38–39; 16:1–2, 4; 1 Cor. 6:15–17; 2 Cor. 11:1–3; James 4:4; Rev. 2:14, 20–23). Raymond C. Ortlund, Jr. has captured the breadth of this truth in his work, *Whoredom: God's Unfaithful Wife in Biblical Theology*, New Studies in Biblical Theology (Grand Rapids: Eerdmans, 1996).

28. Richard D. Patterson, "Metaphors of Marriage as Expressions of Divine–Human Relations," *Journal of the Evangelical Theological Society* 51, no. 4 (2008): 698.

29. Later, after Jesus fed the four thousand, these men come to test Him and again demand from Him a sign from heaven. And again, Jesus repeats the same assessment, "An evil and adulterous generation seeks after a sign; and a sign will not be given it, except the sign of Jonah" (Matt. 16:4).

Paul combines the bridegroom/bride metaphor with the husband/wife in 2 Corinthians 11:2. Yet his fulcrum of these images is marital fidelity:

> I wish you would bear with me in a little foolishness. Do bear with me! For I feel a divine jealousy for you, since I betrothed you to one husband, to present you as a pure virgin to Christ. But I am afraid that as the serpent deceived Eve by his cunning, your thoughts will be led astray from a sincere and pure devotion to Christ. For if someone comes and proclaims another Jesus than the one we proclaimed, or if you receive a different spirit from the one you received, or if you accept a different gospel from the one you accepted, you put up with it readily enough. (2 Cor. 11:1–4)

Again, rather than pure and intimate fellowship with Paul and Christ, they are being led astray. Instead of moving toward Christ, they are moving away from Him to another suitor. These suitors, the false teachers infiltrating Corinth, are not only undermining Paul's apostolic authority, but the Corinthians' faithfulness to Paul, his gospel, and the Lord Jesus Christ.

Paul views this in the same vein as Israel's unfaithful idolatry, which we saw above. He uses a biting sarcasm to try to cause the Corinthians to see the irony of their "openness" to new and different teachings and people. And yet their view of an "open marriage," so to speak, was nothing other than spiritual adultery. Paul is personally wounded and "jealous" like God is, when His people are unfaithful to Him. Paul's goal of ministry is to present them "as a pure virgin to Christ" (11:2).

In Ephesians 5:22–33, the husband-and-wife imagery used by Paul is essential to certain truths about the nature of Christ's relationship with the church. As Christ is the head of the church and she is to submit to Him, analogously, the wife is to be submissive to her husband since He not only is her head but her Savior (5:22–24). In a sense, He earned this special role in their relationship by His giving Himself up for her (5:25). While there is obvious love and amazing depth to this analogy, there does not seem to be any emotionally romantic element to the submissive role the church is to assume. On the contrary, the "ranking oneself under another" concept behind "submit" (*hupotassō*) in this context merely calls the wife and the believer to yield their own rights in the relationship in loving trust and respect.

As Christ sacrificially loved the church by sacrificing Himself on the cross for us, husbands by analogy are to consistently love their wives (5:25–29). This love, while intimate, is primarily sacrificial. It is a love that recognizes imperfections in another but assists them in achieving personal purity before God (5:26–27).[30] Therefore, husbands should emulate Christ's love for the church. He loves us as His own body, since "we are members of His body" (5:30). Paul connects this to Genesis 2:24 with husbands and wives leaving, cleaving, and becoming one flesh. Yet he declares the similar union Christ has to the church a great mystery.

METAPHORICAL SEXUAL UNION?

At this point, we have to answer a crucial question concerning intimacy. Because these images include sexuality, is the sexual union within marriage a mysterious metaphor for intimacy with Christ? For biblical scholars, this is not a new connection. In most cases,[31] they do not mean anything untoward by this. They simply see ultimate intimacy as being sexual. At least a hint of this can be attained spiritually with Christ, either in this age or in the one to come.

---

30. Even though Abbott goes to a more stoic extreme when he claims, "there is no emotion in self-love," he does aptly describe its leading the husband to "regard her welfare as his own, and to feel all that concerns her as if it concerned himself." This conjugal love may be based in affections, but is "reinforced by reflection, and made firm by the sense of duty." T. K. Abbott, *A Critical and Exegetical Commentary on the Epistles to the Ephesians and Colossians*, The International Critical Commentary (Edinburgh: T & T Clark, 1897), 171.

31. From a liberal feminist perspective, Keefe traces this sexual union to Israel's cultural surroundings. She maligns the traditional view that "The God of Israel may exercise power over the realm of fertility but is not in any way implicated in that realm. He may bring fertility, but he is not a fertility god." Alice A. Keefe, "Hosea's (In)fertility God," *Horizons in Biblical Theology* 30 (2008): 26. To be sure, many scholars have bifurcated God too radically, separating His transcendent provision from His immanent and personal interaction with His creation. But her solution is to make Him the high god over all fertility gods, in keeping with the evolution of religion school of thought. Ibid., 22–23, 35–38. Most importantly at this juncture, God participates not only in blessing His people with fertility, but fertilizes them personally. She translates Hosea 2:25 as "and I will inseminate her in the land for myself" (24). This is directly opposed to the consensus translation "and I will sow" that fits the agricultural context much better. She, like others, views the statement that God "knows" His people as some sort of metaphorical sexual union. See, for example, John Piper's use of this language in his "Sex and the Supremacy of Christ: Part 1," *Sex and the Supremacy of God*, edited by John Piper and Justin Taylor (Wheaton, IL: Crossway, 2005) 31–32. Keefe's motivation for this is from her feminism that sees women as wrongly characterized in the Bible. She claims, "In the metaphysical dualisms of Western thought, women and all things feminine have long been associated with the debased pole of matter, along with nature, sexuality, temptation and sin, while men and maleness, along with mind, reason, free will and moral action in history have symbolically associated with the exalted pole of spirit" (24). At the same time, her point is well taken that the prostitute imagery is not meant to communicate only the infidelity of female Israelites against the Lord; males within the society were equally adulterous. This would include the priests who, like with Aaron and the golden calf debacle in Exodus 32, led the people into adulterous idolatry.

A view common in church history is that sexual intercourse is a metaphor throughout the Bible for Christ's intimate union or consummation as
groom or husband with His bride or wife. A striking example of this is in a
blog by Marvin Olasky (the editor-in-chief of *World Magazine*) entitled, "20
Thoughts on Intimacy with God: A Holy Experience."[32] He lists numerous
examples of this metaphorical sexual intimacy in what he claims to be the
language of Scripture and historical Protestant Christianity.

Olasky seems to gain further permission to do this from the last chapter
of Ann Voskamp's deeply moving New York Times best seller, *One Thousand
Gifts: A Dare to Live Fully Right Where You Are.*[33] The first sentence of this
chapter simply states, "I fly to Paris and discover how to make love to God."[34]
As she describes her experience of being alone in Paris, she claims that God
woos her as she sheds her fear and is drawn into closer communion with Him.
Upon citing 1 Corinthians 6:17, "But the person who is joined to the Lord is
one spirit with Him," she enters into an erotic description of her encounter
with the Lord:

> I run my hand along my loft bed, wood hewn by a hand several hundred
> years ago. I can hear Him. He's calling for a response; He's calling for
> oneness. *Communion.* Jesus says there is no other way to take up the faith
> but complete union: "I am in my Father, and you are in me, and I am in
> you" (John 14:20). I am stilled. . . . I lay thinking. This invitation to have
> communion with Love—is this the edge of the mystery Paul speaks of? "A
> man leaves his father and mother and is joined to his wife, and the two are
> united into one." This is a great mystery, but it is an illustration of the way
> Christ and the church are one' (Ephesians 5:31–32). The two, Christ and
> the church, becoming one flesh—the mystery of that romance. Breath fall-
> ing on face, Spirit touching Spirit, the long embrace, the entering in and
> being within—this is what God seeks? With each of us? . . . Mystical union.
> This, the highest degree of importance. God as Husband in sacred wedlock,
> bound together, body and soul, fed by His body, quenched by His blood—

32. Marvin Olasky, "20 Thoughts on Intimacy with God: A Holy Experience," Ann Voskamp,
    http://www.aholyexperience.com/intimacy-with-god.
33. Ann Voskamp, *One Thousand Gifts: A Dare to Live Fully Right Where You Are* (Grand
    Rapids: Zondervan, 2011), 201–22.
34. Ibid., 201.

this is where *eucharisto* leads. Lover bestows upon the Beloved, gifts, the Beloved gives thanks for those gifts and enters into the mystical love union.[35]

She then reaches a climax of her mystical love of God:

> God, He has blessed—caressed.
> *I could bless God*—caress with thanks.
> It's our making love.
> God makes love with grace upon grace, every moment a making of His love for us. And He invites the turning over of the hand, the opening and the saying Yes with thanks. Then God lays down all of His fullness into all the emptiness. I am in Him. He is in me. I embrace God in the moment. I give him thanks and *I bless God* and we meet and couldn't I make love to God, making every moment love for Him? To know Him the way Adam knew Eve. Spirit skin to spirit skin. . . . The intercourse of soul with God is the very climax of joy.[36]

Olasky's response to this is simple: "I once taught a course on Puritan writing, and I recall that they used imagery in the same way Voskamp does, without people doubting their orthodoxy."[37] This is racy spirituality.

We can imagine the Puritans allegorizing Christ and the church in this way, but Olasky cites two other extremely influential evangelicals. First, Tim Keller claims,

> Sex is for fully committed relationships because it is to be a foretaste of the joy that comes from being in complete union with God. The most rapturous love between a man and woman is only a hint of God's love for us (Rom. 7:1–6; Eph. 5:21–33). . . . Positively, we are called to experience the spousal love of Jesus.[38]

---

35. Ibid., 211–13.
36. Ibid., 216–18, italics in original.
37. Olasky, "20 Thoughts on Intimacy with God."
38. Tim Keller, "The Gospel and Sex," Christ 2R Culture, http://www.christ2rculture.com/resources/Ministry-Blog/The-Gospel-and-Sex-by-Tim-Keller.pdf (originally from The Gospel and Life conferences of 2004 and 2005). Peter Kreeft also claims that "sex is a sign and appetizer" of the mystical union with God. Peter Kreeft, "A Refutation of Moral Relativism—Transcription," http://www.peterkreeft.com/audio/05_relativism/relativism_transcription.htm.

Second, John Piper develops this in Hosea 2:14–23:

> But the most daring statement of all is the last one in verse 20: "And you shall know the Lord." To see what this means recall the peculiar use of the word "know" in the Bible. For example, Genesis 4:1, "Adam knew Eve his wife and she conceived and bore Cain." And Matthew 1:25, "Joseph knew her [Mary] not until she had borne a son." In the context of a broken marriage being renewed with the fresh vows of betrothal must not the words, "and you shall know the Lord" (v. 20), mean, you shall enjoy an intimacy like that of the purest sexual intercourse. When the wife of harlotry returns to her husband, he will withhold nothing. He will not keep her at a distance. The fellowship and communion and profoundest union he will give to his prodigal wife when she comes home broken and empty.[39]

Piper later boldly but carefully develops this idea in one of his essays in the book *Sex and the Sovereignty of God*:

> Now I don't mean that every time the word know is used in the Bible there are sexual connotations. That's not true. But what I do mean is that sexual language in the Bible for our covenant relationship to God does lead us to think of knowing God on the analogy of sexual intimacy and ecstasy. I don't mean that we somehow have sexual relations with God or he with man. That's a pagan thought. It's not Christian. But I do mean that the intimacy and ecstasy of sexual relations points to what knowing God is meant to be.[40]

He is clear that knowing God is not merely intellectual. He rightly argues, "I think it is virtually impossible to read this and then honestly say that knowing God, as God intends to be known by his people in the new covenant, simply means mental awareness or understanding or acquaintance with God."[41] However, as passionately as he proclaims this, is this the best way to illustrate this? Is this the best interpretation and application of the marriage metaphor in Hosea and Ezekiel? I don't think so.

---

39. John Piper, "Call Me Husband, Not Baal," Sermon, Bethlehem Baptist Church, December 26, 1982, http://www.soundofgrace.com/piper82/122682m.htm.
40. John Piper, "Sex and the Supremacy of Christ: Part 1," *Sex and the Supremacy of Christ*, eds. John Piper and Justin Taylor (Wheaton, IL: Crossway, 2007), 31.
41. Ibid., 32.

So what are we to think? Is sexual intercourse between husband and wife a metaphor for intimacy with Christ and His Church? Often interpretations of "one flesh"[42] set the course toward or away from this as a sexual metaphor elsewhere. However, one flesh is more than sex. It is a covenant kinship that is culminated in intimate marital sex.[43] Paul even argues this in 1 Corinthians 6 when he cites Genesis 2:24. He forbids them to "join" themselves to temple prostitutes, because Christians are joined to Christ (1 Cor. 6:17). Yet their union with prostitutes is not merely a sexual reference but a covenant-kinship one. They are not to break their covenant vow with Christ and join another relationship. They are members of His body. The Corinthians' Neoplatonism allowed them to believe their physical bodies are separate and less valuable than their spiritual sides, so sex with the temple prostitutes doesn't affect their relationship with Christ. Paul dismantles this thinking quickly. We are members of Christ, joined to His body, that is, the Church. He cites Genesis 2:24 to further demonstrate that we are joined together just like husbands and wives are joined together in a one-flesh relationship. Being "joined" to Christ in 6:17 is not a sexual metaphor. It is our being one in spirit with Him, since we are temples of the Holy Spirit (6:19). This is made possible by His payment of our redemption (6:20). As we will see, Paul describes this union in Ephesians as well.[44]

---

42. Whichever view one takes, it makes sense that "one" is *echad*, used for compound unions (Num. 13:23; Deut. 6:4), vs. *yahid* (singular unity). There is something unique to this relationship. Furthermore, Adam's use of *ishah* from *ish* demonstrates their "unique 'genetic' relationship" (David Shepherd, "'Strike His Bone and His Flesh': Reading Job from the Beginning," *Journal for the Study of the Old Testament* 33 [2008]: 86).

43. Tasuto takes a slightly different approach. However, he still decidedly favors "one flesh" as being marriage itself over against it being "love," which he views as a consequence of marriage. Angelo Tasuto, "On Genesis 2:24," *The Catholic Biblical Quarterly* 52 (1990): 404–5.

44. However, the one-flesh union is more than simply a business transaction. Adam truly rejoices in his new relationship with Eve. "The way the author builds suspense in Genesis 2:18–23 also expresses his approval. . . . If we are reading this for the first time, we wonder who is the fit helper; and then we see how far God will go to produce one—anesthesia and surgery, verse 21—we are prepared to agree with the man's satisfied declaration." Nakedness in verse 25 implies the possibility of sexual intercourse in marriage. However, sexual intercourse is not the beginning of marriage, just the consummation or completion of it. It is an expression of a benefit and purpose of the covenant itself. C. John Collins, *Genesis 1-4: A Linguistic, Literary, and Theological Commentary* (Phillipsburg, NJ: P&R Publishing, 2006), 139. In Matthew 19:5–6 (Mark 10:8), Jesus claims that God joins a couple in marriage. In His appeal to Genesis 2:24, is He declaring this occurs when people join sexually on wedding day? That is a forced insertion into the context. He is declaring that God joins when people join under a covenant, and that no one should separate them and break the covenant.

So "one flesh" is both the covenant kinship and its pleasurable procreative sexual consummation. To claim "either/or" is reductionistic. However, does this give us the license to apply this sexual aspect of the "one flesh" element of marriage metaphorically to Christ and the church? I would say yes and no. We should affirm that the Bible uses adultery as a metaphor for spiritual infidelity through idolatry. This is clearly a violation of the essence of marriage. To leave Christ for idols is not only a violation of the covenant-kinship bond between us as members of His family, but also it is as if we joined ourselves to another for the satisfaction of our urges (power, sex, etc.).

However, we may not logically reverse the sexual aspect of the metaphor to pursue or wait for an ultimate one-flesh intimacy with Christ. We do not pursue a deeper covenant-kinship bond with Him, because we already have that in the New Covenant (Jer. 31:31–33; Heb. 8:7–9:28; 10:15–25). We are to remain faithful to the covenant bond we are in. Unlike Keller, we may not reverse the metaphor to say that it teaches us to pursue a deeper union with Christ like intimate "rapturous sex" with our spouse. Earlier, Piper struggles with being consistent to the clear covenant element of the marriage metaphors when he claims that "sexual language in the Bible for our covenant relationship to God does lead us to think of knowing God on the analogy of sexual intimacy and ecstasy." Why should this lead us to this analogy? Metaphors like parables are meant to have one main point and application.[45] The marriage/adultery metaphor is only that.[46] It is primarily a prohibitive analogy. Obviously, maintaining our faithfulness to Christ amidst worldly temptations is a legitimate assertive application.

To add any sexual innuendo is beyond the intent of the metaphor and must be avoided. It causes Christians, including Piper, to connect the verb "to know" in Hosea 2:20, Ezekiel 16:62, etc. to sexual intimacy, just because it is used for Adam knowing or having sexual relations with Eve. To be consistent this would have to mean that when Paul desires in 2 Corinthians 11:2 to "present" the Corinthians "as a pure virgin to Christ," he intends for them to

---

45. It is interesting to note that Patterson's study sees little if any reversal of sexual imagery in these marital metaphors. Patterson, "Metaphors of Marriage as Expressions of Divine-Human Relations." See especially his conclusions on pp. 701–2.

46. Stauffer is indeed correct when he observes that the Old Testament has no hint of any actualization of this relationship in mysteries, or of any sensually perceptible union with the deity. On the contrary, marriage is simply a symbol for the covenant between God and the people which is to be kept in all fidelity and renewed with passion (Hos. 2:19; Isa. 54:4ff.; 62:4f.; Ezra. 16:7ff.). Ethelbert Stauffer, "*gameo, gamos,*" in Kittel, ed., *Theological Dictionary of the New Testament*, 1:653–54.

have intimate oneness like a metaphorical sexual union with Him. That is not what Paul is ascribing.

Who wants to be the one to parse out what is sexually appropriate and inappropriate of this metaphor? What is taking it too far? Is it kissing Jesus? Is it the ultimate coitus itself? Is Ann Voskamp biblically justified in claiming, "I fly to Paris and discover how to make love to God"?[47] How is that to help in our intimacy with Christ? Or is it something more? These questions demonstrate the difficulty of going down the path of reversing the metaphor and allowing for any sort of sexual nuancing.

METAPHORICAL MYSTERIOUS UNION WITH CHRIST

Another key issue for the intimacy of the marital imagery used for Christ and the church in this passage is wrapped up in what Paul means by "this mystery is great" in Ephesians 5:32:

> So husbands ought also to love their own wives as their own bodies. He who loves his own wife loves himself; for no one ever hated his own flesh, but nourishes and cherishes it, just as Christ also does the church, because we are members of His body. FOR THIS REASON A MAN SHALL LEAVE HIS FATHER AND MOTHER AND SHALL BE JOINED TO HIS WIFE, AND THE TWO SHALL BECOME ONE FLESH. This mystery is great; but I am speaking with reference to Christ and the church. (Eph. 5:28–32)

These words have been used to open up the marital imagery of the whole Bible, and thus to further elaborate and intimately be applied to Christians and their relationship with Christ. It is imperative to clarify what Paul means here. There are three main views as to what "mystery" means here.[48]

The first view believes the mystery is human marriage mentioned in Genesis 2:24.[49] This is the Roman Catholic view. They understand the institution of marriage as a church sacrament to be a conveyor of God's grace. It is not that they deny the metaphoric nature of human marriage for Christ and the Church. His sacrifice for the Church is what gives Christian marriage its

---

47. Voskamp, *One Thousand Gifts*, 201. See also 216–18.
48. Andreas J. Köstenberger, "The Mystery of Christ and the Church: Head and Body, 'One Flesh,'" *Trinity Journal* NS 12, no. 1 (1991): 79–94; and Harold W. Hoehner, *Ephesians: An Exegetical Commentary* (Grand Rapids: Baker, 2002), 776–78.
49. *Catechism of the Catholic Church*, 2nd ed. (Libreria Editrice Vaticana, 1994), 400 [1602], 406 [1624].

"mystery" and thus the redemptive value it has always had. Support is drawn from the Vulgate's translation of *mustērion* as *sacramentum*.[50] These are the principles undergirding Jessica Hayes's view of marriage as a Catholic and her commitment to marrying Jesus.

This cannot be Paul's view here. It would make marriage a means of God's grace contributing to the ultimate salvation of believers only. Thus only marrying in the church merits this grace. Yet there is no distinction of "Christian" marriage versus secular marriage stated or implied in Genesis 2:24. This mystifies marriage even though it is a human institution, albeit created by God, throughout all societies.[51] Barth is indeed correct in claiming that human marriage is "not a semiheavenly repetition of Christ's romance."[52] Furthermore, there is no evidence of this view being a part of first-century thinking after this in Western Asia Minor, but only in later second- or third-century Gnostic sources.[53] Thus marriage partners should not use each other to become closer to God.[54] In addition, we are not married to Christ individually, but as a corporate entity. Otherwise, Christ has multiple wives. And, those called to singleness must either have no access to this sacrament, or they must marry Christ. This is a view from implication not from Scripture.

The second view is the union of Christ and the church as the deeper typological meaning of marriage in Genesis 2:24.[55] However, this cannot be the

---

50. Some argue that this view is connected to pagan marriage rituals (*hieros gamos* or "holy wedding"). Hoehner, *Ephesians*, 776; and Richard A. Batey, "Jewish Gnosticism and the '*hieros gamos*' of Eph. 5:21–33," *New Testament Studies* 10, no. 1 (1963): 121–27.
51. Some cite 1 Corinthians 7:12–16 for marriage being a sacrament, due to the sanctifying effects of a Christian spouse being married to a nonbeliever. This is merely God's common grace and not the institution itself.
52. Markus Barth, *Ephesians 4–6*, Anchor Bible Commentary, 34A (New York: Doubleday & Co., 1974), 748.
53. Hoehner, *Ephesians*, 777.
54. Köstenberger summarizes Barth on this well, when he adds, "There is a syncretistic element introduced from pagan religion where partners use each other to come closer to the divine." Kostenberger, "The Mystery of Christ and the Church," 86; Barth, *Ephesians 4–6*, 748–49.
55. An example of this is found in Pol Vonck, "This Mystery Is a Profound One (Ephes. 5:32): A Biblical Reflection on Marriage," *African Ecclesial Review* 24, no. 5 (1982): 278–88 (287): "What is the mystery? It is the depth-dimension of 'one flesh', the *beyond* in human sexuality. In light of Jesus's story (in Matt. 19:1–10), Gen. 2:24 acquires a new dimension. Men and women try to become one flesh, but they never fully succeed. The Church on the contrary *is* the body (Eph. 1:23); the Christian community is the flesh of Christ (v. 29). This deepened meaning of 'one flesh' illumines what human marriage is called to be." See also F. F. Bruce, who sees the mystery as referring to Christ and the church, but in light of Christ's saving work: "the hidden meaning of Gen. 2:24 now begins to appear: his people constitute his bride, united to him in 'one body'. The formation of Eve to be

case since *mustērion* does not have this deeper meaning in Ephesians or the New Testament.[56] More importantly, the context of verses 30 and 33 speaks of believers as members of Christ's body. This spiritual union is merely illustrated by the human union in Genesis 2:24.

The third and best view is the union of Christ and the church specifically.[57] This fits with how Paul argues his case here and in 1 Corinthians 6. Hoehner rightly notes that when Paul cites Genesis 2:24 in 1 Corinthians 6:16, he uses it in a similar way. Since believers are members of Christ's body, they should not commit sexual immorality with temple prostitutes because a man then is joined to the prostitute and becomes one body with her. Paul proves his point by citing Genesis 2:24. He parallels this one body concept with the reality that the believer joins himself to the Lord, thus they are one spirit with Him (6:17). He uses the same pattern in Ephesians 5 arguing from the spiritual realm (5:30) to the physical (Gen. 2:24 in 5:31) and then returning to the spiritual (5:32). Earlier Paul argues that Christ is the loving model for the husband. The church is the trusting and submissive model for the wife (5:24–27). So the one flesh union of the husband and wife is a model for the union of Christ and the church (5:31–32). Thus the "mystery" is clearly the union of Christ and the church.

If this is what Paul means, then what is the essence of this intimate union he is referring to? It is not a metaphoric intimacy like sexual intercourse. Throughout Ephesians Paul tells us that it is our identifying with and obtaining "Christ's fullness." In 1:22–23 he makes a staggering claim that we as the church are not only the body of Christ, but we are "the fullness of Him who fills all in all" (*plēroumenou*). This is Old Testament temple language, when it was filled with God's presence (Jer. 23:24; Ezek. 44:4).[58] We are "the dwelling place of Jesus

---

Adam's companion is seen to prefigure the creation of the church to be the bride of Christ. This seems to the be the deep 'mystery' contained in the text, which remains a mystery no longer to those who have received its interpretation." He sees Paul using contemporary Qumran interpretational methods (a hidden sense). F. F. Bruce, *The Epistles to the Colossians, to Philemon, and to the Ephesians*, The New International Commentary on the New Testament (Grand Rapids: Eerdmans, 1984), 394–95. Kostenberger rightly objects to this and states, "The difference between Paul's usage and Qumran's, however, is that Paul does not resort to the often far-fetched 'contemporizing' hermeneutic methodology so common in the Dead Sea Scrolls." "The Mystery of Christ and the Church," 81.

56. See Andrew T. Lincoln's conclusive research in "The Use of the OT in Ephesians," *Journal for the Study of the New Testament* 14 (1982): 31–33.

57. Köstenberger, "The Mystery of Christ and the Church," 79–94. See also Lincoln, "The Use of the OT in Ephesians," 32–33, 36.

58. Clinton E. Arnold, *Ephesians: Power and Magic: The Concept of Power in Ephesians* (Cambridge: Cambridge University Press, 1989), 83–85.

Christ, the place where his 'fullness' resides."[59] Like in the temple, Christ's fullness is specially chosen to abide in the church,[60] even though he universally "fills all in all" (1:23). In this intimate union we experience the fullness of the Spirit's power, Christ's love and God's glory (3:14–21). Through this we can gain confidence that Christ has chosen us and given us an amazing ability to mediate His presence to the world.[61] This fullness is brought to fruition in His body's growth toward being like Him (4:12–16). That is, we experience and take on the perfection and magnitude of His character (4:13, 15).[62]

Isn't this a profound union we have with Christ? He loves His own body as husbands are to love their wives as their own bodies. It is a great mystery how as His church we are His body, of which He is our very head. Yet we are joined to Him as a unit to enjoy His fullness. Just like the temple in the Old Testament, He fills us with His presence. We are filled with the Spirit's power, Christ's own love, and God's glory. This is how God in Christ can join into a mysterious union with humans.

This is the same union Christ prayed for to His Father (John 17:21, 23). It is the same the union believers have when they abide or remain in Christ as branches to the vine (John 15:4, 7). This abiding union is again based on salvation (15:3), appropriation of the truth of Christ and His teachings (John 15:7; 1 John 2:21–24), and acceptance and modeling of Christ's love (15:8–10).

In summary then, the Bible's metaphors of the divine Bridegroom and bride, Husband and wife are a part of an unfolding story in the Old and New Testaments that calls us ultimately to an intimate relationship with Christ Himself. The bridegroom/bride image is used to communicate our need to prepare

---

59. Timothy G. Gombis, "Being the Fullness of God in Christ by the Spirit: Ephesians 5:18 in Its Epistolary Setting," *Tyndale Bulletin* 53, no. 2 (2002): 260.

60. Paul actually prays for us to discern this through our experience of the powerful fullness of the salvation Christ provides us all by faith (1:18–19). For example, in Romans 6:3–6, this same union is founded upon the uniting of us as believers in the death and resurrection of Christ. Paul argues there, "For if we have become united with Him in the likeness of His death, certainly we shall also be in the likeness of His resurrection" (6:5). The old sin nature we inherited from Adam dies when we entrust ourselves to Christ and His sacrificial death on our behalf. Sin then is no longer our master, but we are able to "walk in newness of life" since we are now "alive to God" (6:4, 11–14). There does not seem to be any fuller way to be united to Christ in our salvation.

61. Robert L. Foster, "A Temple in the Lord Filled to the Fullness of God: Context and Intertexuality (Eph. 3:19)," *Novum Testamentum* 49, no. 1 (2007): 94–95.

62. In Ephesians 5:18, we experience our union with Christ's fullness when we obey Paul's call for us to be "filled with the Spirit" (5:18). This is our yielding to God's will and influence. This filling will transform our relationships (5:19–6:9), including our very marriages that serve as the analogy of Christ's union with His church (5:22–33). We will develop the Holy Spirit's role in intimacy with God in the next chapter.

ourselves for Christ's imminent return. It is joyful for the pure (Rev. 19:7–10; 21:2, 9), but it is mostly a call for serious repentance (Matt. 25:1–13; 2 Cor. 11:1–3). The husband/wife imagery may be viewed from two vantage points. On one side, the marital image itself stresses how we are to love God/Christ and be faithful to Him (Ezek. 16:8–43; 23:1–49; Hosea 1–3; James 4:4). On the other, like Christ, the husband's role initiates love and sacrifice for his wife (Eph. 5:25–33). Like the church, the wife's role is responsive to her husband in trust, respect, and submission (Eph. 5:22–24, 33). At the same time, these vantage points overlap to stress in both testaments the unique union of marriage itself, but not the intimacy of sexual intercourse. The mysterious union of Christ and His body is in our experiencing His fullness, love, and sanctifying power (Eph. 5:32).

However, we need to move on to how to apply these images. In light of our history as the church, this is where we must tread lightly. Many feel we are justified in connecting the metaphors for Christ's wedding and marriage to His people to a variety of allegorizings and contemporary Western concepts. Many loudly proclaim that we ought to be pursuing some sort of divine romance with Him. But as we assess the legitimacy of a biblical application, it is not intended to question the sincere devotion people have for Christ. It can be an intervention into a stream of thinking that has become polluted with ideas foreign to the texts of Scripture.

WESTERN ROMANCE: A FOREIGN BODY APPLIED

Applying romance to these metaphors of Christ and the church is like adding more of an ingredient to a cooking mixture because if the recipe calls for some, more must be better. It is a matter of degrees. An extra quarter-cup of flour to a biscuit recipe that calls for four cups may not be disastrous. An extra quarter-cup of diced habanero chilies into a four-egg omelet will demand a call to the fire department. Christ indeed loves us and we are to love Him. However, adding romantic love to this mixture is too much. Adding this is often applying a foreign body. Let's look at the characteristics of this so that we can know if it is a foreign concept or just too much of a good thing.

The Concept of Romance

Romance is an energizing positive feeling that does have noble aspects. It makes us feel alive and vibrant.[63] It is something that God uses for good

---

63. John Townsend, *Loving People: How to Love and Be Loved* (Nashville: Thomas Nelson, 2008), 174.

purposes. As such it is a part of natural human experience that brings people together into a marital relationship. Managing and experiencing relational intimacy, dealing with change, communicating needs and feelings,[64] interpersonal union, and self-sacrifice are some of the positive aspects of romance. These ingredients can even help stabilize people who struggle with depressing, anxiety, and insecurity.[65]

However, because romance is also a powerful feeling or emotion, it has significant problems when not under control. It is at times irrational when it seeks an exclusive attachment or union with another person.[66] Christian psychologist Dr. John Townsend defines romance as "a temporary idealization of the other person that increases passionate and sexual attraction."[67] When people make romance equal to love, they can become romance addicts. Townsend adds:

> These people live for romance and only feel alive when they are in love. They love the intensity of the passion, but it is based upon some idealization either of the person or of the entire process. Then, when reality comes in the form of a conflict or weakness, they feel disappointed and search for the next romance. It is a tough existence, having serial romances and watching the years pass by with no direction, purpose or progress in finding deep and lasting love.[68]

Increasing trends of individualism show it will continually grow as a personal and cultural force.[69] Bergler provides a very helpful summary of the famous anthropologist Helen Fisher's study of romantic love:

---

64. S. Grey, "Positive Effects of Dating for Teenagers" Livestrong.com, October 19, 2013, http://www.livestrong.com/article/154840-positive-effects-of-dating-for-teenagers.

65. Jaleesa Baulkman, "Romantic Relationships Have a Positive Effect on Personality Development," University Herald, May 9, 2014, http://www.universityherald.com/articles/9331/20140509/romantic-relationships-have-a-positive-effect-on-personality-development.htm.

66. See for example, Bergit Brogaard, *On Romantic Love: Simple Truths about a Complex Emotion*, Philosophy in Action (New York: Oxford University Press, 2015), 12–163.

67. Townsend, *Loving People*, 174.

68. Ibid., 177.

69. Susan Hendrick and Clyde Hendrick, "Romantic Love," in *Oxford Handbook of Positive Psychology*, eds. S. J. Lopez and C. R. Snyder (New York: Oxford University Press, 2009), 447–54.

The person who is "in love" thinks obsessively about the beloved. She idealizes that person and ignores his flaws. He may believe that he would be willing to die for her. Lovers experience "extreme energy, hyperactivity, sleeplessness, euphoria, mood swings." Obstacles or adversity can heighten their passion. Many become emotionally dependent on the relationship and rearrange their life to spend more time with that person. They will neglect other obligations and relationships in order to pursue their beloved. Above all, the lover "craves emotional union" with the beloved. But all this passion is "involuntary and difficult, if not impossible to control." And it inevitably fades.[70]

Thus the romantic lover may tend to value their feelings above all else and thus find it difficult to sustain commitment in place of infatuation. Bergler entitles this "romantic spirituality"[71] when it is joined with one's Christianity.

An Example of the Romantic Intimacy View

A good example of justifying a romantic relationship with Christ is found in Frank Viola's book *From Eternity to Here: Rediscovering the Ageless Purpose of God*.[72] This popular author develops this as one of his biblical themes concerning the church.[73] When he admits that his favorite movie genre is the romance film with an element of mystery,[74] it becomes quite clear that he develops his theology through this lens. So let's look at how Viola calls us to experience intimacy with Christ through Scripture's romantic images of marriage.

---

70. Thomas E. Bergler, "A Pastoral Process for Leading Churches toward Spiritual Maturity" *unpublished manuscript, 2009), 14–15. See Helen Fisher, *Why We Love: The Nature and Chemistry of Romantic Love* (New York: Henry Holt and Co., 2004), 1–25. See also her *Anatomy of Love: A Natural History of Mating, Marriage, and Why We Stray*, completely revised and updated with a new introduction (New York: W. W. Norton and Co., 2016), 19–42, 147–67, 265–80.

71. Thomas E. Bergler, *From Here to Maturity: Overcoming the Juvenilization of American Christianity* (Grand Rapids: Eerdmans, 2014,) 23–25, 126–39, 167–69.

72. Frank Viola, *From Eternity to Here: Rediscovering the Ageless Purpose of God* (Colorado Springs: David C. Cook, 2009). Others see the metaphor as the love story of the Bible. See Paul E. Billheimer, *Destined for the Throne: How Spiritual Warfare Prepares the Bride of Christ for Her Eternal Destiny* (Bloomington, MN: Bethany House, 2005 [1975]): "The author's thesis is that the primary purpose of the universe from all eternity is the production and preparation of an Eternal Companion for the Son, called the Bride, the Lamb's Wife. Since she is to share the throne of the universe with her Divine Lover and Lord, privileged to judge the world with Him, she must be trained, educated and prepared for her role" (from the introduction, p. 15). "The secret . . . effective prayer" (p. 18).

73. Although he develops the marital imagery only in part one of the three of his book (the house of God and the body of Christ being the others), it is the first and it leaves a lasting impression on the reader. His narrative approach to theology draws the reader in.

74. Viola, *From Eternity to Here*, 26.

For Viola, believers must grasp how God sees them through the grand love story of the Bible.[75] From its very beginning, the love stories of Adam and Eve, Abraham and Sarah, Jacob and Rachel, and even Asenath and Joseph are patterned after the heavenly romance.[76] Therefore, the very purpose for the Eternal Son becoming human was so that He could "obtain a wife for Himself," so that He could "obtain the passion that burned within His bosom from before time."[77] The terminology Viola uses for God's love is decidedly romantic. For example, he claims, "The Lord Jesus is the greatest lover under God's heaven. No creature can match Him as a passionate romantic."[78] When Jesus prays, "Father, You love them just as much as You love Me," it is here and other places in John's Gospel that we supposedly find the "unstoppable passion of a love sick God."[79] In referring typologically to the Samaritan woman, Viola exhorts believers that "you are part of that matchless woman with whom Christ has fallen hopelessly in love. Yes, Jesus Christ, the king of the universe, has fallen irreversibly in love with you."[80]

What does Viola mean by falling in love? It is a hyper-emotional idealization designed to possess the loved one. In his section entitled, "The Divine Frustration," he describes it this way:

> When a man falls in love with a woman, he will walk over cut glass for her. His mind becomes occupied, consumed, and even obsessed with the thought of her. He becomes a driven man, driven to find ways of express-

75. More recently see also Brant Pitre's *Jesus the Bridegroom: The Greatest Love Story Ever Told* (New York: Image, 2014). A Catholic scholar, Pitre is professor of sacred Scripture at Notre Dame Seminary in New Orleans, Louisiana. To him, the passion of Christ is the fulfillment of a Jewish wedding ceremony, where God weds Himself to humanity. Then he shows that the key to unlocking this mystery can be found by going back to Jewish Scripture and tradition and seeing the entire history of salvation, from Mount Sinai to Mount Calvary, as a divine love story between Creator and creature, He shows how this schema can transform familiar images in the Bible, like the Exodus, the Song of Solomon, the wedding at Cana, the woman at the well, the Last Supper, the Crucifixion, and Christ's Second Coming at the end of time. They are none other than pieces in the greatest love story ever told.
76. Viola, *From Eternity to Here*, 91, 93–94.
77. Ibid., 41.
78. Ibid., 61, 282.
79. Ibid., 74. In referring typologically to the Samaritan woman, Viola exhorts believers that "you are part of that matchless woman with whom Christ has fallen hopelessly in love. Yes, Jesus Christ, the king of the universe, has fallen irreversibly in love with you." Ibid., 128.
80. Ibid., 128.

ing his affection for his beloved. When the heart has been infected by the passion of human love, there's simply no cure in sight.[81]

He likens this to God's love for His people. Like any lover whose advances are shunned, He is truly a frustrated lover. But Christ also sees His bride through the eyes of a lover. There are no faults in her. So Viola chides believers to not "make the mistake of diluting this wonderful reality by calling it 'positional truth'. This is toxic thinking clothed in theological rhetoric."[82]

Song of Solomon is a rich resource of romantic imagery for Viola.[83] For example, he notes how the king is charmed by and praises his bride's beauty. Song of Solomon chapters 4 and 7 go into great detail about parts of her body. Viola applies this to the church. "As the king vividly describes each portion of his bride's body, we are given insight into how you and I look in the eyes of our king, the Lord Jesus Christ."[84] He then argues, "One of the greatest truths that the Song of Solomon presents to us is that the Lord's love is not only for the whole, His bride, but it's also for all of her individual parts."[85] Then with Ephesians 5:32, Viola claims, "Behold a mystery: Christ loves His bride corporately. But also He loves the individual parts of her body. In fact, He loves each part just as much as He loves the whole. In case you don't understand, *those individual parts are you and me*."[86] Thus, that divine love, for Viola, is equivalent to marital romance.

What, then, is Viola's purpose behind his passionate use and development of this romantic marital imagery? It is not only his obsession that believers are to grasp and respond to God in an intimately romantic sense but his assertion that true love is devoid of the torment of fear. So he candidly confides with his readers, "I ache when I meet Christians who are terrified of God. If you are His child, there is no reason to be afraid of your Lord. The 'fear of the Lord' that Scripture often enjoins is not terror or dread. It is a holy reverence for God and an awe and respect for His power." However, he feels that "many believers relate to God out of fear and trepidation." God is a "'Soup Nazi' in the sky."[87] We have already addressed this shame that is a problem among

---

81. Ibid., 55.
82. Ibid., 59.
83. Popular women's author Nancy Leigh DeMoss is one of many who develop these same concepts from Song of Solomon. See her curriculum, *How to Fall and Stay in Love with Jesus: A Study of the Song of Songs* (Niles, MI: Revive Our Hearts, 2013).
84. Viola, *From Eternity to Here*, 113.
85. Ibid., 115.
86. Ibid., italics his.
87. Ibid., 74.

God's people. However, a romantic conception of God's love for His people is not the biblical precedent, and thus not the solution, for this fear factor.

Problems with the Romantic Spirituality View

Viola is a helpful example because he often shows us his hand to reveal his motivations and presuppositions. This makes it clear where we can begin to challenge the inadequacies of this attempt to legitimize the romantic intimacy view of the Bible's marital imagery. First, we need to address the foundational hermeneutical issues. Second, we need to evaluate the legitimacy of using romance for the Bible's teaching on the intimate love between Christ and His people. Third, we need to revisit the analogical intent of the Bible's imagery of marriage. Finally, we cannot overlook the practical implications of holding a romantic view, which is essential to one's mental conception and personal pursuit of intimacy with Christ.

THE CHRISTOCENTRIC/ALLEGORICAL/SPIRITUAL INTERPRETATION OF THE MARITAL IMAGES

Authors like Viola have an allegorical or spiritualizing hermeneutical approach. Viola states that he uses the "Christocentric interpretation" of Scripture to glean his ideas from both Testaments. He claims, "This is the very interpretation that the New Testament authors used to expound in the Old Testament. Scholars in the field of canonical criticism use it today as well."[88] Furthermore, he claims, "A Christian hermeneutic is a Christological hermeneutic. Jesus Christ is *the* subject of *all* Scripture."[89] He associates this hermeneutic with *sensus plenior*, which he defines as "the deeper meaning, intended by God but not clearly intended by the human author, that is seen to exist in the words of Scripture when they are studied in light of further revelation."[90] Although advocates of the *sensus plenior* hermeneutic claim it has parameters and controls, it does overlap considerably with allegory, at least how Viola uses it. Furthermore, seeking a deeper or hidden spiritual meaning as opposed to its original human or carnal meaning has it overlapping considerably with those who use a method seeking the "spiritual sense."

---

88. Ibid., 16. Esp. Brevard Childs, and the narrative theology approach of Hans Frei. Frank Viola, "Beyond Bible Study: Finding Christ in Scripture," 2007, www.ptmin.org/beyond. pdf.
89. Viola, "Beyond Bible Study."
90. Ibid. See a nearly identical definition by the Catholic scholar Raymond E. Brown in his *The 'Sensus Plenior' of Sacred Scripture* (Baltimore: St. Mary's University, 1955), 92, which Viola does not credit.

Is this legitimate in order to gain clarity in describing the intimacy between God and His people? Garrett provides a helpful summary of trends in allegorical interpretation. First, the whole process is often driven by the imagination of the individual interpreter. Second, the allegorizer usually views their religious tradition in the text. Third, simple psychological associations are what suggest the allegorical interpretation. Fourth, the interpretations of the allegorizer are based on word associations to other biblical passages, with theirs being the best.[91] However, there are numerous problems with allegorical interpretation. First, true allegories do not hide their nature as such. Longman notes that *Pilgrim's Progress*, for instance, has clearly identifiable elements of an allegory. The main character is a person named Christian on a journey to the Celestial City, etc.[92] The Song of Solomon, for example, has no such identifiable elements, nor hints that there is another level of meaning.[93] There are also no indications that the Lover represents God or Christ and the that the Beloved represents the Church or the soul of the individual believer.[94] The fact that Jews and the Church adopted a Neoplatonic view of sex and thus asceticism[95] does not justify allegorizing this beautiful love poem.[96]

---

91. Duane Garrett, *Song of Songs*, Word Biblical Commentary, 23B (Nashville: Thomas Nelson, 2004), 74.
92. Tremper Longman III, "Song of Solomon," in *Dictionary for Theological Interpretation of the Bible*, gen. ed. Kevin Vanhoozer (Grand Rapids: Baker, 2005), 759.
93. The opposite is true. Allegory fails to explain its detailed descriptions of concrete allusions to the body parts of the lovers and their erotic experiences. Daniel C. Fredericks and Daniel J. Estes, *Ecclesiastes & the Song of Songs*, Apollos Old Testament Commentary, 16 (Downers Grove, IL: IVP, 2010), 280.
94. Interpreting Song of Solomon has a long history of allegorization. However, Phipps is right in saying, "It is one of the pranks of history that a poem so obviously about hungry passion has caused so much perplexity and has provoked such a plethora of bizarre interpretations." William E. Phipps, "The Plight of the Song of Songs," in *The Song of Songs*, ed. Harold Bloom (New York: Chelsea House, 1988), 5–6. Mitchell, as a Lutheran, claims as a result of his Christological hermeneutic that "it is the most difficult book in the sacred Scriptures." Christopher Wright Mitchell, *The Song of Songs*, Concordia Commentary (St. Louis: Concordia, 2003), 2.
95. The church in its first millennia and a half often faced an embarrassing dilemma of interpreting the Song of Solomon as the lyrics of human love. "If, on the one hand, the book's prima facie meaning was acknowledged, then the established assumption about the superiority of those persons in the church devoted to lifelong sexual abstinence is called into question. On the other hand, if the book was renounced, what would prohibit Christians from calling into question other biblical books which had been appealed to as authoritative? Given these practical problems, it is easy to understand why allegory was brought to the rescue even though there is no clue within the Song to suggest it was originally composed with another meaning in mind." Phipps, "The Plight of the Song of Songs," 22.
96. Or love poems that comprise the whole. See Roland E. Murphy, O. Carm., *The Song of Songs: A Commentary on the Book of Canticles or The Song of Solomon* (Minneapolis: Fortress, 1990), 57–60. Hess's general interpretive advice is very helpful: "The best

A second problem is its overshadowing and even eradication of the biblical author's intended meaning by the supposed "spiritual" or "Christological"[97] meaning. If the main focus of a given text is another allegorical concept, the literal meaning is suppressed or buried. This does not allow God's own words to be accepted and heeded in their own context. To be sure, it is argued that individual texts of Scripture should be read in light of the context of the whole Bible, and rightly so. Biblical theology would be impossible without such an approach.[98] However, progressive revelation demonstrates God has chosen not to reveal everything about a topic all at once but as He deemed necessary and appropriate. At the same time, any text must be allowed to speak for itself. Otherwise, finite human reasoning and imagination becomes the standard for what a biblical text can or cannot communicate. As a result, "No single interpretation has any more claim to legitimacy or makes any more sense than another."[99]

A third problem is its lack of objective controls. This causes it to be open to abuse. Granted, this doesn't falsify the presupposition behind the approach that God can communicate more than what the original author understood at the time. However, it does cause one to wonder what the basis is for deciding what the Holy Spirit might be saying through the words of a given text.[100] It is also true that Jesus demonstrated to the men on the road to Emmaus that the Scriptures spoke of Him (Luke 24:27) and He said to the Jews that the Scriptures testify of Him (John 5:39) and Moses wrote about Him (John 5:46). The crucial issue is whether Jesus is giving them the green light to find Him

---

interpretation is to remain sensitive to the language of imagery and attempt to follow its contours without imposing too much demand on specifics of interpretation." Richard S. Hess, *Song of Songs* (Grand Rapids: Baker, 2005), 34.

97. Some even claim that Song of Solomon was brought into the canon of Scripture because of an allegorical interpretation of it. E.g., Otto Eissfeldt, *The Old Testament: An Introduction*, trans. Peter R. Ackroyd (New York: Harper and Row, 1965), 485. However, Garrett shows why this cannot be true and concludes by saying, "If the Song were not already Scripture, it is hard to imagine why anyone would allegorize it in the first place." Garrett, *Song of Songs*, 15.

98. Years ago, Bernard Ramm rightly claimed that it is the "profound similarity of the two Testaments which makes predictive prophecy and typology a possibility." *Protestant Biblical Interpretation*, 3rd rev. ed. (Grand Rapids: Baker, 1970), 228.

99. Garrett, *Song of Songs*, 74.

100. Douglas Moo, "The Problem of *Sensus Plenior*," in *Hermeneutics, Authority, and Canon*, eds. D. A. Carson and John D. Woodbridge (Grand Rapids: Zondervan, 1986), 202. The more extreme continuity (vs. discontinuity) approaches are known for their attempts to justify extended typology. This is not only seen in Seventh Day Adventism, but other continuity positions on a variety of issues from Christological interpretive methods. See Hans K. LaRondelle, *The Israel of God in Prophecy: Principles of Prophetic Interpretation* (Berrien Springs, MI: Andrews University Press, 1983), especially chapters 1–5.

wherever they may.[101] Even though there may be examples of the New Testament writers explaining a fuller sense of an Old Testament text (say, Joel 2 in Acts 2)—a sense or meaning not clearly seen but compatible with the human author's intent—they were inspired and had a unique stance in God's revelatory history.[102] That is a long way from justifying the presupposition that now every believer has the ability and thus should search the Old Testament for a sense other than the original author's.[103] More extreme continuity (versus discontinuity) approaches are known for their attempts to justify extended typology (Roman Catholic, Puritan Reformed, etc.).[104]

Again we are back to allegorizing the sexual intercourse alluded to in the Song of Solomon (4:6, 12, 16; 7:8, 12; 8:1–3, 5) and finding some sort of intercourse between Christ and His bride. Why is this off-limits to many like Viola, but not to a raft of others? [105] We have seen why is this an unwarranted image of intimacy with Christ.[106] At the same time, Viola's approach

---

101. The same can be said of Paul's allegorization in Galatians 4:24. Not only is this rare for Paul, but also a limited use different from Song of Solomon. The challenge is to know whether Paul is using typology or allegory or if these terms are synonymous. Gignilliat provides more careful nuancing of these difficult issues. He summarizes Paul's approach to this text: "Paul's figural reading of the Sarah/Hagar story is not like a certain type of Alexandrian exegesis that tears apart the narrative coherence of the text. Rather, Paul respects the textual coherence of the story, or the way the words go, while recognizing that it has the potential within the divine economy to function figurally as an eschatological indicator of God's future action in Christ." Mark Gignilliat, "Paul, Allegory, and the Plain Sense of Scripture: Galatians 4:21–31," *Journal for Theological Interpretation* 2, no. 1 (2008): 141.

102. Moo, "The Problem of *Sensus Plenior*," 210.

103. There is much debate on this issue and especially on this passage, which to many is a crux text that demonstrates one's position in this area. See Gregory V. Trull, "The Use of Psalm 16:8–11 in Acts 2:25–32" (PhD diss., Dallas Theological Seminary, 2002) for a good summary of the views and an example of the most scripturally consistent view of Peter's use of this specific text.

104. Some claim that "my beloved" is a numerically coded reference to YHWH. Peter J. Leithart, "The Poetry of Sex," *First Things*, January 13, 2012, http://www.firstthings.com/web-exclusives/2012/01/the-poetry-of-sex.

105. Many of allegories of the church fathers did not even approach attempting to see any sexual union in Song of Solomon. See for some examples, J. Robert Wright, ed., *Proverbs, Ecclesiastes and Song of Solomon*, Ancient Christian Commentary on Scripture: Old Testament, 9 (Downers Grove, IL: InterVarsity, 2005), 337–39, 341–42, 359–64.

106. It is quite surprising to find D. A. Carson, on the one hand, rightly argue against seeing sex as "an intrinsically soiled or at best morally inferior" activity, and then go on to typologically overextend the Bible's marital imagery. He argues the final consummation of the marriage "can be thought of as the marriage supper of the Lamb." His next line of reasoning is oddly stated: "It is as if the only pleasure and intimacy in this life that comes close to anticipating the pleasure and intimacy of the church and her Lord being perfectly united on the last day is the sexual union of a good marriage." He offers no real support for this other than how Hosea is a typology of Yahweh and Israel. He then argues the reverse: "And, conversely, that invests each marriage with a kind of typological value that should make thoughtful

is nearly unbridled. Almost anything is possible. But what does the text say? His approach is simply a highly allegorical narrative theology of the marriage images in the Bible that he uses to justify his romance themes.

We need to remember at this point that many Christians like Viola have a sincere desire to draw close to God in Christ. They have grasped that God clearly invites His people to an intimate relationship with Him. They seem to be fully aware that biblical imagery of marriage appears to communicate a close intimacy with God. Yet they have perhaps unknowingly not only struggled with the accuracy of interpreting this imagery, but with applying it to the believer's relationship with God. These metaphors are to be interpreted literally or in keeping with the authorial intent rather than allegorically. God is not a literal husband or bridegroom to a literal wife or bride with all its human aspects. The marital image of the relationship God has with His people is an analogy that describes faithfulness and preparation.

So some may ask what harm there is in inserting or overlaying a certain biblical concept into or onto other texts where it is not warranted. Should it really matter, as long as it is already taught in the Bible? First, it is not only a serious hermeneutical error to not allow God's own words to be heeded in their own context, but it brings shame and dishonor to the interpreter and thus to God's people. The teachers of God's Word are to be zealous to demonstrate that they are proclaiming an interpretation that God would approve of and would not cause Him to disapprove of them and cause shame (2 Tim. 2:15).

Second, what is used to overshadow the intended meaning of these marital images is a concept that is mostly foreign to the Bible itself. In this case, love is often equivalent to romance, passion, or emotion. This is mixing metaphors. Laying cultural images over biblical ones shrouds the believer's ability to appropriately conceive of the Lord's intimate love for them and therefore their love for Christ.[107] It shrouds the truth of the nature of the relationship itself, which is crucial to intimacy itself.

Christians all the more eager for the Lord's return, for the coming of the Bridegroom, for the consummation. Hence the spectacular intertwining of the pairs husband/wife and Christ/church in Ephesians 5:25–33." Is the sexual union of marriage really the only good explanation of what it will be like when believers experience their union with Christ at His return? Does the image of the marriage supper imply the pleasure of sexual intercourse? Is that what John was describing in Revelation 19? Isn't the imagery primarily focusing on the celebration of the wedding and the joyous though ceremonial joining of the couple? D. A. Carson, *Love in Hard Places* (Wheaton, IL: Crossway, 2002), 191.

107. "To speak of rapture and consummation and so on uses the vocabulary of love, but the metaphysical relationship between the believer and Christ is at an entirely different level from that between two lovers. To confuse the two types of relationship can lead to

Third, and related, this mixing of metaphors is an illegitimate contextualization[108] of the Scripture's teachings. Rather than translating the biblical truth of the intimate love between God and man in appropriate and corresponding concepts, Viola and others transform this concept into a love foreign to the biblical worldview. Granted, while this culturally captive love may resemble certain aspects of the Bible's marital imagery (devotion, passion, sacrifice, etc.), those who adopt it as a direct correspondence do so uncritically.[109] To equate love with romance is indeed a reductionism of contemporary culture.[110]

More serious theological reflection is needed with respect to the biblical concept of love and intimacy with the Lord in order to ground them sufficiently in truth si that they can be articulated for believers and pursued with legitimate means.[111] It is clear that many like Viola are affected by cultural and theological conceptions of love. Could it be that they are a part of the ebb and flow of post-Enlightenment debates on the impassibility of God? Are they reacting to the same static impassible God that the process theologians abhor? At the same time, do they allow the pendulum to swing so far that God's love is merely His "passion"?

> So now God comes to us and says, "I love you." What does he mean? Does he mean something like this? "You mean everything to me. I can't live without you. Your personality, your witty conversation, your beauty, your smile—everything about you transfixes me. Heaven would be boring without you. I love you!" That, after all, is pretty close to what some therapeutic approaches to the love of God spell out. We must be pretty wonderful because God loves us. And dear old God is pretty vulnerable, finding himself in a dreadful state unless we say yes. Suddenly serious Christians unite and rightly cry, "Bring back impassibility!"[112]

---

heretical notions and spiritual disaster." Tom Gledhill, *The Message of the Song of Songs: The Lyrics of Love* (Downers Grove, IL: IVP, 1994), 33.

108. Lints defines contextualization as "the manner in which the expression of a biblical passage is shaped in and by the native conceptuality of a given culture." Lints, *The Fabric of Theology*, 101. This helps to clarify the shaping process that is taking place here.

109. Carson, *Love in Hard Places*, 11.

110. Other cultural reductionisms are truth is equal to public scientific facts vs. private/personal values; morality is culturally relative, etc.

111. Part of this discussion could be around the issue of whether God's love is one of His attributes to be categorized and described or how He relates. See Kevin J. Vanhoozer, *First Theology: God, Scripture & Hermeneutics* (Downers Grove, IL: InterVarsity, 2002), 80.

112. Carson, *The Difficult Doctrine of the Love of God*, 62–63.

These cultural pendulum swings concerning the love of God can only be brought back closer to the center through accurate theological reflection on the Scriptures as the "norming norm."

A final caution needs to be given concerning infusing a romantic spirituality into the love inherent in the Bible's marital images. While they do engender a certain kind of intimacy with the Lord, this popular understanding of love and intimacy is often associated with the experiences and emotions of being in love as well as falling out of love. Again, Bergler summarizes the psychological research that demonstrates that

> especially for younger adolescents, romantic relationships are primarily about the individual's status, emotional needs, and identity search. The ability to develop genuinely mutual romantic relationships with staying power develops later. For some people, this ability is only just developing during young adulthood. Some never get there.[113]

A significant danger of a romantic approach is that love for Christ can be reduced to emotional infatuation.[114] We as the church must help its members develop intimacy with the Lord with the staying power of a maturity founded in an accurate interpretation of Scripture. They must "get there."

BIBLICAL IMAGES OF MARRIAGE AND INTIMACY WITH CHRIST

We should now be compelled to ask ourselves how we arrive at appropriately applying these images today. In this process, we should seek to stay focused on the main point of the metaphor. There is much to apply here. Like so many believers before us, we should reflect upon and meditate deeply on this image. May we hear Christ's voice speaking a specific message to His church.

First, we should consistently rejoice that Christ has given us this metaphor to communicate His love for us as His unique people. In this church age, Christ is our bridegroom and we are His bride. Initially, this means we are His chosen ones. Like His choice of Israel out of all the nations of the earth, He chose us because He loves us and not because of our noble qualifications

---

113. Bergler, "A Pastoral Process for Leading Churches toward Spiritual Maturity," 14.
114. Jesus is being reduced to the boyfriend, fiancé, or husband of Christian women. See Angieszka Tennant, "Dating Jesus: When 'Lover of My Soul' Language Goes Too Far," *Christianity Today* (December 2006): 56.

(Deut. 7:7–8; Eph. 1:4). It is a profound mystery of how and why Christ would want to tie Himself to people like us for all eternity. Yet He sacrificed His own life so that each of us could be a part of His people (His bride, ultimate wife, family, sheep, body, building, temple, etc.). This calls for a great celebration of His loving loyalty to the covenant He has made with His people. Nothing can separate us from His love (Rom. 8:31–39).

As His bride, we need to experience His fullness in the mysterious union of being a part of His body. The church as the bride of Christ is not an organization, but a unique group of people who are filled with His presence, glory, and love. This union with Christ is never only individual and personal. It is corporate. When we pray and sing, we should see Christ as the center of all of us as His bride and His body. When we celebrate the Lord's Supper, we partake of the one loaf and one cup together as His bride and body (1 Cor. 10:16–17). Our mental picture is to draw us all together and draw us to Him. We are drawn together in thanksgiving, in love, in sacrifice, in purity, in service. We are His bride, *not* I am His bride. It's not about *me*, it's about *we*. Our chance meetings and planned gatherings should be filled with the joy of the bride who knows her Bridegroom's intentions for us all.

Second, Christ's love for us as His bride must compel us not to drift away from Him. Intimacy with Christ is conditioned upon our faithfulness to Him. We must not love anything or anyone more than Christ. We must diligently pursue devotion to Him alone (2 Cor. 11:2). We must remain pure, loyal, and faithful. Anything else is impurity, disloyalty, and infidelity. How do we commit spiritual adultery against Christ? It is when we love the world (1 John 2:15–17). It is craving its substitutions for what only He can provide. For Christians, loving the world can be adopting elements of non-Christian worldviews.[115] We may drift away from Christ to nationalism when we have our ultimate loyalty in our country and find our meaning and deliverance in it. We may love the world more than Christ as consumerists, when we determine our identity and worth in what we own. We may have become loyal to the truths of culture rather than the authoritative truth of Christ when adopting relativism. We are no longer exclusive with our Groom when we conceive Him as being just one of many valid paths to salvation and morality. We then do not think it necessary to want others to stay loyal to Christ, or become loyal to Him. We start to feel ashamed and lose our passion for Christ when

---

115. See Wilkens and Sanford, *Hidden Worldviews*.

confronted with postmodern claims that we are really losing our individuality in our exclusive mindless subservience.

The ultimate test for the church as Christ's bride is when Satan will do everything he can to destroy our loyal love for our Groom. He will even inspire the Great Whore of Babylon (Rev. 17–18). She desires every earth-dweller to become drunk with her adulteries (Rev. 17:2, 5; 18:3; 19:2). She is the base of operations for the Beast/Antichrist and loyalty to them is mandatory for everyone on pain of death (Rev. 17:6; 18:24). Every age and the one to come has this "spirit of antichrist" (2 Thess. 2:3–7; 1 John 2:18; 4:3) that wants Christ's bride to play the harlot. But we must heed the call to "come out of her, my people, so that you will not participate in her sins and receive of her plagues" (Rev. 18:4). We must prepare ourselves until our Groom comes for us.[116] We must anticipate and run from these temptations. Then one day we may rejoice in the righteous deeds we have done for Him, which are symbolized in the bright and clean fine clothes we will wear in His presence (Rev. 19:7–8).

Finally, like a bride before her wedding day, we long to be with Christ. Even though He is in heaven with His Father until He returns, we long to be in His presence. This is not in a romantic sense. We know Christ better than that. The point of the metaphor is the hope in our suffering for Christ. To be absent from our physical bodies at our deaths is to open our eyes into the face of Christ (2 Cor. 5:6–10; Phil. 1:23). And the place He is preparing for us is beyond description (Rev. 21:3, 22–27; 22:1–5, 17, 20). But all that matters is being with Him. So we eagerly wait for Him (Phil. 3:20).

---

116. A trend of rapture-ready Bride of Christ books is emerging. See Patricia King, *The Bride Makes Herself Ready: Preparing for the Lord's Return* (Maricopa, AZ: XP Publishing, 2010); Anita W. Jones, *Calling Forth the Bride of Christ: A Personal Account of End-Time Signs and Synchronicities Pointing to the Rapture* (CreateSpace Independent Publishing Platform, 2016); Sheryl Pellatiro, *The Bride of Christ: Being Rapture* (CreateSpace Independent Publishing Platform, 2015); Dr. Patricia Venegas, *The Bride of Christ without Spot or Wrinkle* (N.p.: Xulon Press, 2015); Elizabeth Paige, *He's Looking for a Bride: Preparing the Bride of Christ for Holy Intimacy with Jesus*, Kindle ed. (Colorado Springs: Moldable Clay Publishing, 2015); Audrey Drummonds, *Rising to Royalty: Manifesting the Bride of Christ Jesus* (Bloomington, IN: AuthorHouse, 2015).

NOW WHAT?

1. Has someone shared with you romantic imagery used for intimacy with God or Christ? If so, what do you think they were actually trying to communicate? What would you say to them, now that you have read this chapter?

2. Are you committing spiritual adultery against God? If so, what do you think you need to communicate to Him?

3. What can deep loyalty to Christ look like in your life?

4. Do you long for Christ to return? If so, how? If not, how could that change?

CHAPTER 7

INTERPRETING INTIMACY WITH THE HOLY SPIRIT

The Holy Spirit is central to God's mission in this age of the church. We are such a needy people. We all have specific relational needs. Some we easily trust will be met, like falling back onto a bed at the end of a long day. Trust for other certain needs is much more difficult. Even attempting to leave them at God's feet, we immediately experience the tightening of a vice around our hearts, the swelling of our throats, the scattering of our thoughts, the sleeplessness of our nights. It is about not knowing what to do, fearing doing something, being unable to do something. The Spirit apparently knows all of this.

However, when "studying" the Holy Spirit and His intimate role in our lives, there are certain challenges. I certainly relate to Francis Chan's comment in his *The Forgotten God: Reversing Our Tragic Neglect of the Holy Spirit*: "As I wrote this book, the question that kept burning in my mind was how can any human being write well on the sacred topic of the Holy Spirit of God?"[1] Yes! Since He is the *Holy* Spirit, the Third Person of the Triune God, we must tread carefully and respectfully with a sense of awe. We can experience His nearness and relationship, but we must not become too casual and

---

1. Francis Chan, *The Forgotten God: Reversing Our Tragic Neglect of the Holy Spirit* (Colorado Springs: David C. Cook, 2009), 17.

treat Him in a pedestrian way.[2] Since He is the Holy *Spirit*, we must be careful to walk by faith and not by sight. Attributing the seen "manifestations"
of the Spirit's presence to His unseen spiritual work is precarious and can
lead to superstition or exaggeration.[3] On the other hand, we must avoid an
all-too-clinical approach to studying the Holy Spirit. Kärkkäinen cautions
us in this regard:

> Approaching the topic of the Spirit and pneumatology from the perspec-
> tive of experience is the only way to do justice to the "object" of our study.
> It is one of the rules of scientific inquiry that the methodology has to fit
> the object, not vice versa. However, a word of warning is in order here: The
> Spirit is not an "object" of human study in the same way that, for instance,
> the objects of the physical sciences are. In fact, we can say that the Spirit,
> rather than being an object of our scrutiny, is the One who searches us. Paul
> was quite emphatic about that. . . . (1 Cor. 2:10b–11).[4]

And a more specific challenge for this study is to maintain focus on the Holy
Spirit's intimacy and not on broader considerations of pneumatology.

In this chapter, we need to examine the Holy Spirit's intimate provisions
for believers. While there are transition issues between the Old and New
Testaments there is continuity of His closeness with God's people. Jesus Christ
made an astounding promise of the Paraclete, Who provides intimate disclosure of the truth of Christ's sustaining presence. The book of Acts demonstrates the Spirit's intimate ministry to the growing church and its leaders.
Yet it is in the Epistles that we find how the apostles, especially Paul, bring a
measure of clarity to the provision of the Holy Spirit and His intimate role in
our lives. In sum, He truly is a provision and we must have faith in Him as a
member of the Trinity to meet our needs.

---

2. I think I understand Hernandez's legitimate desire for believers to understand and
   experience the Holy Spirit's role in their lives. However, his approach can weaken the
   majesty of the Holy Spirit. David Diga Hernandez, *The Carriers of Glory: Becoming a
   Friend of the Holy Spirit* (Shippensburg, PA: Destiny Image, 2016).
3. See Benny Hinn, *Good Morning, Holy Spirit* (Nashville: Thomas Nelson, 1997); Michael
   Koulianos, *Holy Spirit: The One Who Makes Jesus Real* (Shippensburg, PA: Destiny
   Image, 2017).
4. Veli-Matti Kärkkäinen, *Pneumatology: The Holy Spirit in Ecumenical, International, and
   Contextual Perspective* (Grand Rapids: Baker, 2002), 15–16.

Old Testament vs. New Testament?

The role of the Holy Spirit in the Old Testament is deep and wide. While we have seen that God's relationship to His people of that era is often described as an intimate one, the Holy Spirit's relationship is more functional. For instance, He filled, was endowed, was put on, rested, came upon, stirred, entered, departed, lifted up, and fell upon people.[5] Men even spoke by the Holy Spirit (2 Sam. 23:2; Zech. 7:12). Yet our goal is to investigate intimacy with the Holy Spirit,[6] and data on this is less prominent in the Old Testament.

This doesn't mean that the Holy Spirit is not personal in the Old Testament. Job understood the intimacy of the Spirit's function as the Creator when he said, "The Spirit of God has made me, and the breath of the Almighty gives me life" (Job 33:4). David knew God's intimate presence in his life as united with the presence of His Spirit. After being confronted by Nathan for his adultery and murder, he pleaded with God, "Do not cast me away from Your presence and do not take Your Holy Spirit from me" (Ps. 51:11). Similarly, he asked God rhetorically in Psalm 139:7, "Where can I go from Your Spirit? Or where can I flee from Your presence?" He also viewed the Holy Spirit as his teacher and leader. In Psalm 143:10 he asked the Lord, "Teach me to do Your will, For You are my God; Let Your good Spirit lead me on level ground." Negatively, Isaiah viewed Israel's rebellion against God as something that "grieved His Holy Spirit" (Isa. 63:10–14). In all of this we see that God's Spirit has parallel qualities and functions that human spirits have.[7] Thus the Holy Spirit's activity in the believer's life has always been an intimate one regardless of the Testament. So let's grapple with the major themes in the New Testament concerning the close relationship He has with us.

---

5. Exod. 28:3; 31:3; 35:31; Num. 11:25, 26, 29; 24:2; 27:18; Judg. 3:10; 6:34; 11:29; 13:25; 14:6, 19; 15:14; 1 Sam. 10:6, 10; 11:6; 16:14; 19:20; 1 Chron. 12:18; 2 Chron. 15:1; 18:23; 24:20; Isa. 11:2; 42:1; 59:21; 61:1; Ezek. 2:2; 3:12, 14, 24; 8:3; 11:24; 37:14; 43:5; Mic. 3:8; Zech. 4:6; 7:12. He is also spoken of as being poured out (Isa. 32:15; 44:3; Joel 2:28, 29; Zech. 12:10). Yet some spoke by Him (2 Sam. 23:2; Zech. 7:12).

6. The name "Holy Spirit" is surprisingly only used three times in the Old Testament (Ps. 51:11; Isa. 63:10, 11).

7. Averbeck demonstrates that this point of continuity is "one of the most obvious, simple, and helpful ways of approaching the subject of God's Spirit in the Old Testament in relation to the Holy Spirit in the New Testament." That is, "*Just as people have a 'spirit', so does God*" (italics his). Richard E. Averbeck, "The Holy Spirit in the Hebrew Bible and Its Connections to the NT," in *Who's Afraid of the Holy Spirit: An Investigation into the Ministry of the Spirit of God Today*, eds. M. James Sawyer and Daniel B. Wallace (Dallas: Biblical Studies Press, 2005), 21, cf. 36.

THE HOLY SPIRIT AS THE PARACLETE AND INTIMACY

The richness of the Holy Spirit's intimacy with us as our Paraclete (Helper, Comforter, etc.) is stunning. However, the term *parakletos* is only used five times in the Bible, and so understanding the context of the four times it is used in the Upper Room Discourse in John's Gospel is essential.[8] Jesus promised Him because He would be leaving the world and His disciples. He was aware of how they were taking this news. They had a form of separation anxiety. While most think that separation anxiety is only experienced by children when they feel excessive fear or stress about separation from their home or a person they are attached to, according to new versions of the DSM, "The diagnosis is now categorized as an anxiety disorder that can be present at all stages of life."[9] The functional consequences of this disorder in adults may be not leaving the parents' home, not traveling, not working outside the home.[10] If the disciples continued to spiral down into a full manifestation of this disorder, without God's transforming aid there is the possibility that the Great Commission would end with Christ's ascension. Thus the Holy Spirit's role as the Paraclete sent by Jesus is the ultimate prescription for all believers.

We start to see the disciples' separation crisis begin to unfold in the Upper Room.[11] John introduces this evening's Passover meal in this way: "Jesus, knowing that His hour had come that He would depart out of this world to the Father, having loved His own who were in the world, He loved them to the end" (John 13:1). It is full of close relationships. Jesus, the Son of God, was about to return home to God His Father in heaven (13:3). He was also leaving behind the very followers who He loved to the very end (13:1). He expressed His love by washing their feet (13:5). This was followed by an intimate Passover meal where He reiterated that He was more than a Lord and Teacher to them (13:12–14). Jesus revealed His troubled spirit because of His impending betrayal, while John, the disciple Jesus's loved, was leaning back on Jesus's chest (13:23, 25). After Judas left, Jesus began to reveal

---

8. It is used once for Christ as our "advocate," in 1 John 2:1: "My little children, I am writing these things to you so that you may not sin. And if anyone sins, we have an Advocate with the Father, Jesus Christ the righteous."
9. "Separation Anxiety," *Psychology Today*, https://www.psychologytoday.com/conditions/separation-anxiety; *Diagnostic and Statistical Manual of Mental Disorders (DSM-5)*, 5th ed. (Washington, DC: American Psychiatric Publishing, 2013), 190–94.
10. *DSM-5*, 194.
11. Their crisis was not mentioned in the previous intimations of His death around that time in 11:50–53; 12:7–8, 23–34.

His personal legacy, His life's mission, with them as His "little children" (13:33). However, the tipping point was when Jesus told them, "Where I am going, you cannot come" (13:33). Peter questioned this immediately and Jesus had to reveal to him the harsh reality of Peter's own impending denials (13:36–38). So Jesus put His finger on their difficulty in processing the unthinkable: "Do not let your hearts be troubled; believe in God, believe also in Me" (14:1). His departure was causing a form of separation anxiety, and Jesus knew it, so He, like their wise Master, Teacher, Parent, and Friend, gave them the crucial knowledge that would carry them past perhaps the most difficult trial they would ever face. That was why they needed to know where He was going, what He was going to be doing, and what their responsibilities would be while they were separated from Him. Yet even more important was the fact that they would not be left alone . . . ever. He was going to send the Paraclete to them.

The Meaning of Paraclete

Before we move on to the Holy Spirit's intimate role as Paraclete, we should try to understand the term or name itself. The problem is that it is an elastic term that is difficult to connect solely to one English word. "Helper" (NASB) is indeed part of what His role is, but it is too general and "could carry for readers the misleading implication that a human could be in charge of the relationship with the Spirit and the Spirit would then be demoted to the role of an assistant."[12] "Comforter" partly conveys what the Spirit would bring to the disciples, but it is too narrow: He also provides assistance, teaching, etc. "Advocate" is closer, since it is how the term is used for Christ in 1 John 2:1 and is consistent with the word's religious history[13] and use in John 16:8–11. Yet it is a bit too restrictive in light of His role as comforter and helper. Further, the context does not emphasize His role as a defender against God, but more of the role of a prosecutor's defense against the disobedient world on behalf of God and believers as witnesses for Him.[14] So Paraclete appears to be one who helps, comforts, and advocates for believers after Christ's ascension. We must add that He is also a successor to Jesus Himself, carrying on the work and relationship

---

12. Gerald L. Borchert, *John 12–21*, The New American Commentary, 25B (Nashville: Broadman & Holman, 2002), 123.
13. Johannes Behm, "Παράκλητος," in Kittel, Bromiley, and Friedrich, eds., *Theological Dictionary of the New Testament*, 814.
14. Borchert, *John 12–21*, 123.

that He has had with His disciples while on earth.[15] The Paraclete alone is uniquely qualified as the *allon paracletos* ("another One of the same kind," 14:16) to provide all of this as an exact representation of the Son and the Father's will, plan, and love.

So the concept of the Holy Spirit as Paraclete is that He is Christ's substitute or representative. He is His alter ego in the best possible sense. By this, I do not mean "alter ego" in a deceptive sense like Bruce Wayne is Batman's alter ego, or in a creepy negative sense where Gollum is Smeagol's worst self. Cicero coined the term as one's better "second self" or "trusted friend."[16] We couldn't ask for anyone better. However, we must be careful not to overapply this section of Scripture on the Holy Spirit. Cole is correct in his cautions:

> Much of the promise connected with the coming of the Paraclete has to do with those gathered in the upper room and is not as easily generalized. Thus there is a good case for seeing part of the fulfillment of the teaching about the Paraclete in the formation of the New Testament but not for some notion of a magisterium as found in the Roman Catholic Church, nor for wild claims to special Spirit-granted knowledge in the present based on an appeal to these texts in John.[17]

While the formation of the New Testament and the first-century fulfillment of the *missio dei* are in view here, we can appreciate His ongoing intimate ministry as Paraclete.

---

15. "Judaism was also familiar with the idea of a 'successor' who carries on a predecessor's work." Craig S. Keener, *The IVP Bible Background Commentary: New Testament* (Downers Grove, IL: InterVarsity, 1993), John 14:16. Cf. Keener, *The Gospel of John: A Commentary, Volume 2* (Peabody, MA: Hendrickson, 2003), 966–69.

16. "Alter ego," Dictionary.com. *Online Etymology Dictionary*, http://www.dictionary.com/browse/alter-ego. Pompey would later call Cicero his "alter ego in all things." David L. Stockton, *Cicero: A Political Biography* (New York: Oxford University, 1971), 195.

17. Cole, *He Who Gives Life*, 187.

The Intimacy of the Paraclete

What is the intimate role of the Holy Spirit as Paraclete in our lives? First, he is the means by which we can move to intimacy with the Trinity. Christ asked the Father to send Him to His followers and He gave Him. This is so "that He may be with us forever" (14:16). Christ made it clear that He would not "leave you as orphans" (14:18). Rather than that kind of hopeless separation, the Spirit is the means by which Christ could say, "I will come to you" (14:18). He clarified this by saying, "After a little while the world will no longer see Me, but you will see Me; because I live, you will live also" (14:19). His opening our eyes is His movement in us so that we can see and experience the risen Lord through the Spirit. Thus Christ's departure has been to our advantage: "for if I do not go away, the Helper will not come to you; but if I go, I will send Him to you" (16:7; cf. 1 John 4:13).

Second, the Paraclete provides intimate knowledge of God to us. Christ called Him "the Spirit of truth" (14:17; 15:26; 16:13; cf. 1 John 5:6). This knowledge is exclusive—"the world cannot receive because it doesn't see or know Him; but we know Him" (14:17; cf. 1 John 4:2). Christ by means of the Paraclete discloses Himself to us out of love (14:21). Thus a tell-tale sign of one of Christ's followers is that they keep His words, in contrast to the world which doesn't love Him and keep His words. The words or truths the Spirit reveals to us are not only Christ's words, but the Father's as well (14:24). Such intimate sharing of intimate knowledge of the Father's desires and plans! (15:26). All of it is by means of the Paraclete who "proceeds" from the Father, like the sword that will come from Christ's mouth (Rev. 1:16; 19:15) or from one's very feelings, affections, deeds, and sayings (Matt. 5:44; cf. Matt. 7:15, 20). Furthermore, the Paraclete will work with us to aid in our understanding of this knowledge. Christ promised, "He will teach you all things, and bring to your remembrance all that I said to you" (14:26). But again, this is not mere knowledge of facts, but "He will testify about Me" out of intimate experience like Christ's disciples had while He was with them (15:26–27).[18] So it is clear that the Holy Spirit does not have intimacy with us on His own. He mediates for the other members of the Trinity. In Christ's attempts to explain this to them, He knew they wouldn't fully grasp the role of the Paraclete in their lives. "I have many

---

18. "What Jesus was in thought, word, and deed is precisely what the 'other Paraclete' will be in Jesus's stead." V. George Shillington, "The Spirit-Paraclete as Jesus's Alter Ego in the Fourth Gospel (John 14–16)," *Vision* 13 (2012): 35.

more things to say to you, but you cannot bear them now" (16:12). Yet He guaranteed the Paraclete's intimate role in helping their separation anxiety:

> But when He, the Spirit of truth, comes, He will guide you into all the truth; for He will not speak on His own initiative, but whatever He hears, He will speak; and He will disclose to you what is to come. He will glorify Me, for He will take of Mine and will disclose it to you. All things that the Father has are Mine; therefore I said that He takes of Mine and will disclose it to you. (16:13–15)

They would ever be hearing the collective voice of the Trinity.

Third, the Paraclete would provide an intimate connection for Christ's followers while He was in heaven. This connection is the Spirit's intimate location or place as well as contact with the believer. Christ's departure would guarantee the Paraclete's presence with them. As Köstenberger puts it, "just as God was present with them through Jesus, he will continue to be with them through his Spirit."[19] This is so "that He may be with you forever" (14:16). In other words, His presence is an abiding one, that is, "He abides with you and will be in you" (14:17; cf. 1 John 3:24). And then Christ promised them, "I will not leave you as orphans; I will come to you" (14:18). Borchart synthesizes the Paraclete's role well:

> Thus the picture presented in this context is that of a Paraclete who will function as a replacement and a strengthening companion who will be a kind of alter ego for Jesus. Jesus had been leading them, advising them, teaching them, empowering them, and critiquing them. But his time with them would thereafter be limited, and his followers needed a new companion who could function in all those ways.[20]

The movement He makes to bring the Trinity close to us, the intimate and personal knowledge He carefully shares with us, and the place He has in our

---

19. Andreas J. Köstenberger, *A Theology of John's Gospel and Letters* (Grand Rapids: Zondervan, 2009), 397.
20. Borchert, *John 12–21*, 123–24.

lives touches our souls,[21] especially when we struggle with our own separation anxieties.[22]

THE HOLY SPIRIT, INTIMACY, AND BUILDING THE CHURCH IN ACTS

What intimate role did the Holy Spirit play in building the church in the book of Acts? It is here that we see His role as Paraclete, the alter ego of Christ, minister in uniquely personal ways. His initial ministry of His baptizing Christ's followers into His body, the Church, in Acts 2, while not necessarily intimate as we have been defining it in this study, does demonstrates His power and unifying force. We first see how His ministry is very personal. Peter's assessment of the hoarding of Ananias and Sapphira was that they were lying to and putting the Spirit to the test (Acts 5:3, 9). The consequences of their collusion were the same as lying to God,[23] who takes violations of a

---

21. It is striking how believers interpret the proof of presence of the Holy Spirit in our lives. Revivalist Todd Bentley provides an interesting charismatic example of anecdotal evidence.

    Now we sure want the "with you" presence of the Holy Spirit in our lives! But do we know the *with you* presence? Everyone who is saved has the "in you" presence, but if we want to feel and know the Holy Spirit is with us, hovering over us in everything we do and everywhere we go, then we need to know Him. It's about nurturing intimacy. Then you can't help but have the *with you* presence of God on your life. And what an impact that has on the people around you! Look at how God's *with you* presence affected people through the lives of Kathryn Kuhlman, Charles Finney, and Smith Wigglesworth.

    - Kathryn Kuhlman carried so much of the presence on her that when she stepped out of her hotel room and she walked by, people they would fall down under the power. Then when she got to the crusade and stepped out on the platform, the power of God would ramp up 10 levels because of the glorious presence of God that she carried.
    - Charles Finney carried such a powerful presence of God that one day when he walked into a factory it was like God Himself stepped in with Him. All the workers got saved even though he said nothing.
    - Smith Wigglesworth was sitting on the train going somewhere minding his own business and people would come up to him and ask, "What can I do to be saved?" He was so saturated, filled and controlled by the Holy Ghost that when the lost got in his presence they felt another Presence.

    Todd Bentley, "Intimacy with the Holy Spirit: Part 2," Identity Network, http://www.identitynetwork.org/apps/articles/default.asp?articleid=43634&columnid=.

22. Christ would symbolically promise the presence of the Spirit in an intimate commissioning of the disciples as His ambassadors in John 20:21. This reference to Jesus breathing on them is not a pre-gifting of the Spirit or the actual gifting at Pentecost fifty days later. See Köstenberger's helpful development of the purpose of this event in his *A Theology of John's Gospel and Letters,* 399–400.

23. Their dishonesty for the sake of ill-gotten gain is parallel to Judas's betrayal of Christ. Cf. also Isa. 59:13; Jer. 27:16; 29:31; 43:2; Ezek. 13:8; Rev. 3:9.

close relationship with Him very personally.[24] Yet the Holy Spirit provided emotional support to the young believers. In Acts 9:31, the churches throughout all Judea and Galilee and Samaria not only enjoyed peace and growth, but they were able to continue on "in the fear of the Lord and in the comfort of the Holy Spirit."

The most common intimate role of the Holy Spirit in Acts was when He gave specific instructions of God's will to the leaders of the early church. In these cases He would be communicating to them as He was "directing events in accordance with the will of God."[25] In Acts 8:29, "the Spirit said to Philip" to go up and join the Ethiopian eunuch's chariot. In Acts 10:19, while Peter was reflecting on the vision he had received of the sheet of animals, "the Spirit said to him, 'Behold, three men are looking for you.'" The Spirit later "told" him to go to Cornelius in Caesarea (11:12). In these instances, the Spirit helped them violate cultural conventions and expectations at crucial junctures to fulfill God's overall mission.[26] When the prophets and teachers in Antioch were "ministering to the Lord and fasting," the Holy Spirit gave them detailed instructions, to commission for Him Barnabas and Saul for their first missionary journey (Acts 13:2, 4). At the Jerusalem Council, James and the apostles found that "it seemed good to the Holy Spirit and to us to lay upon you no greater burden" than certain essentials (Acts 15:28). Paul and his missionary team experienced the Spirit's close guidance forbidding them from sharing the Word in certain places (Acts 16:6–7). Yet the most personal of information given Paul by the Holy Spirit was of his impending "bonds and afflictions" that awaited him in Jerusalem. He said that, "the Holy Spirit solemnly testifies to me in every city, saying that bonds and afflictions await me" (Acts 20:23) and that certain disciples informed him by the Spirit that he shouldn't set foot in Jerusalem because of it (Acts 21:4). All this was confirmed in the Spirit's object lesson to Paul through Agabus in Acts 21:11. He prefaced it by declaring, "This is what the

---

24. The Holy Spirit's convicting work as Paraclete promised by Christ in John 16:13–15 was exemplified in Stephen's accusation of the unbelieving Jews: "You men who are stiff-necked and uncircumcised in heart and ears are always resisting the Holy Spirit; you are doing just as your fathers did" (Acts 7:51).

25. C. K. Barrett, *A Critical and Exegetical Commentary on the Acts of the Apostles: Volume 1, I-XIV* (Edinburgh: T & T Clark, 1994), 427.

26. Craig S. Keener, *Acts: An Exegetical Commentary: Volume 2, 3:1–14:28* (Grand Rapids: Baker, 2013), 1581: "It may be that Philip would need specific instructions before approaching a person of (presumably) higher social standing." See also Barrett, *A Critical and Exegetical Commentary on the Acts of the Apostles: Volume 1*, 427.

Holy Spirit says," giving it divine authority by replacing the more common, "This is what the Lord says."[27] Thus it is clear that the Holy Spirit's speech was not frivolous or subjective. Luke's choice of these cases demonstrates that the Holy Spirit directly and indirectly provided crucial intimate knowledge to the early leaders for the growth of the church. In so doing, He led them outside of their cultural comfort zones to fulfill the Great Commission of Acts 1:8 in ways they probably never thought possible. This would lead Paul to great discomfort but for the sake of the call. And so we may be able to hear the Spirit's voice most clearly today when we are willing to sacrifice everything for the "outsiders" God wants us to reach with His gracious and merciful good news.

THE HOLY SPIRIT, INTIMACY, AND THE CHRISTIAN

As Paul and others wrote letters to the early churches, they clarified intimacy with the Holy Spirit in at least three significant ways. However, before we move to these ways, it is clear that the Spirit has a personal relationship with us as Christ-followers. He is not an "it" (as some of my students in the past have written).[28] His personal attributes and interactions with believers is the continual theme in the aspects of intimacy we will investigate further. He intercedes for us in our prayers, provides help and guidance, and provides intimate knowledge of God for us. His personal connection to us can even cause His emotions to change. Paul exhorted believers not to break the unity of relationships within the church by our attitudes or "unwholesome speech," and thus, "Do not grieve (*lupeite*) the Holy Spirit of God, by whom you were sealed for the day of redemption" (Eph. 4:29–31). The Spirit's deep emotional pain and sadness appears to be the result of His investment of intimate personal and emotional capital in His relationship with us.[29]

---

27. Eckhard J. Schnabel, *Acts*, Zondervan Exegetical Commentary on the New Testament (Grand Rapids: Zondervan, 2012), 857.
28. Porter calls Him "itself" when commenting on this section of Romans. Stanley E. Porter, *The Letter to the Romans: A Linguistic and Literary Commentary* (Sheffield: Sheffield Phoenix, 2015), 170. For a helpful summary of the personhood of the Holy Spirit, see Cole, *He Who Gives Life*, 65–69.
29. Eckman argues that since the same term for grief is used of what Christ went through in the garden in Matthew 26:37, "In a sense, we can say that Jesus the Messiah had his passion in the Garden and on the cross, but the Holy Spirit has his continual passion within us." This comparison—simply due to the same term being used in both cases—while interesting, seems a bit overstated. David Eckman, "The Holy Spirit and Our Emotions," in Wallace and Sawyer, eds., *Who's Afraid of the Holy Spirit?*, 210.

The Spirit's Providing Intimate Knowledge for Us

A foundational way the Epistles bring focus to the Holy Spirit's intimate role in our lives is how they show that he provides us intimate knowledge of God. There is a monumental difference between the human understanding of how the grand epic of history factors into human purpose and destiny and what followers of Christ have had revealed to them by God. In this regard, Paul experienced the Athenian sages mocking him as a "babbler" (Acts 17:18) and scoffing at his teaching on the resurrection (17:32). In Corinth, Gallio, the proconsul of Achaia, deemed the volatile debate between Paul and the Jews as merely inconsequential wrangling about "words and names and your own law" (18:14–15). Later in Caesarea, Festus publically declared Paul out of his mind and mad (26:24). It isn't surprising that human wisdom seeps into the church. The church at Corinth had gathered many "wise" teachers that were actually undermining the truth of the gospel, the authority of Paul as an apostle, and even the reality of the resurrection. So Paul was compelled to challenge their arrogant worldly thinking by contrasting human wisdom and wisdom from the Spirit. He argued in 1 Corinthians 2:10–16:

> For to us God revealed them through the Spirit; for the Spirit searches all things, even the depths of God. For who among men knows the thoughts of a man except the spirit of the man which is in him? Even so the thoughts of God no one knows except the Spirit of God. Now we have received, not the spirit of the world, but the Spirit who is from God, so that we may know the things freely given to us by God, which things we also speak, not in words taught by human wisdom, but in those taught by the Spirit, combining spiritual thoughts with spiritual words. But a natural man does not accept the things of the Spirit of God, for they are foolishness to him; and he cannot understand them, because they are spiritually appraised. But he who is spiritual appraises all things, yet he himself is appraised by no one. For WHO HAS KNOWN THE MIND OF THE LORD, THAT HE WILL INSTRUCT HIM? But we have the mind of Christ.

His point? Human wisdom, that is, natural reason and intuition, is completely powerless to gain access to and understanding of divine realities without God's help.[30] Thus the key role of the Holy Spirit is to provide intimate knowledge of God.

---

30. David E. Garland, *1 Corinthians*, Baker Exegetical Commentary on the New Testament, (Grand Rapids: Baker, 2003), 100.

The striking nature of God's wisdom is that it is revealed to us (v. 10).[31] Paul's teachings to us were preached and written "in demonstration of the Spirit and power" (2:4). And so verses 4 and 10, where we see the first two instances of the word "Spirit" used in his letter, provide a foundation for the rest of his teachings on the Spirit in chapters 12–14 and 15:42–57. In sum, the Spirit's ministry is inseparable from Christ[32] and His church. Furthermore, we know this revelation, *apekalupsen*, is special and intimate because it is provided by "the Spirit that searches all things, even the depths of God" (2:10). The Spirit searches (*ereunaō*) not to find new information but so that he penetrates all[33] that can be known as a member of the Godhead.[34] This includes "the depths (*bathē*) of God." This term is not only used for the unfathomable depths of the sea, but is a part of apocalyptic literature. To the finite and shallow human mind, this knowledge is unattainable and mysterious. At the invitation of God, however, the teachings and writings of His apostles are a way to remove the veil to experience the inexhaustible riches and wisdom and knowledge of God (Rom. 11:33), which most importantly include His gift of salvation to mankind, the spread of the gospel in every age and generation, and the coming of Christ's kingdom.[35] The Spirit reveals the crucial facts about the Lord Jesus Christ, and so Paul declared, "Therefore I make known to you that no one speaking by the Spirit of God says, 'Jesus is accursed'; and no one can say, 'Jesus is Lord,' except by the Holy Spirit" (1 Cor. 12:3).[36] The

---

31. Even if this is the supernatural revelation only given to Paul and the other apostles in light of the "we" of verse 6 (so Ciampa and Rosner), it is still given to us "who love Him" (v. 9) by God from them and interpreted by the Holy Spirit. See Roy E. Ciampa and Brian S. Rosner, *The First Letter to the Corinthians* (Grand Rapids: Eerdmans, 2010), 129.

32. Anthony C. Thistleton, *The First Epistle to the Corinthians*, The New International Greek Testament Commentary (Grand Rapids: Eerdmans, 2000), 256.

33. Leon Morris, *The First Epistle of Paul to the Corinthians: An Introduction and Commentary* (Grand Rapids: Eerdmans, 1985), 56.

34. Bloesch communicates the Spirit's Trinitarian role well in light of this passage: "I do not see the Father as the only actor in the Trinity, nor is he the sole source of action (monopatrism). The Father presents a plan and the Son carries through the plan with the aid of the Spirit. But the Son and the Spirit also contribute to this plan. The Spirit not only receives from the Father and the Son but also responds creatively. The Spirit is not only acted upon by the Father and the Son, but forges the bond of unity between Father and Son. He searches the depths of God and brings the intentions of God to fruition and realization (1 Cor. 2:10–11)." Donald G. Bloesch, *The Holy Spirit: Works & Gifts* (Downers Grove, IL: IVP, 2000), 273.

35. Simon J. Kistemaker, *Exposition of the First Epistle to the Corinthians* (Grand Rapids: Baker, 1993), 87.

36. Paul also indicated to Timothy, "But the Spirit explicitly says that in later times some will fall away from the faith, paying attention to deceitful spirits and doctrines of demons" (1 Tim. 4:1). The writer of Hebrews recognized the Spirit's imparting crucial knowledge

Spirit also opens the eyes of our minds and hearts to empower them for a transforming relationship with Jesus Christ. Paul later told the Corinthians, "But we all, with unveiled face, beholding as in a mirror the glory of the Lord, are being transformed into the same image from glory to glory, just as from the Lord, the Spirit" (2 Cor. 3:18).

It should be noted at this point that there is no enlightened spiritual elite among believers today. John is quite clear that every one of God's children receives "the anointing from the Holy One" (1 John 2:20), which is the illumination given by the Spirit.[37] John appears to be making a play on words with *antichristos, Christos,* and *chrisma* (anointing) (2:18–22). So the anointing specifically refers to the same revelation of the truth about Christ and the gospel of 1 Corinthians 2:10–16 and what is recorded in the Scriptures.[38] This is in contrast to any cult-like people who secede from the true body of Christ and follow a parody of who Christ really is (1 John 2:18–20).[39] Thus John could genuinely claim, "you all know" (2:20). Since the Holy Spirit provides intimate knowledge for us, we don't need extra outside teachers to provide the "real" truth about Christ and the gospel (2:27).

The Spirit's Leading Us

Another significant way in which intimacy with the Holy Spirit is clarified is how He leads us. Paul's section on the Spirit's leading and interceding in Romans 8 is undergirded by the fact that He indwells us as believers.

> However, you are not in the flesh but in the Spirit, if indeed the Spirit of God dwells in you. But if anyone does not have the Spirit of Christ, he does not belong to Him. . . . But if the Spirit of Him who raised Jesus from the dead dwells in you, He who raised Christ Jesus from the dead will also give life to your mortal bodies through His Spirit who dwells in you. (Rom. 8:9, 11)

That the Spirit indwells us (*oikeo*) is in contrast to the sin that indwells in 7:20. However, Christ's victory on the cross provides the Spirit who frees us from that bondage. When He indwells or resides in us, He is not a welcome guest

---

through the Scriptures when he said, "And the Holy Spirit also testifies to us; for after saying . . ." (Heb. 10:15) and he quoted Jeremiah 31:33.

37. Morris, "1 John," 1403.
38. The common Pentecostal/charismatic view of the anointing equates this passage with receiving the "fullness" or "baptism" of the Holy Spirit that overcomes us with an electrical feeling and emotion.
39. Akin, *1, 2, 3 John,* 117.

but the master of the house. So the Spirit's intimate location within our inner being provides Him a base of operation to lead us as God's children. "For all who are being led by the Spirit of God, these are sons of God" (Rom. 8:14).

Being led by the Spirit is an activity of our interpersonal relationship with God. The *ago* ("lead") word group emphasizes the ability "to so influence others as to cause them to follow a recommended course of action."[40] Thus there is a distinction here between leading and governing/ruling, and yet it is not demonstrating or "showing." In other words, the Spirit does not simply go ahead like a scout to see if things are safe or is not just the most distinguished person in the group.[41] He leads us to a victorious life by helping us put "to death the deeds of the body" rather than "living according to the flesh" (8:12–13). Furthermore, Paul phrased "being led" by the Spirit as a present passive indicative. In other words, besides being an inherent quality of the Christian's inherited position ("these are sons/children of God"), it entails our consistent willingness to be influenced by the Spirit at the internal juncture of our spirituality and morality. This may cause us to reflect on the exodus[42] and how God not only freed His people from slavery (8:15) and gave them the law that set them apart from the pagan nations (Exod. 19:5–6), but how He led them by His glorious cloud and fire through the wilderness (Exod. 13:21–22). Until our ultimate redemption, we must allow God to influence us, to lead our lives, through the Holy Spirit, since He has provided Him as the deposit of our inheritance (8:17; Eph. 1:13–14).

The Spirit leads us to the intimate knowledge of our loving relationship as God's children and helps us move away from a fearful slave mentality and morality. Paul assures us, "The Spirit Himself testifies (*summartureo*) with our spirit that we are children of God" (Rom. 8:16). He also notes in Galatians, "But if you are led by the Spirit, you are not under the Law" (Gal. 5:18). Slavery to obedience to any external standard cannot establish the family relationship God desires for His creatures. Only legitimate children can cry out to God "Abba, Father!" (Rom. 8:15). In fact, it is only due to Christ's sacrifice that our justification and adoption are possible (Gal. 4:5). This new family relationship causes God to send forth "the Spirit of His Son into our hearts, crying, 'Abba! Father!'" (Gal. 4:6). It is interesting to speculate on how first-century Jews would grapple with their conscience at being

---

40. Johannes P. Louw and Eugene Albert Nida, *Greek-English Lexicon of the New Testament: Based on Semantic Domains* (New York: United Bible Societies, 1996), 464.
41. Ibid.
42. Keener, *Romans: A New Covenant Commentary*, 102.

told they could now call God their "Abba."[43] They might feel a great sense of unworthiness and presumption at first. But as they reflect upon what Christ the Son of God has done for them, and as they began to trust in Christ's teachings and their explanation by the apostles, they would begin to experience being God's child. They would feel God drawing them into an intimacy that they had never dared even to dream of. They now had welcome access into the love of God.[44] We can reflect on this reality and experience God drawing us to Himself by the leading of the Spirit. We can walk away from fear and shame and rest in the Spirit's leading.

It is telling that Paul uses a derivation of *martureo* here as he moves his readers to understand that as a close spiritual family who are fellow heirs with Christ, we will suffer with Him in order to be glorified with Him (8:17). The testimony or witness of the faithfulness of believers amidst their persecution would cause them to be called martyrs. It is clear that the close family of Christ suffers together.

We must be aware that in Galatians 5 Paul uses four distinct verbs for the life of the believer that is intimately led by the Holy Spirit. In 5:16, he tells us that we are to walk (*peripateō*) in or by means of the Spirit, "and you will not carry out the desire of the flesh." Similarly, according to Paul, we are not to walk or conduct our lives the way the world does (Eph. 4:17; cf. 2:2; Col. 3:7), but walk by faith and not by sight (2 Cor. 5:7) and newness of life (Rom. 6:4).[45] The case here of our walking by means of the Spirit in Galatians 5:16 and being led by him in 5:18 means we personally are to choose "to go where the Spirit is going, to listen to his voice, to discern his will, to follow his guidance."[46] Believers will then live a fruitful virtuous life that is produced by the Spirit Himself. Thus this manner of living cannot be governed or chained to a series of legalistic commands (5:18, 23), but it joyfully and spiritually lives out the whole Law, loving our neighbors (5:14). The third and fourth verbs are in 5:25: "If we live by the Spirit, let us also walk by the Spirit." Paul's first class conditional "if" shows he wanted them to reckon with the reality of their new life (*zōmen*) in the Spirit that resurrected their spirits when they were cruci-

---

43. John Bligh, *Galatians: A Discussion on St. Paul's Epistle*, Householder Commentary 1 (London: St. Paul's, 1969), 355.

44. Timothy George, *Galatians*, The New American Commentary, Vol. 30, (Nashville: Broadman & Holman, 1994), 308.

45. See Heinrich Seesemann, "Πατέω, Καταπατέω, Περιπατέω, Ἐμπεριπατέω," *Theological Dictionary of the New Testament*, edited by Gerhard Kittel, Geoffrey W. Bromiley, and Gerhard Friedrich (Grand Rapids: Eerdmans, 1964), 945.

46. George, *Galatians*, 386.

fied with Christ (Gal. 2:20; cf. 3:3; 6:8; Rom. 6:4). Since this new life in the Spirit is a reality, we should follow after the Spirit. *Stoichōmen* here means to keep in step with, be in harmony with, to be in agreement with. It is used of a military marching cadence. Witherington puts the force of this well:

> [T]he Galatians do not need to place themselves under any elementary prin-
> ciples of the universe, either pagan or Jewish ones, precisely because they
> already live in and by the Spirit of God and should follow the Spirit's lead,
> staying in line or step with the Spirit, not the Law.[47]

We must also refuse to listen to or follow the lead of the urges of our flesh. Heeding the intimate words of the Spirit will help us fulfill Paul's exhorta-tion, "Let us not become boastful, challenging one another, envying one another" (5:26), and thus guard against destroying the closeness of the body of Christ.

I love Francis Chan's answer to the question, "Who is the most Spirit-filled person you know?" The summary of his description of Joni Erickson Tada is of a paraplegic woman indwelt by the Spirit, who walks with Him keeping in step with His cadence. Chan is careful to note that it is not for her great accomplishments that she came to mind when he answers:

> It has to do with the fact that you can't spend ten minutes with Joni before
> she breaks out in song, quotes Scripture, or shares a touching and timely word
> of encouragement. I have never seen the fruit of the Spirit more obviously
> displayed in a person's life as when I am with Joni. I can't seem to have a conver-
> sation with Joni without shedding tears. It's because Joni is a person whose life,
> at every level, gives evidence of the Spirit's work in and through her.[48]

She has allowed the Spirit to meet her deepest and most intimate needs. And so the Spirit does lead and when we follow, it is apparent.

The Spirit's Help in Our Prayers

Continuing on in Romans 8, another way the Epistles bring focus to our intimacy with the Holy Spirit is that He helps us pray to God the Father. In 8:26–

---

47. Ben Witherington III, *Grace in Galatia: A Commentary on St. Paul's Letter to the Galatians* (Grand Rapids: Eerdmans, 1998), 413.
48. Chan, *The Forgotten God*, 41.

27, one of the most profound declarations of the Spirit's intimacy in the Bible, Paul gives hope to believers who struggle with praying in the midst of suffering:

> In the same way the Spirit also helps our weakness; for we do not know how to pray as we should, but the Spirit Himself intercedes for us with groanings too deep for words; and He who searches the hearts knows what the mind of the Spirit is, because He intercedes for the saints according to the will of God.

The Holy Spirit helps us (8:26). His "help" is an intensified form of the verb that means to take hold of someone at their side so as to support them.[49] This is what Martha wanted Mary to do for her when Jesus was with them in their home (Luke 10:40). Thus the intimacy with God here is palpable because Paul has already shown that the Spirit hears our groanings in that He indwells us as a firstfruit (Rom. 8:23). Creation itself groans in agony (*sustenazo*), suffering the radical effects of bondage to sin with its droughts, destructive storms, diseases, and death (8:22). This sinful bondage also crushes in on the human soul. Therefore, as believers we wait in eagerness for the suffering of this world to give way to a radically new age and place (8:24–25). This is where the intimate ministry of the Spirit is essential.

In our lack of hope amidst our suffering, the Spirit ministers to us in our weakness, which in this case is due to our ignorance.[50] Praying "as we should" (8:26) and the Spirit's intercession "according to the will of God" (8:27) dictates that our lack of knowledge is not about the right way or perfect technique[51] of praying but the content of God's will. Schreiner is right about suffering believers: "they do not have an adequate grasp of what God's will is when they pray. Because of our finitude and fallibility we cannot perceive

---

49. *Sunantilambanetai.* Willam Sanday and Arthur C. Headlam, *A Critical and Exegetical Commentary on the Epistle to the Romans*, 5th ed. (New York: Charles Scribner's Sons, 1899), 213.
50. Schreiner shows that verse 26 is a chiasm and its focal point defines our weakness:
    A The Spirit helps
    B   in our weakness.
    B`   For we do not know what to pray for as we ought,
    A`   but the Spirit intercedes with unspeakable groanings.
    "It is weakness in prayer that Paul zeroes in on, and the Spirit's help in prayer is the answer to our weakness." Thomas R. Schreiner, *Romans*, Baker Exegetical Commentary on the New Testament (Grand Rapids: Baker, 1998), 443.
51. Ernest Best, *The Letter of Paul to the Romans* (New York: Cambridge University Press, 1967), 100..

fully what God would desire." He adds that this is because "the totality of God's will is hidden from them."[52] Osborne interprets this further:

> When I pray for healing, financial aid, social relationships and so on, I do not know what is the actual will of the Lord in the circumstance. This is a very important qualification, especially for those who think that faith always gets its request from God. God is clearly sovereign over our prayers and knows when to say no to them. In fact, from the perspective of true faith, God's no is actually a yes, for it is an affirmation of his love in giving us what we need rather than what we want.[53]

Paul himself struggled with this ignorance when praying for his thorn in the flesh (2 Cor. 12:7–10). Yet Schlatter is right that God does not remove the believer's inadequacy: "Through the process of prayer one experiences simultaneously futility and the Spirit's help, since we do not know what the content of our prayer should be."[54]

The Spirit's help is in the form of intercession "with groanings too deep for words." While this speaks to profound intimacy, two issues need to be clarified. First, who is doing the groaning? Some take the groanings to be ours as believers. A key support is simply that the Spirit does not groan anywhere else in the Bible. The phrase "with groanings" (*stenagmois alalētois*) is also in the dative, which may be translated as "in" the believer's groanings. If we cannot find the right words to say to God in prayer, then the only thing we have left is our groanings.[55] Since unbelievers cannot groan in this way, it makes sense that they are prompted by the Spirit. However, it is best to see the scales tipping in favor of the groanings of the Holy Spirit. We should expect Paul to insert "our" (*hēmen*) to clarify them as human, but he doesn't. They are associated with the one interceding, "the Spirit Himself." The Spirit-prompted human groaning doesn't fit the context, because the focus throughout verses 26–27 is on the Spirit and His intentions. God understands and responds to His mind, and He is the one who intercedes on our behalf.[56] It is true that

52. Schreiner, *Romans*, 443.
53. Grant Osborne, *Romans*, The IVP New Testament Commentary Series (Downers Grove, IL: IVP, 2004), 216–17.
54. Adolf Schlatter, *Romans: The Righteousness of God*, trans. Siegfried S. Schatzmann (Peabody, MA: Hendrickson, 1995 [1935]), 190.
55. Morris, *The Epistle to the Romans*, 328.
56. William Hendriksen, *Exposition of Paul's Epistle to the Romans* (Grand Rapids: Baker, 1980), 275–76; Moo, *The Epistle to the Romans*, 525 n.95.

there is a linguistic connection between the groanings of creation, believers, and the Spirit in Romans 8. Yet the Spirit's groanings have a different source in His intercession rather than the frustration in suffering.[57] If the Spirit grieves (Eph. 4:30) then He surely can groan.

Second, what are the groanings? Are they inexpressible groanings, or are they unspoken? The word *alalētois* is only here in the Bible, and yet its word origin is obviously from "wordless" or "unspoken." Yet does it mean inarticulate audible sounds and thus groans, or simply unspoken feelings and thoughts? I lean toward the latter.[58] Paul uses a different phrase for the inexplicable or unspeakable words (*arrēta rēmata*) he heard in his vision in the third heaven (2 Cor. 12:4). This language for the Spirit's expression of emotion for and with us may well be anthropomorphic, but as we have seen in an earlier chapter, no less genuine and real. The issue here is that the Spirit intimately empathizes with our suffering and our ignorance of how to pray for God's will in it.

Some have tried to argue that the groanings are not only that of the believer, but they are tongues. Käsemann claims, "it can only be a matter of ecstatic cries," thus "the praying in tongues."[59] Schreiner summarizes best the case for and against groanings being believers speaking in tongues.[60] The charismatic position reasons that the language of unspeakable groanings fits with praying in/with the Spirit elsewhere (1 Cor. 14:14–15; Eph. 6:18; Jude 20) and with vocalizing mysteries (1 Cor. 14:2). In that first-century world, supposedly no one prayed silently. They further argue that a blending of our groaning (8:23) and the Spirit's groaning (8:26) best explains these texts as well as places where our spirits mingle with the Holy Spirit (Rom. 8:15–16; 1 Cor. 14–15; Gal. 4:6). *Alalētois* doesn't necessarily mean wordless, silent, or unspoken, because *aneklalētos* is the term used for that idea. So *alalētois* in 8:26 may mean something uttered without words. Yet groaning must involve the ability to be heard by definition. Our inability to understand the content of this praying makes sense because the text states that only the Spirit understands it. Furthermore, speaking in tongues is the only common early church experience that fits this passage.

---

57. Colin G. Kruse, *Paul's Letter to the Romans*, The Pillar New Testament Commentary (Grand Rapids: Eerdmans, 2012), 352.
58. See Moo, *The Epistle to the Romans*, 524–25
59. Ernst Käsemann, *Commentary on Romans*, trans. Geoffrey W. Bromiley (Grand Rapids: Eerdmans, 1980), 240, 241. See also Gordon D. Fee, *God's Empowering Presence: The Holy Spirit in the Letters of Paul* (Peabody, MA: Hendrickson, 1994), 580–85.
60. Schreiner, *Romans*, 444–45.

While this is, at first glance, a good case for the groanings of Romans 8:26 being tongues-speaking, there are significant reasons for rejecting this explanation. The context mitigates against the groanings being human. They are the Spirit's groanings while He intercedes, not while believers pray in an unknown language. Further, while the meaning of *alalētois* cannot be the most important argument, it is still better to take it in its most natural sense of "without speech" and thus with the absence of any vocalization at all. And again, the Spirit's *stenagmois* or groanings do not appear to be literal, but a metaphorical anthropomorphism. Thus His groanings are inaudible in the same way that creation's groanings are (8:22). And even if the groanings refer to all believers (which I do not think they do), tongues is a gift that is not given by the Spirit to every believer (1 Cor. 12:12, 30). Yes, Paul desired all Christians to speak in tongues (1 Cor. 14:5), but not any more than he wanted them to all be celibate (1 Cor. 7:7). This would mean that the Spirit's aid described in Romans 8:26–27 is only available to those with the gift of tongues, which clearly is not what Paul is saying. In some instances, the claim that Romans 8:26 is tongues appears to be experience looking for biblical support. This is what is done with the statements in Jude 20, "praying in the Holy Spirit,"[61] and Ephesians 6:18, "With all prayer and petition pray at all times in the Spirit." Again, these verses refer to all believers, rather than just those with the gift of tongues. While tongues may be a minute application of these passages, the context of each mitigates against that.[62]

What about Paul's instructions for praying in tongues in 1 Corinthians 14? At the outset I have to say that this cannot be dealt with in depth, because it would take us afield of intimacy with and by the Holy Spirit. At the same time, Paul's emphasis in the broader context is the Spirit's sovereignty over the gifts as to their distribution (12:7–11) and manifestation (12:7, 11). Yet overemphasizing one gift over another violates the very fruit the Spirit desires to produce in the church, especially love and self-control (Gal. 5:22–23). Furthermore, praying in tongues (1 Cor. 14:2, 14, 28) is not meant for all believers since only certain members of the body of Christ possess the gift of tongues (1 Cor.

---

61. For praying in tongues, see for example Richard J. Bauckham, *Jude, 2 Peter,* Word Biblical Commentary, 50 (Waco, TX: Word, 1983), 113; James D. G. Dunn, *Jesus and the Spirit* (London: SCM, 1975), 239–40.

62. Richard C. Lucas and Christopher Green, *The Message of 2 Peter and Jude: The Promise of His Coming* (Downers Grove, IL: IVP, 1995), 222; Thomas R. Schreiner, *1, 2 Peter, Jude,* The New American Commentary, 37 (Nashville: Broadman & Holman, 2003), 482–83; Douglas J. Moo, *2 Peter and Jude,* NIV Application Commentary (Grand Rapids: Zondervan, 1996), 285.

12:30). Thus it is also not meant to be the exclusive means of intimate prayer for them or anyone. Its primary purpose is as a sign to the unbelieving, especially Jews, that God has indeed turned from the Jews exclusively and has opened the doors to the Gentiles to be His people as well (14:20–22). In 14:2, when one speaks in a tongue, they speak to God (cf. Acts 2:11). Yet no one understands because they are speaking mysteries. In 14:14, praying in a tongue, while not discouraged, is not an individualistic practice, nor is it a justification of one's spirituality over others. It is not the primary or special means of prayer. It also must be managed with self-control and cognitive awareness and communication with God (14:13–19). Similarly, therefore, performing or leading music in the church, for example, must not be only an affective experience in our deepest spiritual being, nor only a cognitive technical one. The Spirit would want us to minister in the church with our spirits and our minds. We must interact intimately with God by means of the Spirit regardless or our ministries, because the Spirit speaks through it and He produces the spiritual fruit in our lives and those ministered to by the gift He has given (1 Cor. 12:4–7). May all this accomplish the ultimate purpose of the spiritual gifts of serving and speaking: to bring God glory through Jesus Christ (1 Peter 4:10–11).

Nevertheless, most agree that the Spirit's intercession (*uperentugkano*) associated with groanings is in some way His expression of deep love and concern for us amidst our sorrows in this age.[63] In one sense, whatever is going on is imperceptible to us.[64] In another sense, the very knowledge of His intercession brings confidence that our prayers are not only being heard, understood, and rightly interpreted, but are being answered according to God's perfect and overall will. This is the fulfillment of His role as Paraclete

---

63. Some assume the Spirit groans because He wants a relationship with us, but we are ignoring Him:

> The Spirit of God longs to have a closer intimate relationship with each and every person in the body of Christ. As I type this I hear the groaning of the Spirit! I hear the Spirit of God longing for a personal relationship with you. Even though we seek Him for all the so called right biblical reasons such as His gifts, anointing & His power, however by ignoring the part of knowing Him as an individual we have indirectly ignored Him completely!

Guarding the Heart, "Intimacy with the Holy Spirit," August 13, 2008, https://revivenations.org/blog/2008/08/13/intimacy-holyspirit (accessed April 14, 2019).

64. Stuhlmacher thinks that those speaking are those in heaven who make intercessions before God for the suffering faithful. Yet he still adds, "This language is closed and forbidden to to earthly people, but, according to Paul, the Spirit assists the justified who are still suffering on earth so that their prayers are heard in heaven in the way that corresponds to God (cf. Rev. 8:3)." Peter Stuhlmacher, *Paul's Letter to the Romans: A Commentary*, trans. Scott J. Hafemann (Louisville: Westminster John Knox, 1994), 133.

that Christ promised (John 14:16, 26; 15:26; 16:7, 13). Christ prays and intercedes for us at God's right hand (Rom. 8:34; Heb. 7:25; 1 John 2:1), but the Spirit intercedes within us.[65] His intercession is very effective because of the perfect union of mind and heart of the members of the Trinity. It may be intimacy with the Trinity that is a "foretaste of the future glory that will be ours" in heaven.[66] Yet Osborne is so right: "When we feel that somehow God has forgotten us . . . at that moment the Spirit is closer to us than at any other time."[67] Our great example is the Lord Jesus in the garden of Gathsemene. He prayed, "And He was saying, "Abba! Father! All things are possible for You; remove this cup from Me; yet not what I will, but what You will" (Mark 14:36). Christ's intimate prayer for God's will in the midst of His struggle was acceptable to the Father. We can trust in the Spirit's intercession as much as Christ's. Romans 8:28 follows, so we know that God's plans and desires will be accomplished!

The reality of the Spirit's intercession amidst the heartache believers bear reminds me of the song by Mark Schultz entitled, "He's My Son." He was inspired to write this song by the grieving couple in his church whose son was suffering through leukemia.[68] Schultz observed their struggles and noted that the mother Louise often stayed up with her son Martin until he fell asleep. "She would rub his back and try to comfort him, but she felt helpless. Some nights, John would wake up and walk down the hall to Martin's room and watch him sleep. As he stood there, he would try to imagine what life would be like without his son." Schultz tried "for several months to write a song for this dear couple, but nothing seemed to capture what they were going through. I couldn't begin to understand the depth of pain John and Louise faced every day—but God did." He eventually recognized that "the only thing I had to do with this song is that I just happened to be there when God sat it in my lap." This song captures the desperate groanings of a diseased creation and the human groanings of suffering parents longing for some understanding and comfort from a God who seems hidden. We must trust at minimum that Paul's words are true and the Spirit was interceding for them with groanings of His own according to the perfect desires and plans of God. They were never alone, and years later, God still uses the song "He's My Child." In fact, in 2001

---

65. Morris, *Epistle to the Romans*, 327; Craig S. Keener, *Romans: A New Covenant Commentary* (Eugene, OR: Cascade, 2009), 108.

66. Osborne, *Romans*, 218.

67. Ibid., 217.

68. Mark Schultz, "He's My Son," Songfacts, http://www.songfacts.com/detail.php?id=12351.

Schultz was awarded the Leukemia and Lymphoma Society Beacon Award for his awareness-raising efforts. We can rejoice that we do not know what all of God's desires and plans have been through their prayers for young Martin. We do know that he went into remission and on to college.[69]

CONCLUSIONS

Paul gives an important conclusion to the Holy Spirit's intimate role in the lives of believers in the benediction of his second letter to the Corinthians: "The grace of the Lord Jesus Christ, and the love of God, and the fellowship of the Holy Spirit, be with you all" (2 Cor. 13:14). It is a helpful conclusion to this chapter because it reminds us of several key points. First, the intimate role of the Spirit is Trinitarian. He is the Paraclete, the One sent by the Father and the Son, as an alter ego/representative of Christ for us until His return. Second, the Spirit is a gift of grace from the Father and the Son out of their love for us. Third, the Spirit provides the *koinonia* we need as relational beings in God's family. Paul prayed here "for the Corinthians [to have] a deepening of their participation in the Holy Spirit; he also wishes for the unity which the Holy Spirit gives to the community."[70] That church struggled to locate the Spirit in His rightful place in their lives. At times He needed to be acknowledged as the only true source for divine wisdom (1 Cor. 2:4, 10–16). At times His role needed to be clarified to cultivate and protect the unity of the church (1 Cor. 12–14).

Our participation with the Spirit is through His guidance and our following. He will guide us to what we need: to the truth about Christ, to fruitful living, and effective service to the church. Jonathan Edwards captures the unique quality of our communion with the Spirit:

> The Spirit of God dwells in the hearts of the saints as a seed, or spring of life, that exerts and communicates His own sweet and divine nature. The soul is made a partaker of God's beauty and Christ's joy so that the saint has true fellowship with the Father and His Son, Jesus Christ. This

---

69. "I'm amazed to go into concerts around the concert and people come after the concerts just in tears and say, 'You may think you've written that song for the Bairds or thought you did, but you wrote the song for our son or our daughter or for my husband.' So, I'm amazed." Sandy Engel, "Mark Schultz: God's Instrument," Christian Broadcasting Network, http://www1.cbn.com/700club/mark-schultz-gods-instrument (accessed April 14, 2019).
70. David E. Garland, *2 Corinthians*, The New American Commentary, 29 (Nashville: Broadman & Holman, 1999), 556.

> communion is the participation of the Holy Spirit. The grace that is in the hearts of the saints is of the same nature as the divine holiness. It is the same nature as the brightness of the sun but it cannot compare with the sun in its fullness. Therefore Christ says, "That which is born of the Spirit, is spirit" (John 3:6). But it is infinitely less in degree. It is like the brightness that is in a diamond that the sun shines on.[71]

This is vastly different than anything natural humanity can experience. This participation with the Holy Spirit is most necessary in our times of greatest need when we feel the tightening of our hearts, the swelling of our throats, the scattering of our thoughts, the sleeplessness of our nights. The Spirit will provide intimate knowledge, supernatural leading, and compassionate intercession for us when we don't know what to do, fear doing something, or feel unable to do something.

I hesitate to provide illustrations of the Spirit's activities outside of biblical ones. Too often we do not see clearly. Wanting to justify the authenticity of Christianity, many have claimed the Spirit's intimate presence in their lives, when in truth the experience may be self-validating or misinterpreted. We do know from our digging into the theology of the Spirit's intimacy that He is always present in our lives and His most prominent activities are life transformation and edifying service. Without His presence, believers will follow their own cravings and be indistinguishable from the world. The church will wither.

It is appropriate to call upon those whose grasp of the Spirit's nearness and ministries is greater than mine. May we pray with the author what is true and liberating.

O HOLY SPIRIT,
As the sun is full of light, the ocean full of water,
    Heaven full of glory, so may my heart be full of thee.
Vain are all divine purposes of love
  and the redemption wrought by Jesus
  except thou work within,
    regenerating by thy power,
    giving me eyes to see Jesus,
    showing me the realities of the unseen world.

---

71. Edwards, *Faith beyond Feelings*, 108–9.

Give me thyself without measure,
  as an unimpaired fountain,
  as inexhaustible riches.
I bewail my coldness, poverty, emptiness,
  imperfect vision, languid service,
  prayerless prayers, praiseless praises.
Suffer me not to grieve or resist thee.
Come as power,
  to expel every rebel lust, to reign supreme and keep me thine;
Come as teacher,
  leading me into all truth, filling me with all understanding;
Come as love,
  that I may adore the Father, and love him as my all;
Come as joy,
  to dwell in me, move in me, animate me;
Come as light,
  illuminating the Scripture, moulding me in its laws;
Come as sanctifier,
  body, soul and spirit wholly thine;
Come as helper,
  with strength to bless and keep directing my every step;
Come as beautifier,
  bringing order out of confusion, loveliness out of chaos.
Magnify to me thy glory by being magnified in me,
  and make me redolent of thy fragrance.[72]

---

72. Bennett, ed., *The Valley of Vision*, 28.

NOW WHAT?

1. How does it help you to know that the Holy Spirit intercedes for you with groanings concerning God's ultimate will and purposes?

2. How has the Spirit given testimony that you are God's child?

3. Read Paul's personal words in Romans 9:1–3: "I am telling the truth in Christ, I am not lying, my conscience testifies with me in the Holy Spirit, that I have great sorrow and unceasing grief in my heart. For I could wish that I myself were accursed, separated from Christ for the sake of my brethren." How might these words help us understand the Holy Spirit's intimate understanding of our motives and emotions?

4. How can you commit yourself to ministering to others in the Spirit's presence and power?

5. How will you walk by the Spirit and keep in step with the directions He provides you from the Scriptures?

6. Who needs you to pray that the Spirit will be more real to them?

CHAPTER 8

INTERPRETING SUFFERING AND INTIMACY WITH GOD

When I think of the title of John Feinberg's book, a lump begins to form in my throat. A book on the problem of evil and suffering can do this. The book is not especially graphic in its depiction of suffering. Rather, it simply is a courageous and well-crafted reflection written by a mentor. John Feinberg was one of my theology professors and dissertation-readers. His lectures and books continue to speak to me as I teach my own students and as I write. His book on suffering, *Deceived By God? A Journey through Suffering*, describes his struggle as husband, father, and Christian philosopher-theologian who confronts his wife Pat's incurable, genetically transmitted Huntington's Disease. While I watched from a distance as the disease that causes the brain to deteriorate took its toll on her, I discovered my mentor was by no means exempt from despair. In fact, he has described part of his turmoil as "the feeling of abandonment":

> Invariably when news like this [i.e., Pat's diagnosis] comes, people are very concerned; but because they are afraid they will say the wrong thing, they tend to stay away. Nobody wants to be like Job's comforters. Better to stay away than take the chance of sticking your foot in your mouth. However, remaining at a distance only confirms the worst fears of the person suffering. One already feels abandoned, and when family and friends keep their

distance, they communicate that this apparently is true. The deeper fear is not just that one feels abandoned by family and friends, but that God is no longer there. It doesn't matter how much one has sensed God's presence before, for at times like this, he seems absent. And when one knows that God is the only one who can do anything about the problem, it is especially painful to sense his departure.[1]

The seeming abandonment of God can bring the harshest of sufferings, the loss of hope and the realization of "how dismal life can seem."[2]

And so in fairness to God and His Word, this book must embark on a journey. This chapter is perhaps the most relationally intense, as it attempts to grapple with the seemingly uncaring absence of God that appears to haunt many instances of suffering. Tim Keller rightly argues that a visceral argument against God arises in the face of unimaginable or unconscionable suffering and makes Him "implausible and unreal to the heart."[3] This is why we will seek to understand the sufferer's feelings and perspectives toward God in Scripture. And then we will examine how God not only has intimate knowledge of our trying circumstances, but also provides in Himself the necessary intimate place of security and safety amidst the suffering, no matter how terrifying it might be. It is here that His people can bring others near to God.

GOD'S DISTANCE OR ABSENCE IN SUFFERING

The absence of God's presence is indeed a paradox for the believer and unbeliever alike. By His very nature and promises, God is supposed to be intimately involved in the lives of His people. This is so commonly known that even the unbeliever has foolishly mocked God's people with the simple question, "Where is your God?" (Job 35:10). In Psalm 42, the writer, amidst his emotional anguish, claims, "My tears have been my food day and night" in verse 3, and "as a shattering of my bones, my adversaries revile me" in verse 10, and both verses say, "while they say to me all day long, 'Where is your God?'" (Ps. 43:3, 10). After pleading with God for His salvation, Asaph argues, "Why should the nations say, 'Where is their God?'" (Ps. 79:10; cf.

---

1. John S. Feinberg, *Deceived by God? A Journey Through Suffering* (Wheaton, IL: Crossway, 1997), 27.
2. Ibid., 26.
3. As examples of the visceral argument, he cites the deep moral and emotional wrestling with evil suffering of Elie Wiesel, Victor Frankl, and J. Christian Beker amidst the Holocaust. Timothy Keller, *Walking with God through Pain and Suffering* (New York: Penguin Random House, 2013), 101–2.

115:2). Because God's presence is obviously united with His blessings, the psalmist asks God, "Where are Your former lovingkindnesses, O Lord?" (Ps. 89:49; cf. Isa. 63:11, 13). Jeremiah added to his request for healing and salvation the agonizing reality that he was continually being mocked as a suffering prophet. Thus he called to the Lord, "Look, they keep saying to me, 'Where is the word of the LORD? Let it come now!'" Micah believed that after the Lord would deliver him, "Then my enemy will see and shame will cover her who said to me, 'Where is the LORD your God?'" (Mic. 7:10a).

As foolish as these mocking questions are, they can still sting us. Why do they? God can seem anything but close to the believer. After the death of his wife, C. S. Lewis intimated his frustration with this in terms of God's chosen location:

> Where is God? This is one of the most disquieting symptoms (of grief). When you are happy, so happy that you have no sense of needing Him, so happy that you are tempted to feel His claims upon you as an interruption, if you remember yourself turn to Him with gratitude and praise, you will be—or so it feels—welcomed with open arms. But go to Him when your need is desperate, when all other help is vain, and what do you find? A door slammed in your face, and a sound of bolting and double bolting on the inside. After that, silence. You may as well turn away. The longer you wait, the more emphatic the silence will become. There are no lights in the windows. It might be an empty house. Was it ever inhabited? It seemed so once. And that seeming was as strong as this. What can this mean? Why is He so present a commander in our time of prosperity and so very absent a help in time of trouble?[4]

It is interesting to note that Lewis didn't think he was in danger of ceasing to believe in God, but coming to believe things about God that were in his words, "dreadful."[5] To understand this struggle, let's first look at two places God appears to be in times of trouble.

God Is Distant

One way the Scriptures describe this relational distance in suffering is that God appears to be far off or away. Even modern Jews struggle with feel-

---

4. C. S. Lewis, *A Grief Observed* (New York: Bantam, 1963, 1976), 4–5.
5. Ibid., 5.

ings that God has abandoned them. One young Jewish woman wrote in to the website Jew in the City, describing her tragic dilemma:

> Hi Jew in the City,
>
> I grew up in a religious environment, but in the last few years I've pretty much left religion: I don't *daven* (pray) at all (too lazy), Shabbat (what's that ???), but still keep kosher [hmm…]. Although I still dress like a religious Jew, I don't really practice much and the reason for that is [I think]: God left me.
>
> However there's a reason I'm contacting you, and you probably know the answer already. I'm planning to leave the community for a completely non-Jewish one . . . so what's your advice. . .
>
> Toda (thanks) in advance,
>
> Sorry I've gotta leave my name out

While this is common among Christians as well, it is sad that the advice given this woman was to keep God's commandments, remember why you love Him, and pray prescribed prayers.[6] We observe God's distance in the Scriptures when the psalmist pleads with the Lord, "Why do You stand afar off, O LORD?" (Ps. 10:1). This term for far off or distant (*rachoq*) is used in a secretive sense, for example to describe the place in Exodus 2:4 where Moses's sister positioned herself after she put him in the basket in the Nile, or it can refer to a distant or far-off country or sea (1 Kings 8:41; Ps. 65:5), or a distant place but still within earshot (1 Sam. 26:13; Ezra 3:13; Neh. 12:43). In this case, the psalmist actually chides God for choosing to be a bystander or standing in the distance "as an idle spectator"[7] when he is in serious trouble. David cries out in Psalm 22:11, "Be not far from me, for trouble is near; for there is none to help." He sees God's being far off as the closeness of trouble and being alone in his struggle. When trouble is near, God should be near! He is the only one who can help him (v. 19). Further, God may even seem tardy as for the aged psalmist in Psalm 71:12: "O God, do not be far from me; O my God, hasten to my help!"[8] Yet it does not seem right that the words distant, far off, bystander, and tardy, should ever be

---

6. "God Left Me, So Now I'm Leaving Jewish Observance," Jew in the City, http://jewinthecity. com/2011/05/god-left-me-so-now-im-leaving-jewish-observance (accessed April 14, 2019).
7. Carl Friedrich Keil and Franz Delitzsch, *Commentary on the Old Testament*, Vol. 5 (Peabody, MA: Hendrickson, 1996), 109.
8. Cf. 71:18, "even when I am old and gray." Nevertheless in this case all this causes the psalmist to trust in the Lord, who has shown him many past sufferings, will revive him and will bring him up again "from the depths of the earth" (v. 20).

used by a believer for their experience of God during our trials! He should be eager, possibly even excited, to hurry to our aid.[9]

God Hides/Is Hidden

God's hiddenness is another way the Scriptures describe this relational distance. For many it is almost unbearable to go through suffering and feel that God is hiding or is hidden from them. David Brainerd, the godly missionary to the Native Americans during the American colonial period, kept a diary which included his spiritual highs and lows. At one point he was suffering amidst extremely difficult labor, sleeping on straw, and having very little ministry success. However, the worst of it can bee seen in his urgent expression that follows: "God hides His face from me."[10] How could he speak about his relationship with God in those terms? It may be because people in the Bible spoke that way.

The suffering person may conjecture that since God is able to help them, then for some reason He must have hidden Himself from them. For example, one of the questions of Psalm 10:1 is: "Why do You hide Yourself in times of trouble?" In other words, why would God hide (*alam*), that is, veil Himself from our sight, blind us to His presence, or willingly conceal Himself? Similarly, David pleads with the Lord in Psalm 13 by asking,

> How long, O LORD? Will You forget me forever?
> How long will You hide Your face from me?
> How long shall I take counsel in my soul,
> Having sorrow in my heart all the day?
> How long will my enemy be exalted over me?
> Consider and answer me, O LORD my God;
> Enlighten my eyes, or I will sleep the sleep of death. (vv. 1–3)

Notice his repetition of "How long?" (*Ad amah*) four times in a row. *Ad* is often the word for "where" and thus he is asking "to what point" in time[11] does God

---

9. From Hebrew *chus*, meaning "hasten." See Pss. 22:19; 38:22; 40:13; 70:1, 5; 141:1; Isa. 5:19.
10. David Brainerd, *The Life and Diary of David Brainerd*, 91 (May 18, 1743), Grace-eBooks.com, http://grace-ebooks.com/library/David%20Brainerd/DB_Life%20and%20Diary%20of%20David%20Brainerd%20The.pdf (accessed April 16, 2019).
11. Francis Brown, Samuel Rolles Driver, and Charles Augustus Briggs, *Enhanced Brown-Driver-Briggs Hebrew and English Lexicon* (Oxford: Clarendon, 1977), 33. God asks the same question of Moses and ties it to trust in Exodus 16:28 and Numbers 14:11; see also Joshua 18:3 and Job 18:2; 19:2.

want him to keep trusting that He will no longer be distant and hidden (cf. Hab. 1:2). He views the Lord's keeping Himself concealed (*satar*) as a sign that He has forgotten all about him (Ps. 44:24) and thus he has to figure a way out by himself. However, he goes on to ask for his eyes to be enlightened or opened to God's presence, because if He doesn't he will surely die. These are life and death issues. In Psalm 55:1 he asks that the Lord not hide Himself from his supplication because of the terror and horror he has because of his enemies (v. 5). In fact, he himself wants to be in a place far from there:

> I said, "Oh, that I had wings like a dove!
> I would fly away and be at rest.
> Behold, I would wander far away,
> I would lodge in the wilderness." (vv. 6–7)

And so God's hiddenness may feel like rejection. The psalmist unites these when he asks, "O LORD, why do You reject my soul? Why do You hide Your face from me?" (Ps. 88:14).

God Abandons?

When believers express feelings of rejection in the Scriptures they often use terminology of abandonment. In Psalm 27:9 David not only thinks that the Lord has hidden Himself and turned away from him, but cries out: "Do not abandon me nor forsake me, O God of my salvation." To him being abandoned (from *natash*) is for God to cut or cast him off like unnecessary baggage (1 Sam. 17:22) or to let him fall to the side like the slain in battle (Num. 11:31). For him to be forsaken (from *azab*) is for God to leave him for dead like when the defeated men of Israel left the bodies of Saul and his sons to be horribly dishonored by the Philistines (1 Sam. 31:7–9). In Psalm 71:9–11 the vulnerable psalmist asks the Lord, "Do not cast me off in the time of old age; Do not forsake me when my strength fails." His enemies mock him, saying, "God has forsaken him; Pursue and seize him, for there is no one to deliver." David elsewhere simply implores the Lord to be near: "Do not forsake me, O LORD; O my God, do not be far from me!" (Ps. 38:2; cf. Jer. 14:8–9). These feelings are exactly what our Lord cried out on the cross, "My God, My God, why have You forsaken Me?" (Matt. 27:46; Mark 15:34; cf. Ps. 22:1).

The challenge at this point is our response to God's hiddenness. Philip Yancey admits his own instinctive response: "I retaliate by ignoring him. Like a child who thinks he can hide from adults by holding a chubby hand over his eyes, I try to shut God out of my life. If he won't reveal himself to me, why should I acknowledge him?"[12] If we don't go down that route, we may expend a great amount of energy attempting to figure out exactly why God chooses to be hidden.

Why Is God Absent?

A common biblical perception of God's hiddenness is that it results from His displeasure. Many have asked Him, "What did I do wrong for You to hide Yourself from me?" It is true that God can be absent from His unfaithful and disobedient people. He even abandoned Israel into the hands of their enemies for periods of time.[13] Early in Israel's history, in Numbers 32:14–15 when the tribes of Gad and Reuben abdicated their responsibility to go to their brothers and help them conquer the land across the Jordan, Moses promised God would abandon them as well:

> Now behold, you have risen up in our fathers' place, a brood of sinful men, to add still more to the burning anger of the LORD against Israel. For if you turn away from following Him, He will once more abandon them in the wilderness, and you will destroy all these people.

One of the last words the Lord spoke to Moses before he died was that His people would forsake Him, and so He would forsake them and hide His face from them (Deut. 31:17, 18). Moses would repeat this in his song (32:20). Manasseh's idolatry would prompt God to declare, "I will abandon the remnant of My inheritance and deliver them into the hands of their enemies" (2 Kings 21:14). Micah prophesied of the impending judgment of Israel as such:

> Then they will cry out to the LORD,
> But He will not answer them.
> Instead, He will hide His face from them at that time
> Because they have practiced evil deeds. (Mic. 3:4)

---

12. Philip Yancey, *Disappointment with God* (Grand Rapids: Zondervan, 1988), 283.
13. While the Lord would hand over His people to their enemies in His judgment, He would never completely cut off every one of His children, because of His faithfulness and promises to the patriarchs. At the beginning of the monarchy, Samuel told the Israelites, "For the LORD will not abandon His people on account of His great name, because the Lord has been pleased to make you a people for Himself" (1 Sam. 12:22).

God promised in His judgment of idolatrous Judah, "I will abandon you to the wilderness" to be food for beasts (Ezek. 29:5). When our Lord Jesus defines discipleship, He promises the double principle: when we confess Him before others, He will confess us before His Father, and yet when we deny Him before others, He will deny us before His Father (Matt. 10:32–33; Luke 12:8–9; cf. Mark 8:38; Luke 9:26; Rev. 3:5). The Apostle Paul reminds Timothy of this principle when enduring persecution when he says, "If we deny Him, He also will deny us" (2 Tim. 2:12b; cf. 1 Tim. 5:8).

Similarly, the Jews claim to have experienced what they call *hester panim*, meaning the "hidden face" of God. The name Esther comes from *satar* or hidden, probably related to the fact that God's name is not mentioned in the book that bears her name. Jews have struggled with *hester panim* since the fall of Jerusalem in A.D. 70. There have been a variety of explanations by Jewish scholars of *hester panim* in the Holocaust, which some scholars have argued[14] was God's judgment and yet an opportunity to exercise one's faith in Him.[15]

Thus the "innocent" especially recognize this principle of God's abandonment of the unrighteous. David calls out to God in Psalm 143:7, saying, "Answer me quickly, O LORD, my spirit fails; Do not hide Your face from me, or I will become like those who go down to the pit." Those who die in God's judgment will be separated from Him. Job's protests to God reveal this recognition: "Why do You hide Your face and consider me Your enemy?" (Job 13:24). In Psalm 89:46, Ethan the Ezrahite sees God's hiddenness as directly related to the fury of His judgment: "How long, O LORD? Will You hide Yourself forever? Will Your wrath burn like fire?" And again, David in Psalm 27:9 unites God's anger to His hiddenness, turning away, and forsaking:

> Do not hide Your face from me,
> Do not turn Your servant away in anger;
> For You have been my help;
> Do not forsake me,
> O God of my salvation!

---

14. For a very helpful survey of the range of Jewish reflection on the Holocaust, see Elizabeth Pinder-Ashenden, "How Jewish Thinkers Come to Terms with the Holocaust and Why It Matters for This Generation: A Selected Survey and Comment," *European Journal of Theology* 20, no. 2 (2011): 131–38.

15. Norman Lamm, "The Face of God: Thoughts on the Holocaust," in *Theological and Halakhic Reflections on the Holocaust*, eds. Bernard Rosenberg and Fred Heuman (New York: Ktav, 1992), 121.

In Lamentations 3:56, Jeremiah just wanted relief from the judgment he was experiencing in the fall of Jerusalem: "You have heard my voice, 'Do not hide Your ear from my prayer for relief, From my cry for help.'"

Yet for contemporary rabbi Rav Tamir Granot, the issue is very personal:

> Even if God's decree is just, and even if we believe that we will be redeemed, how can God abandon us to such degradation and affliction? Is He not interested in us? Is He not here at all?
>
> This is not a theological question. It is obvious that God watches over His world and guides it. Likewise, it is not a matter of theodicy—that is, the justification of God's actions. Obviously, God is righteous and we are wicked, or alternatively, we do not understand Him. But even if God is watching His world, and even if He is righteous—it is not sufficient. The question is: Does He love us? Are we precious to Him?[16]

Thus, as the people of the Book, Christians and Jews recognize the visceral and existential crisis of faith we can have when our intimate God is not close. Yet Elihu reminds Job and us, "When He keeps quiet, who then can condemn? And when He hides His face, who then can behold Him, that is, in regard to both nation and man?" (Job 34:29). In other words, Hill is right that this is "the residual mystery of the transcendent God, who is free to remain hidden."[17] That is, since He is above and beyond us, so are His purposes and actions. C. S. Lewis recognized something along these lines when he admitted,

> I have gradually been coming to feel that the door is no longer shut and bolted. Was it my own frantic need that slammed it in my face? The time when there is nothing at all in your soul except a cry for help may be just the time when God can't give it: you are like the drowning man who can't be helped because he clutches and grabs. Perhaps your own reiterated cries deafen you to the voice you hoped to hear.[18]

---

16. Rav Tamir Granot, "Lecture #16a: 'Hester Panim' and God's Presence in the Holocaust Part 1," VBM—The Israel Koschitzky Virtual Beit Midrash, https://www.etzion.org.il/en/lecture-16a-hester-panim-and-gods-presence-holocaust-part-1 (accessed April 14, 2019).
17. Andrew E. Hill, "rts," in *The New International Dictionary of Old Testament Theology and Exegesis*, Vol. 3, ed. Willem A. VanGemeren (Grand Rapids: Zondervan, 1997), 301.
18. Lewis, *A Grief Observed*, 53–54.

And this is why His gracious revelation of Himself should be that much more precious to us.

GOD'S PRESENCE/NEARNESS IN SUFFERING

So we are not left in our suffering with an absent God. There is an abundance of instances when God's people trust in His deliverance and experience His presence and protection. He promises to do no less. In Psalm 3:1–4 we can feel David's angst as well as his trust, amidst his fleeing from his own son Absalom:

> O Lord, how my adversaries have increased!
> Many are rising up against me.
> Many are saying of my soul,
> "There is no deliverance for him in God." Selah.
> But You, O Lord, are a shield about me,
> My glory, and the One who lifts my head.
> I was crying to the Lord with my voice,
> And He answered me from His holy mountain. Selah.

He likens the Lord's intimate presence to a shield that is round about him, protecting him from evil, harm, and dishonor. And in an intimate act of comfort, strengthening, and deliverance, the Lord lifts his head that had bowed in shame and helplessness so that David could see God's blessed countenance. God does not hide forever and often provides intimacy with Him amidst and beyond our suffering.

In spite of our feelings to the contrary, the Bible is abundantly clear that God will not forsake us in our suffering. While we saw in Numbers and Deuteronomy God's promise to hide from and forsake Israel if and when they rejected Him, His faithful presence with His people was remembered a thousand years later. In Nehemiah 9:17–19 after their return from exile, the Levites, while recounting the rebellion of their forefathers in the wilderness, blessed the Lord!

> But You are a God of forgiveness,
> Gracious and compassionate,
> Slow to anger and abounding in lovingkindness;
> And You did not forsake them. (Neh. 9:17)

Even after the golden calf debacle, they praised Him:

> You, in your great compassion,
> Did not forsake them in the wilderness;
> The pillar of cloud did not leave them by day,
> To guide them on their way,
> Nor the pillar of fire by night, to light for them the way in which they were
> to go. (Neh. 9:19)

Then the Levites repeat the same concepts of 9:17 in 9:31 about the time of the prophets later. What a flawless track record God has for never ultimately forsaking His people!

In addition, the same section in Deuteronomy 31 of God's hiddenness and forsaking Israel for their rebellion has Moses providing Joshua with tremendous assurance of God's presence for him personally. Moses called him to lead with strength and courage rather than be afraid or trembling at the sight of their enemies moving forward. From where came his motivation to do this? Moses added, "For the LORD your God is the one who goes with you. He will not fail or forsake you" (Deut. 31:6). Then in sight of all Israel Moses told Joshua, "The LORD is the one who goes ahead of you; He will be with you. He will not fail you or forsake you. Do not fear or be dismayed" (Deut. 31:8). In case Joshua was to doubt this or forget it, the Lord declared to him after Moses died, "No man will be able to stand before you all the days of your life. Just as I have been with Moses, I will be with you; I will not fail you or forsake you" (Josh. 1:5). With the challenges of the flooded Jordan River, the walled city of Jericho, and the slaughter at Ai because of Achan ahead of him, he needed absolute confidence in the Lord's abiding presence.

It shouldn't surprise us that the Psalms are replete with trust that God will never forsake His people. In Psalm 16:10 David gives the reason for his strength in the midst of what would attempt to shake him: "For You will not abandon my soul to Sheol; nor will You allow Your Holy One to undergo decay." Paul would show that this would ultimately be true of Jesus the Christ when God in His faithfulness would not abandon His sacrificed Son to the grave but would resurrect Him (Acts 13:35).[19] Even when David's closest rela-

---

19. For a good summary of the various views of Peter's use of Psalm 16:10 in Acts 13:35, see Gregory V. Trull, "Views on Peter's Use of Psalm 16:8–11 in Acts 2:25–32," *Bibliotheca Sacra* 161 (2004): 194–214. Trull also sorts through the thorny issues in his "Peter's Interpretation of Psalm 16:8–11 in Acts 2:25–32," *Bibliotheca Sacra* 161 (2004): 432–48.

tionships failed, he could say, "For my father and my mother have forsaken me, but the LORD will take me up" (Ps. 27:10). The psalmists root their trust and endurance in the Lord's covenantal vested interest in His people, and so Psalm 94:14 declares, "For the LORD will not abandon His people, nor will He forsake His inheritance" (cf. Ps. 138:8). Yet this is a two-way street in that there is a strong element of personal accountability to living according to the Lord's desires. David appeals to the Lord's love of justice and godliness when he says, "For the LORD loves justice and does not forsake His godly ones" (Ps. 37:28). The psalmist of Psalm 119 feels he can entreat God to "not forsake me utterly!" because he promises to "keep Your statutes" (Ps. 119:8).

The prophets also reassured God's people of His unfailing presence. After being overrun by oppressive enemies how wonderful would these words of Isaiah be to them?

> Although the Lord has given you bread of privation and water of oppression, He, your Teacher will no longer hide Himself, but your eyes will behold your Teacher. Your ears will hear a word behind you, "This is the way, walk in it," whenever you turn to the right or to the left. And you will defile your graven images overlaid with silver, and your molten images plated with gold. You will scatter them as an impure thing, and say to them, "Be gone!" (Isa. 30:20–22)

His intimate knowledge of their tears and His longing to be gracious to them ensures His close care (30:18–19). After the foretelling of the invasion of Israel by Gog from Magog, the Lord promises through Ezekiel the restoration of His people with these intimate words of assurance: "'I will not hide My face from them any longer, for I will have poured out My Spirit on the house of Israel,' declares the Lord GOD" (Ezek. 39:29). Even though He made them go into exile because of their idolatrous rebellion, a remnant of His people would always experience His enduring presence amidst their suffering. In this case, it would be through His Spirit (36:27).

In the New Testament, this tremendous confidence continues in the lives of believers who trust that the Lord will not forsake them. In 2 Corinthians 4:9, Paul claims that God will not forsake the Corinthians especially in the midst of suffering persecution. Why? God has entrusted the treasure of His gospel in the total insufficiency and frailty of humanity as clay jars, "so that the surpassing greatness of the power will be of God and not from ourselves" (v. 7). This power in the life of genuine Christians is manifested in God's presence with them and provision for them amidst persecution. So Paul and all believers have the confidence to claim,

> [W]e are afflicted in every way, but not crushed; perplexed, but not despairing; persecuted, but not forsaken; struck down, but not destroyed; always carrying about in the body the dying of Jesus, so that the life of Jesus also may be manifested in our body. For we who live are constantly being delivered over to death for Jesus's sake, so that the life of Jesus also may be manifested in our mortal flesh. So death works in us, but life in you (2 Cor. 4:8–12).

In Hebrews 13:5, the writer uses God's words to Joshua, "I will not fail you or forsake you" (see also Deut. 31:6, 8) to instill contentment and liberate one's character from greed: "Make sure that your character is free from the love of money, being content with what you have; for He Himself has said, 'I will never desert you, nor will I ever forsake you.'" These Jewish believers faced persecution, and the temptation to be selfish would be strong, a kind of "Every one for themselves!" However, they were to "offer God an acceptable service with reverence and awe, for our God is a consuming fire" (12:28–29) by loving other believers as family, showing hospitality, remembering persecuted prisoners, loving only their spouses, and being "free from the love of money" (13:1–5).

With an apparent twist on His absence, God actually hides us within the intimate location of His protection. Under the Lord's wings is just such a place. David prayed for this when he asked the Lord, "Hide me in the shadow of Your wings" (Ps. 17:8; cf. 61:4; 64:2). Like a bird shielding her young from predators, the Lord provides refuge and His people take refuge there (Pss. 36:7; 57:1; 91:4)[20] and sing for joy (Ps. 63:7). His hiding place for His people is a secret location in His presence and away from their enemies. David trusts that he will find refuge from his distressing life in God's presence in the tabernacle: "For in the day of trouble He will conceal me in His tabernacle, in the secret place of His tent He will hide me" (Ps. 27:5). In his desperate, even terrifying crisis brought upon him by his enemies, he still recounts and trusts that the Lord hides His people "in the secret place of Your presence from the conspiracies of man," and He keeps them "secretly in a shelter from the strife

---

20. Donald J. Wiseman, "*chasah*," in Harris, Archer, and Waltke, eds., *Theological Wordbook of the Old Testament*, 307–8.

of tongues" (Ps. 31:20). He has confidence in this even when he appears to be cut off from God's eyes (v. 22). Like opening a piano and yelling into it, there will always be a resonating chord if we listen.

EXAMPLES OF GOD'S NEARNESS IN SUFFERING

It is appropriate now to see if God's closeness rings true amidst the suffering of people in biblical history. Was God indeed present, as He promised? The examples of four men in particular can instruct us: Moses, Elijah, our Lord Jesus, and Stephen. We also can see a pattern emerging where two, Moses and Elijah, run and hide amidst their distress, but in all four God reveals His nearness to them, in order for them to bring others near to Him.

Moses

We see in the life of Moses that our human temptation to run and hide from suffering is very real. Yet when we do, we may be running and hiding from God and our responsibilities. In his case, the people of God were the ones initially suffering under the hands of the Egyptians. Moses's reactionary attempt to intervene and cure their suffering by himself only resulted in his killing of one Egyptian (Exod. 2:11–14). However righteous his indignation may have been, this only succeeded in angering Pharaoh, who put a contract out on his life. So Moses fled to Midian and started a new life on the run, his own witness-protection program (2:15–3:1).

Nevertheless God, in the angel of the Lord, drew near to Moses in the burning bush (even though according to 3:5, Moses could not come too close to the blazing holiness of God). That Moses was leading his flock to "Horeb, the mountain of God" (3:1) wasn't a coincidence in God's sovereign plan for Horeb/Sinai and how God would speak to him later. Yet he shunned God's call for his involvement and responsibility by focusing on himself and his inadequacies. God, on the contrary, moved past his excuses (3:11) and declared that He would be "with" him (3:12, 18) and "with your mouth" and with Aaron's (4:12, 14). And He truly was near to Moses all the way to Mount Nebo at the doorstep to the Promised Land.

Equally significant was how Moses brought the people near to God amidst their suffering. In fact, in an initial step Moses and Aaron approached Pharaoh in Egypt with the request from the Lord that they should go out and worship Him in the wilderness with a feast and sacrifices (5:1, 3). Even though Pharaoh denied their request, this summarized the ultimate purpose of the exit of God's people: drawing near to Him in worship. Then on their journey to the Promised Land, Moses would lead the people to Mount Sinai "to meet God" (19:17).

Moses's relational suffering as a leader culminated in the golden-calf debacle. The people asked Aaron, "Make a god for us who will go before us; for this Moses, the man who brought us up from the land of Egypt, we do not know what has become of him" (32:23). To them, Moses was not with them, near them, close to them, even though he was with the Lord on Mount Sinai. So God actually struck the people because of their movement away from Him to a golden calf (32:35). So the narrative indicates that Moses would retreat to the tent of meeting where "The Lord used to speak to Moses face to face, as a man speaks to his friend" (33:11). Yet the burden of leading them seemed to be proving too much for Moses—to the point that he cried to the Lord that he couldn't do it without His help (33:12–14). In the midst of his crisis, the Lord extended His assurance: "My presence shall go with you and I will give you rest" (33:14). This would culminate in Moses seeing the glory of God (33:18–23; 34:5–7), replacing the two tablets that he had broken, and requesting to "let the Lord go along in our midst, even though the people are so obstinate, and pardon our iniquity and our sin, and take us as Your own possession" (34:9). The Lord's presence amidst Moses's suffering provided his necessary motivation to bring the people to their ultimate destination.

Elijah

A parallel example of the Lord's nearness in suffering may be found in the life of Elijah. His victorious challenge of the prophets of Baal on Mount Carmel resulted in the Lord's presence as He rained fire from heaven on the altar (1 Kings 18:39). Elijah would slay all the prophets of Baal (18:40) and the Lord would bring rain (18:44–45). However, Ahab promised to slaughter Elijah for what he did (19:2). So like Moses, Elijah "was afraid and arose and ran for his life" (19:3; cf. Exod. 2:15). In his case, he ran as far south in Israel as possible. In its wilderness, he had sunk to such a despairing state that he wanted to die and have the Lord take his life (19:4). He then simply wilted under a juniper tree. However, God was near to him in his most desperate moment and sent the angel of the Lord to feed him twice (19:4–8). He then went to Mount Horeb—that is, Mount Sinai—for a fresh experience of the Lord's presence like Moses had (19:8). However, the Lord questioned him by grabbing the root of the problem: "What are you doing here, Elijah?" (19:9).

Elijah's response reveals two false assumptions he had cultivated in his suffering. First, he felt he and God were in some sort of employment contract, and that God was definitely not holding up His end. Consider Elijah's words at this point: "I have been very zealous for the Lord, the God of hosts; for the sons of Israel have forsaken Your covenant, torn down Your altars and killed Your prophets with the sword." In other words, it's as if he was saying, "You owe me, God! I have served you passionately!" He upheld his part with zeal or jealousy (*qana*) for the Lord's honor. It wasn't fair that the Lord was allowing this terrifying result to take place. Second, he assumed not only that God had abandoned him to a certain torturous death, but that would bring an abrupt end to any influence God has among His people. Elijah cried, "And I alone am left; and they seek my life, to take it away" (19:10). He is saying, "Where are You? I'm the only one left and you are letting them try to take my life!"

However, the Lord's presence is never far. While Elijah wanted a mountain top experience to bolster his fading faith, the Lord reoriented him:

> So He said, "Go forth and stand on the mountain before the LORD." And behold, the LORD was passing by! And a great and strong wind was rending the mountains and breaking in pieces the rocks before the LORD; but the LORD was not in the wind. And after the wind an earthquake, but the LORD was not in the earthquake. After the earthquake a fire, but the LORD was not in the fire; and after the fire a sound of a gentle blowing. When Elijah heard it, he wrapped his face in his mantle and went out and stood in the entrance of the cave. And behold, a voice came to him and said, "What are you doing here, Elijah?" (1 Kings 19:11–13)

Despite the Lord's demonstration, Elijah repeated his claim, "You owe me, God! I have served you passionately! I'm the only one left and you are letting them try to take my life!" (cf. 19:14). Yet Elijah missed two important principles when God's people suffer. First, He doesn't have to shake and torch the world in order for His people to experience His presence in suffering.[21] We can hear His resonating chord as we speak into the piano. Second, God's nearness in our suffering should prompt us to bring others to Him. At this point, the Lord's answer can be summarized as if He said, "Elijah, now that you know My presence, go back to work, and I will give you Elisha to help

---

21. The Lord's performance before Elijah "culminates not in the overt accouterments of divine power but in the mystery of darkness and silence that characterized the inner sanctuary of every ancient Near Eastern temple." John Monson, "1 Kings," in *Zondervan Illustrated Bible Backgrounds Commentary*, Vol 3, general ed. John H. Walton (Grand Rapids: Zondervan, 2009), 83.

you" (19:15–21). This shows us again the emerging pattern of experiencing the nearness of God in suffering, and the necessary result of bringing everyone along to His presence.

Jesus Christ

When we examine our Lord Jesus's suffering the pattern continues, but with some differences. Our Lord didn't run away from suffering; He actually set His face toward it (Luke 9:51) and walked all the way through it (Luke 18:31; 19:28). However, His disciples did not and so He was left to suffer alone to experience God's hiddenness as well as His nearness. The first to leave Christ to His suffering was Judas, the initiator with His deceptive kiss that turned Him over to the Roman authorities. But Matthew recounts, "Then all the disciples left Him and fled" (Matt. 26:56). Peter followed from a distance only because of John's connections, but would ultimately deny even knowing Him three times (Luke 22:54, 61; John 18:15–18). Yet we know the worst of Christ's sufferings was the anguish He felt bearing the sin of the world, embracing humanity's condition of suffering,[22] and experiencing the hiddenness of or "loss of contact"[23] with His Father, Who must turn away from sin.[24] Matthew described it in a bit of detail:

> Now from the sixth hour darkness fell upon all the land until the ninth hour. About the ninth hour Jesus cried out with a loud voice, saying, "ELI, ELI, LAMA SABACHTHANI?" that is, "MY GOD, MY GOD, WHY HAVE YOU FORSAKEN ME?" (Matt. 27:45–46)

These feelings are expressed in His quoting of Psalm 22:1, "Eli, Eli, lama sabachthani?"[25] that is, "My God, My God, why have You forsaken Me?"

---

22. Craig S. Keener, *A Commentary on the Gospel of Matthew* (Grand Rapids: Eerdmans, 1999), 683.
23. R. T. France, *The Gospel of Matthew*, New International Commentary on the New Testament (Grand Rapids: Eerdmans, 2007), 1077.
24. Grant R. Osborne, *Matthew*, Zondervan Exegetical Commentary Series on the New Testament (Grand Rapids: Zondervan, 2010), 1038.
25. Berel Dov Lemer translates Jesus's term *sabachtani* as "tangle up" and thus has Him saying, "My God, my God, I thought I was to be spared like Isaac, but now I see you have tangled me up like the horns of Abraham's ram and I will in fact be sacrificed." "Untangling *sabachtani* (Matt. 27:46 and Mark 15:34)," *Novum Testamentum* 56 (2014): 197. However, many take Jesus's citation of the first words of Psalm 22:1 as a traditional way of identifying the whole psalm, which demonstrates His righteous suffering and His role as the Davidic Messiah to the very end, and His ultimate vindication.

(*egkataleipō*; Matt. 27:46; Mark 15:34). But rather than lash out or question God's fairness like Elijah, He entrusted Himself to His Father. Isaiah prophesied:

> He was oppressed and He was afflicted, yet He did not open His mouth; like a lamb that is led to slaughter, and like a sheep that is silent before its shearers, so He did not open His mouth. (Isa. 53:7)

In fact, Jesus carried Himself in that manner throughout His trial (Matt. 26:63; 27:12–14; Mark 14:61; 15:5; Luke 23:9; John 19:9). And even though He was executed next to criminals, He was buried in a rich man's tomb, "because He had done no violence, nor was there any deceit in His mouth" (Isa. 53:9). Peter has called suffering believers to this same trust and submission amidst suffering persecution (1 Peter 2:22). It is striking that Christ's last response to His Father, who was allowing Him to go through such excruciating pain and mocking, was not even silence. His last words are full of continued intimate communication and confidence. Luke described this in this way: "And Jesus, crying out with a loud voice, said, 'Father, into Your hands I commit My spirit.' Having said this, He breathed His last" (Luke 23:46). He knew He could trust Him to receive His spirit back into eternal joyful communion.

Our Lord didn't just endure the cross, however. He brought others who were suffering with Him into God's presence. Just before His final words on the cross, He turned to the repentant thief next to Him, "And He said to him, 'Truly I say to you, today you shall be with Me in Paradise'" (Luke 23:43). Jesus, like Moses and Elijah, trusted that drawing near to God in the middle of suffering is also a means of helping others experience the presence of God. It is a restoration to the paradise of the garden of sorts.[26] There is a place to go where God is. We can see this in His response to the men on the road to Emmaus after His resurrection and before His ascension:

> And He said to them, "O foolish men and slow of heart to believe in all that the prophets have spoken! Was it not necessary for the Christ to suffer these things and to enter into His glory?" (Luke 24:25–26)

Their feelings of abandonment from the supposed Messiah should have been replaced by an experience of God's nearness through the Scriptures. Like

---

26. David E. Garland, *Luke*, Zondervan Exegetical Commentary series on the New Testament (Grand Rapids: Zondervan, 2011), 934.

them we can experience the nearness of God as we hear His voice in the Bible and trust His promises when we don't always know or see what He is doing. The proof and reward of Christ's trust in His Father while He was suffering is in His ascension. "While He was blessing them, He parted from them and was carried up into heaven" (Luke 24:51). He was finally able to go Home.

Stephen

The example of our Lord amidst suffering leads us to the martyrdom of Stephen in Acts 7:54–60. His suffering is almost a mirror to His Lord's. While Stephen was the first Christian martyr, Peter and Paul were bound to the same fate as their Prophet-Messiah. They were all rejected because of their message of repentance to unbelieving Jews.[27] Yet Stephen's suffering is a condensed portrayal of the nearness of God. So like His Lord and the other men, he did not run away, but was seemingly alone in his experience of suffering. The people also rejected his message to bring them back to God and they took him outside the city of Jerusalem to execute him like His Lord (7:54, 57–58). He was seemingly abandoned to impending terrifying mob violence.

Nevertheless, Stephen demonstrated remarkable trust in God in the midst of his suffering, and his dependence was rewarded with an amazing display of God's nearness. The Holy Spirit's supernatural presence had filled him with remarkable grace, power, and wisdom in his witness (7:3, 5, 8–10, 55) in fulfillment of Christ's promise in Acts 1:8. He was like Peter who had already experienced this powerful verbal courage when he suffered persecution by the Jews in Acts 4:8. As a result, Stephen's focus was on his ultimate relationship and home:

> But being full of the Holy Spirit, He gazed intently into heaven and saw the glory of God, and Jesus standing at the right hand of God; and He said, "Behold, I see the heavens opened up and the Son of Man standing at the right hand of God." (Acts 7:55–56)

While filled (present active participle, *huparchon*), "By the help of the Spirit his mortal eyes were enabled to look right into heaven."[28] He fixed his eyes upon (*atenizō eis*) and not only saw presumably the Shekinah glory of

---

27. David P. Moessner, "'The Christ Must Suffer': New Light on the Jesus—Peter, Stephen, Paul Parallels in Luke-Acts," *Novum Testamentum* 28, no. 3 (1986): 226–27.

28. R. C. H. Lenski, *The Interpretation of the Acts of the Apostles* (Minneapolis: Augsburg Publishing House, 1961), 303.

God, but God the Father seated on His throne with Jesus standing at His right hand of authority and power. This is the same reality of Daniel's vision of the Ancient of Days and the Son of Man in Daniel 7:13–14. Jesus had quoted it about Himself to the Sanhedrin at His trial (Luke 22:69). This vision affirmed Stephen's message about Jesus was true. That Jesus was standing appears that He had risen in part to receive Stephen into Their glorious and loving presence.[29] This is possible because the timing of the vision is revealed just at the peak of the Jewish reaction to his message (Acts 7:54). Stephen also seemed to take His standing that way because he asked Jesus, like He Himself did of the Father, to receive his spirit (7:59; cf. Luke 23:46). God the Father and the Lord Jesus Christ revealed Themselves to Stephen by means of the Holy Spirit. He was not alone or forsaken and the truth of his message was vindicated. Again, emulating his Lord on his cross, he prayed for his murderers' forgiveness when he was being stoned by a hateful and frenzied mob.[30] Luke ends the account with the simple words, "Having said this, he fell asleep." We know that he then immediately opened his eyes at his home in heaven in the presence of Jesus Christ and God the Father (2 Cor. 5:6–8).

Stephen's desire was to bring people back into a close relationship with their God. He told the Jews that they were immovable in their relationship with God. He said they were "stiff-necked and uncircumcised in heart and ears always resisting the Holy Spirit" (7:51). In fact, they betrayed and murdered Jesus Christ, the Righteous One God had sent into their midst to restore their relationship (7:52). Yet God would use Stephen to bring a young man named Saul into an intimate relationship with his God. This same man, at whose the feet the witnesses laid aside their robes in order to stone Stephen, would experience a vision of the Lord Jesus Christ. And one day Paul would not only admit to the Jews his complicity in Stephen's murder, but seek to persuade them to receive forgiveness for their sins and to follow Jesus their Messiah like he did (Acts 22:16, 17–21).

---

29. Polhill argues, "The standing position may thus depict the exalted Christ in his role of judge. If so, Stephen's vision not only confirmed his testimony, but it showed Christ rising to render judgment on his accusers." John B. Polhill, *Acts*, The New American Commentary, 2 (Nashville: Broadman & Holman, 1992), 208.

30. "The forgiveness prayer in itself is a dramatic overturning of the expected cry of the martyr for vengeance. As an expression of self-mastery and the ability to refrain from retaliating in the face of undeserved violence, it is an assertion of the ethical superiority of Christianity over Judaism." Shelly Matthews, "Clemency as Cruelty: Forgiveness and Force in the Dying Prayers of Jesus and Stephen," *Biblical Interpretation* 17 (2009): 120.

These four examples demonstrate a recurring theme for us that God is present in our suffering even when we may feel forsaken and alone. However, they are also a call to trust in God's nearness that must overcome our temptation to run and hide from pain and rejection. How many believers have been strengthened and encouraged to persevere in their trials because Jesus and Stephen persevered? How many pushed past their temptations to capitulate to doubt and even apostasy because God met Moses and Elijah in their times of struggle? How many have encouraged others to follow them to God's presence because of their own experience of God amidst their suffering?[31] We see this in Helmut Thielicke, a German pastor during WWII, who composed his book *The Silence of God* during what he called the "extraordinary years" of 1942–1951. When Europe was suffering from fighting, bombings, and atrocities, he pointed people to Jesus Christ's example of suffering and experience of the silence of God:

> What sorry, what condescension, is thus included in the fact that the Son of God enters into our controversy with God and accepts our abandonment! For this reason we may believe in Him, in Him alone, that He has remitted our guilt and that He can make something new of us. We always trust those who share our difficulties. . . . In war the chaplain's message is accepted only when he is ready to go to the very front lines and does not merely offer cheap comfort from the rear. Jesus fights on the very front lines at Calvary. Nothing human is alien to Him. He places, or better, implicates Himself so fully in our lostness that He must call out and cry in our place: "My God, my God, why hast thou forsaken me."[32]

Christ our Brother has shown us the way through suffering to the Father, to our task of bring others to Him, and to our eternal home.

CONCLUSIONS

As we draw this discussion to a close, we are surely recognizing that we have been able to take just a few steps on the journey of understanding our

---

31. See John Foxe, *Foxe's Book of Martyrs: A History of the Lives, Sufferings, and Triumphant Deaths of the Early Christian and the Protestant Martyrs*, Hendrickson Christian Classics (Peabody, MA: Hendrickson, 2003 [1709]). It is available free on Kindle. See also Richard Wurmbrand, *Tortured for Christ*, 50th anniversary edition (Colorado Springs: David C. Cook, 2017 [1967]).
32. Helmut Thielicke, *The Silence of God*, trans. and with an Introduction by Geoffrey Bromiley (Grand Rapids: Eerdmans, 1962), 72–73.

suffering and God's hiddenness and nearness. It has been intense in a visceral and relational way, as we have struggled with the seemingly uncaring absence of God that appears to be welded to many instances of suffering. However, when we consider the weight of the scriptural evidence we have to be struck with how God not only has intimate knowledge of our trying circumstances, but that He also provides in Himself the necessary intimate place of security and safety amidst suffering. In light of all that he is going through, John Feinberg agrees that

> even in the midst of the worst affliction, God is at work to use suffering to draw us closer to him. That does not make the grief and pain any less evil, but it should encourage us to realize that affliction is not a sign that God has turned away. Rather, he is using the pain and suffering to stimulate our growth in Christ.[33]

When we cry out to God asking where He is and how long must we endure, He will never leave us nor forsake us. With this confidence as His people, like the great examples we have seen, we can persevere and bring others near to God past their suffering. Our God is faithful and true.

Our world reasons that a God who is absent when we are suffering is a God who simply doesn't exist.[34] However, Ravi Zacharias points out that if God doesn't exist then we are left to be the solution to our own suffering. Then the heart and soul of the problem is asking what shape the world would be in if we were the only ones in control.[35] We can, like Elijah in a sense, find joyful mirth at the false failing sources of deliverance from suffering: "Call out with a loud voice, for he is a god; either he is occupied or gone aside, or is on a journey, or perhaps he is asleep and needs to be awakened" (1 Kings 18:27). We should, like Peter, be adamant that despite our skeptical mockers our Lord Jesus Christ will return to deliver us:

> Know this first of all, that in the last days mockers will come with their mocking, following after their own lusts, and saying, "Where is the promise

---

33. Feinberg, *Deceived by God?*, 111.
34. See C. S. Lewis, *The Problem of Pain* (New York: Macmillan, 1962), 15; J. L. Mackie, *The Miracle of Theism* (Oxford: Oxford University Press, 1982); Sam Harris, *Letter to a Christian Nation* (New York: Knopf, 2006), 54.
35. Ravi Zacharias, "Existential Challenges of Evil and Suffering," in *Beyond Opinion: Living the Faith We Defend*, ed. Ravi Zacharias (Nashville: Thomas Nelson, 2007), 178–79.

of His coming? For ever since the fathers fell asleep, all continues just as it was from the beginning of creation." For when they maintain this, it escapes their notice that by the word of God the heavens existed long ago and the earth was formed out of water and by water, through which the world at that time was destroyed, being flooded with water. But by His word the present heavens and earth are being reserved for fire, kept for the day of judgment and destruction of ungodly men.

But do not let this one fact escape your notice, beloved, that with the Lord one day is like a thousand years, and a thousand years like one day. The Lord is not slow about His promise, as some count slowness, but is patient toward you, not wishing for any to perish but for all to come to repentance. (2 Peter 3:3–9)

The Lord may seem hidden, far away, or slow to arrive with deliverance. Yet let there be no confusion here: the Lord Jesus Christ will return bringing redemption, restoration, and reconciliation to those who have trusted in God's promises and faithfully overcome the world's mocking doubts (Rev. 21:1–8). Until then, may we have Pat Feinberg's perspective, which she records in the last paragraph of the "Afterword" to *Deceived by God?*

It has been many years since we learned that I have Huntington's. God has been so faithful to me, and I thank him for his faithfulness, love, and comfort. It is my hope that what I have shared will be a comfort and encouragement to you, the readers. I want to say to those who are suffering that God is sufficient!

Amen.

NOW WHAT?

1. What do I need to remember about God's closeness when I am suffering?

2. What does God's hiddenness feel like?

3. How might Psalm 18 help us reckon with God's presence in our suffering?

4. What does God's presence feel like in the midst of my suffering?

5. Who do I need bring along to closeness with God in their suffering? What key points do they need to experience?

But amid all these rejoicings Aslan himself quietly slipped away. And when the Kings and Queens noticed that he wasn't there they said nothing about it. For Mr. Beaver had warned them, "He'll be coming and going," he had said. "One day you'll see him and another you won't. He doesn't like being tied down—and of course he has other countries to attend to. It's quite all right. He'll often drop in. Only you mustn't press him. He's wild, you know. Not like a tame lion.

—C.S. Lewis,
The Lion, the Witch & the Wardrobe

I have passed through fire and deep water, since we parted. I have forgotten much that I thought I knew, and learned again much that I had forgotten.

—J.R.R. Tolkien,
The Lord of the Rings

CHAPTER 9

ASSESSING OUR SONGS OF INTIMACY WITH GOD

When I teach my class on intimacy with God at Corban University, we conclude the semester by acknowledging that the church has a long history of putting the theme of intimacy with God into song. The students then are to choose a Christian song that has the theme of intimacy with God, and then assess it by putting into practice the biblical and theological themes we have studied together all semester. We do this in two parts. First, they are to find an intimacy-with-God song that is inadequate. They often do a simple search of "bad worship songs" and they are off and running. For some, this assignment is a bit more difficult, and we have several conversations about what they should be looking for. The class period that the assignment is due, they are to make copies of their song's lyrics and assessment for the class. Then they are all to put the title of their song on the board in front of the class so that the class chooses which song they want to hear assessed by the student who wrote about it. It is a significant time of sharing and group process.

The second assignment is for them to assess an adequate intimacy-with-God song. Again, every student is to provide the same kind of assessment handout to the class. However, this time each student is given a fifteen-minute time slot to play the song (audio only or YouTube, etc., version) and then assess it for the other students. These moments turn into wonderful times of worship and exposure to a variety of musical styles and themes, all related to intimacy with God. We also bond as a class even more,because we are sharing an intellectual and affective experience focusing on the truth of what God's Word reveals about intimacy with Him. It seems fitting at this point that in a similar way, we should examine the intimate songs of God's people in this chapter.

ASSESSING SONGS ABOUT INTIMACY WITH GOD

At the outset we need to assess what we mean by "assessing." An initial disclaimer is important. This examination cannot and will not be an exhaustive or comprehensive study of all songs either in the history of Christianity[1] or in current contemporary music. There are just too many songs from too many places to even attempt such an exercise. Nevertheless, we need to provide some examples to develop our sense of the assessment process and results. So we will look at some songs from the distant past but focus mainly on contemporary Christian songs. Furthermore, we must ask what we are looking for in these songs in order to evaluate them biblically and theologically. What are key principles that should guide our process? First, we need to recognize that assessing these songs is not always black-and-white. In other words, we should recognize that humans write Christian songs with varying levels of spiritual and theological maturity, reflection on the content and context, and skill. It is safer to say that the adequacy or inadequacy of these songs are more like points on a continuum rather than either the extreme of being branded "heresy" or "divinely inspired."

Second, we need to use the theological elements of intimacy with God that will communicate the intimate nature of God's movement toward or away from us, His presence or place with us, His personal knowledge, and His contact or touch. This means that our moving to or away from God is also part of the equation. We can then compare these elements in a song with the Bible's use of them. This also entails our responsibility to examine the metaphors used by the songwriter. Are they from our present culture? Is a negative metaphor used in a positive way or vice versa?[2] In other words, are they an

---

1. For more complete studies on Christian music, see David Riddle Breed, *The History and Use of Hymns and Hymn Tunes* (London: Forgotten Books, 2015; originally New York: Fleming H. Revell, 1903); Tim Dowley, *Christian Music: A Global History* (Augsburg/Fortress, 2011).
2. The beloved hymn "There Is a Fountain" by William Cowper could be an interesting case study in inadequacies, but it is more difficult to view it as a song about intimacy with God.
   1. There is a fountain filled with blood
   drawn from Emmanuel's veins;
   and sinners plunged beneath that flood

accurate comparison to the Scriptures' themes and texts? All this to say is that we must evaluate while evaluating. Yes, we must assess the songs for biblical and theological accuracy, precision, and clarity. Yet as we noted before, we should attempt to avoid being judgmental of the songwriter's motives and emotions (Rom. 14:4, 10). We need to speak the truth about our assessments in love (Eph. 4:15) for the building up of our brothers and sisters for a mature relationship with God (Eph. 4:13–16). The Lord has given gifted people to write and perform "psalms, hymns, and spiritual songs" to connect believers with their God as an expression of being filled with the Holy Spirit (Eph. 5:18–20) and the indwelling of Christ's words in our hearts (Col. 3:16). Only a certain kind of lyric is befitting of God's people in reference to their God (Pss. 33:3; 47:7; 1 Cor. 10:31–32; Eph. 4:4).

Let's look at a couple of intimacy-with-God songs with inadequacies. We should try to assess the song's assumptions and positive contributions, as well as the concerns we have concerning its accuracy and adequacy. An initial example is the song "Better Than Drugs" performed by the band Skillet.[3] Take a look at the lyrics. The foundational assumption of this song is that a close relationship with God is healthier than drug addiction. It is commendable that the writers want to engage the depths of despair, and indeed this has proved helpful to some who listen and comment on it.[4] However, while many recognize that the song is about God, even though He is not mentioned specifically, others question whether it is referring to a girl or significant other.[5] There are

---

    lose all their guilty stains.
    Lose all their guilty stains,
    lose all their guilty stains;
    and sinners plunged beneath that flood
    lose all their guilty stains.

3. Skillet, "Better Than Drugs," by Brian Howes and John Cooper, recorded February–April 2006, track 4 on *Comatose*, Lava Records, compact disk. For the lyrics, see https://www.azlyrics.com/lyrics/skillet/betterthandrugs.html (accessed March 23, 2019).

4. "Skillet—Better Than Drugs," http://songmeanings.com/songs/view/3530822107858628851 (accessed April 14, 2019).

5. "i feel this song is simply about how the singer's lover is able to help him cope with his struggles of everyday life. i don't think it's about God at all. remember: band themes can change!!!" pratly2, posted April 15, 2009, http://songmeanings.com/songs/view/3530822107858628851 (accessed April 14, 2019). Another comment reads:

    "even though i know that this song is a christian song and i'm not usually into that kind of stuff, this song has a special place in my heart always. i have my own personal experience and personal interpretation of this song. you see i got into some trouble with the law a while back, and i had been doing some pretty stupid stuff. anyway, after my legal trouble i had to slow things down A LOT. most of my friends back then didn't want to hang out with me anymore, because i wasn't as fun to be around and didn't do the same things that they were doing. only

some cautions we should raise. The line that refers to feeling God's heartbeat is not a biblical theme in intimate contact with or the touch of God.[6] The only place in the Bible where contact close enough to God would allow someone to feel His heartbeat may be when John, the disciple Jesus loved, reclined on His chest at the upper room meal. This singular occurrence does not necessarily imply John's ear nuzzling up to Jesus's chest. Since it can be misconstrued as a romantic image for our relationship with God, believers today are not justi-fied in applying that intimacy. One line refers to the claim in Song of Solomon 1:2 and 4:10 that "Your love is better than wine."

The most significant caution is how God's movement toward us is likened to a drug high. The recurring line that describes God coming fast to get him high is an illegitimate metaphor for God's intimate deliverance. A drug-induced euphoric state causes the loss of personal control and grasp of reality.[7] It is true that Paul makes a comparison between being drunk with wine and being filled with the Holy Spirit in Ephesians 5:18. However, drunkenness is expressly forbidden because of its consequences—a reckless and wasteful life (from *asote-ria* or "unsavedness"), whereas being filled with the Holy Spirit is a voluntary yielding to a Person. Paul uses the phrase "let the word of Christ dwell in you richly" in Colossians 3:16 to describe the exact same relational results of being filled with the Spirit (compare its succeeding participles in Eph. 5:19–6:9, 18–20 with Col. 3:16–4:2; singing, giving thanks to God, submitting, etc.). Yes, we can celebrate how God wonderfully delivers people from drug addiction and other vices when they yield wholly to His mercy and grace in Christ by means of the Holy Spirit. God does meet those needs that people seek to fulfil through the abuse of drugs. Yet we must not mix the metaphors like this song does that are

---

one person stayed by my side, helping me through all the tough shit that i was going through. that friend of mine was like my savior. he saved me from myself, he showed me that i had to live every moment to the fullest. he's the love of my life and i am thankful for my own personal savior and angel in him. that's what i think of when i hear this song anyway. Lol," ManicOrganic, posted December 5, 2009, http://songmeanings.com/songs/view/3530822107858628851 (accessed April 14, 2019).

6. Kari Jobe's song "The More I Seek You" has the same imagery of laying back against God, breathing, and feeling His heartbeat. Yet it also does not specifically mention the person of God in the lyrics.

7. For the fuller scope of the effects of drug use and addiction see Cynthia Kuhn, Scott Schwarzwelder, and Wilkie Wilson, *Buzzed: The Straight Facts about the Most Used and Abused Drugs from Alcohol to Ecstasy*, 4th ed. (New York: W. W. Norton, 2014), and Stephen A. Maisto, Mark Galizio, and Gerard J. Connors, *Drug Use and Abuse*, 8th ed. (Belmont, CA: Wadsworth, 2018).

so disparately different in the Bible. Simply, we do not exchange one addiction for another. We exchange one addiction for freedom and wholeness.

Another intimate song with inadequate elements is the very popular "Your Love Is Extravagant" written by Peter Kipley and Jared Anderson, performed by Casting Crowns, and sung in many church worship settings.[8] The foundational assumption of this song is that the love of Christ is beyond what humans can imagine. This initially sounds like His boundless faithful love of certain biblical passages (John 15:12; Rom. 8:37–39; Eph. 3:19). The song refers to intimate friendship that could be based on John 15:13–15, "Greater love has no man than this that he lay down his life for his friends," because of later lines in the song. In the chorus, the inviting open arms of Christ seem appropriate especially since this metaphor is later defined with words that seem to allude to His atonement on the cross.

Our concern should be with the romance theme that is overlaid on top of these legitimate intimate concepts. The friendship Christ has with His disciples results from no longer being called *doulous* or slaves (John 15:15).[9] This new relationship carries with it a new confidence,[10] and a fellowship like they had with Lazarus (John 11:1).[11] We must be careful to acknowledge that their obedience to His commands (15:14) "brings out very sharply the fact that this is not at all a friendship between equals."[12] He remains their Lord (*kurios*). At the same time, His command is defined as one of love (v. 17), which He Himself fulfills perfectly (v. 10), and in so doing, He makes Himself like them.[13] Yet to couple this imagery with "Capture my heart again" is to foist on it an unrelated popular contemporary Western idiom. To capture, win, or steal someone's heart is often synonymous for making someone start to feel love for you, for starting

8. Peter Kipley and Jared Anderson, "Your Love Is Extravagant," Warner/Chappell Music, 2003. For the lyrics, see https://castingcrowns.com/music/your-love-is-extravagant (accessed March 23, 2019).

9. His calling His disciples friends was a direct result of His willingness to lay down His life for them and the intimate knowledge He shared with them from His Father (John 15:13–16).

10. George R. Beaseley-Murray, *John*, 2nd ed., Word Biblical Commentary, 36 (Nashville: Thomas Nelson, 2000), 275.

11. Tenney captures Christ's meaning of friendship, saying that "it is a partnership of mutual esteem and affection." Shared purpose, respect, and affection are essential marks of "friendship" with the Lord Jesus Christ. Merrill C. Tenney, *John*, The Expositor's Bible Commentary, 9 (Grand Rapids: Zondervan, 1981), 153.

12. Gustav Stählin, "Φιλέω, Καταφιλέω, Φίλημα, Φίλος, Φίλη, Φιλία," in Kittel, Bromiley, and Friedrich, eds., *Theological Dictionary of the New Testament*, (Grand Rapids: Eerdmans, 1964–) 165.

13. Stahlin, "Phileo, etc.," 165.

a romantic or sexual relationship.[14] However, the friendship (*philous*) of Jesus emphasizes love (*agapē*), identity, obedience, loyalty, and sacrifice, not feelings of affection. He contrasts the disciple's identity as His chosen ones that are thus hated by the world with those the world loves (vv. 18–25).[15]

The line that has the writer feeling like they are moving to God's grace in a rhythmic way easily brings to mind the contemporary image of the swaying or moving back and forth[16] of a female being led by her male partner in a slow dance. It is one thing to dance before the Lord as David did (2 Sam. 6:16; 1 Chron. 15:29; cf. Ps. 149:3; it is quite another to picture ourselves slow dancing with Jesus. The song indicates the nearly erotic intimacy of this dance, as the next line intimates that in their secret place with Christ, His fragrance is intoxicating. A simple Google search ties "intoxicating fragrance" to other terms such as obsession, seduction, and sensuality. In the Bible, "Fragrance" is the translation given to the positive sense of the term for scent, aroma, or odor (*reach*) in the Old Testament and similarly for *osmē* (John 12:3) and *euōdia* (2 Cor. 2:15) in the New Testament. In this way it is used most often in the sensual sense in Song of Solomon (1:3, 12; 2:13; 4:10, 11, 16; 7:8, 13). All this is to say, these cautions against using such romantic imagery for a close relationship with Christ overshadow any argued benefit.[17]

---

14. "win/capture/steal someone's heart," *Macmillan Dictionary*, https://www. macmillandictionary.com/us/dictionary/american/win-capture-steal-someone-s-heart (accessed April 14, 2019); "win/steal/capture one's heart," *Merriam-Webster Dictionary*, https://www.merriam-webster.com/dictionary/win/steal/capture%20one's%20heart (accessed April 14, 2019); "steal heart," *The Free Dictionary*, https://idioms.thefreedictionary. com/steal+heart (accessed April 14, 2019). Beau Taplin's "The Connection," shows us a more reflective yet culturally consistent understanding of this idiom:

> My heart is not captured easily. I am disinterested in small talk, disillusioned with love, and too focused on my dreams and aspirations to lend anyone my attention for too long. But if we make that connection, if you find your way into my heart, God, I will fall for you like gravity has let go of the earth.

Beau Taplin, "The Connection, Tumblr, http://afadthatlastsforever.tumblr.com/ post/112507453327/my-heart-is-not-captured-easily-i-am (accessed April 14, 2019).
15. There are other valuable songs that celebrate Jesus as the believer's friend. Joseph M. Scriven, "What a Friend We Have in Jesus" (1855), music by Charles C. Converse (1868) and Lizzie DeArmond, "What a Dear Friend Is Jesus," music by Andrew L. Byers (1923).
16. Current synonyms for "sway" include "move back and forth." *Pocket Oxford American Dictionary and Thesaurus*, 3rd ed. (New York: Oxford University Press, 2010), 784.
17. A more explicit reference to dancing with Jesus is found in the song, "We Dance" by Stephanie F. Gretzinger and Amanda Falk, Bethel Music, 2013. For the lyrics, see https://www.lyrics.com/lyric/30812841/You+Make+Me+Brave%3A+Live+at+the+C ivic/We+Dance (accessed March 23, 2019). The lyrics are similar in some ways to the late '70s hit song, "Slow Dancing, Swaying to the Music," sung by Johnny Rivers. Jack Tempchin, Warner/Chappell Music, 1977. For the lyrics, see https://www.lyricsfreak. com/j/johnny+rivers/slow+dancin_10153450.html (accessed March 23, 2019).

SONGS EMPHASIZING THE FOUR ELEMENTS OF INTIMACY WITH GOD

God has blessed the church with volumes of beautiful music that capture the various elements of intimacy with Him. This music seems to come from a convergence of the truths revealed in Scripture, the experiences of life, and the believer's faith, whether it is strong or fragile. Let's examine adequate songs based upon the elements of intimacy with God they emphasize.

Movement toward Intimacy

The reality of intimacy with God is always a movement toward or away from Him.[18] The famous hymn "Just As I Am" has encapsulated this for over 150 years. In her early thirties, Charlotte Elliott contracted a serious illness that left her a semi-invalid for the rest of her life. Within a year she suffered a spiritual crisis and confessed to the Swiss evangelist Henri A. Cesar Malan that she did not know how to come to Christ. His simple answer was, "Come to him just as you are." Reflecting on that experience twelve years later, she wrote "Just as I Am" as a statement of her faith in 1834.[19] Billy Graham recognized this many decades ago when he began to have the audience singing "Just As I Am" at the culmination of his services.

> **"Just As I Am"**
> [1] Just as I am, without one plea,
> but that thy blood was shed for me,
> and that thou bidd'st me come to thee,
> O Lamb of God, I come, I come.
>
> [2] Just as I am, and waiting not
> to rid my soul of one dark blot,
> to thee, whose blood can cleanse each spot,
> O Lamb of God, I come, I come.
>
> [3] Just as I am, though tossed about
> with many a conflict, many a doubt,
> fightings and fears within, without,
> O Lamb of God, I come, I come.
>
> [4] Just as I am, thou wilt receive,
> wilt welcome, pardon, cleanse, relieve;
> because thy promise I believe,
> O Lamb of God, I come, I come.

18. There is a group of songs that emphasize the believer preparing the way for God's movement to or entrance into our lives associated with the Lord's return. A popular congregational worship song is "Prepare the Way" by Jared Anderson, track 3 on *Live from My Church*, released September 22, 2009, Integrity Music, compact disk. There are other worship songs with the name "Prepare the Way," by Charlie Hall (very brief and repetitive lyrics), http://www.lyricsfreak.com/c/charlie+hall/prepare+the+way_21007254.html (accessed April 14, 2019); "Prepare the Way" by Darrell Evans and Eric Nuzum, 1999, Integrity's Hosanna! Music, http://www.higherpraise.com/lyrics/love/love200014.htm (accessed April 14, 2019); Christopher Walker, "Prepare the Way," *Rise Up and Sing,* http://www.spiritandsong.com/compositions/7356 (accessed April 14, 2019); Paul Wilbur, "Prepare the Way," *Your Great Name,* 2013, Messianic Praise and Worship. https://blindcaveman.wordpress.com/2013/05/27/prepare-the-way (accessed April 14, 2019).
19. Charlotte Elliott, "Just as I Am, without One Plea," Lyrics, 1836; William B. Bradbury, Music, 1849, Public Domain, https://hymnary.org/text/just_as_i_am_without_one_plea (accessed March 18, 2019).

Its famous line "O Lamb of God, I come, I come" captures the repentant sinner's movement toward God and His offer of salvation by means of the sacrifice of His Son. While the language of "bidd'st" is archaic, it means that God bids or invites. This is identical to the biblical themes of seeking,[20] turning,[21] and coming to God we discovered in Chapter 1. It also mirrors James 4:8 with its call to "Draw near to God" in humble repentance. Innumerable sinners have used "Just As I Am" to voice their hearts and have come to saving faith in the Lord Jesus Christ. Believers have also returned to God singing this song and now continue to do so with the latest rendition by Travis Cottrell,[22] which adds a new chorus that culminates in intimate contact with God as the Father who welcomes back his repentant prodigal child with open arms.[23]

Another song in this vein is Chris Rice's "Untitled Hymn (Come to Jesus)."[24] Hymns, from *humnos* or song of praise, are not just individual expressions to God, and this particular hymn is a call to any and all believers to move to Jesus in every stage of their spiritual existence and experience.[25] At conversion, Rice uses imagery of the one who was robbed and beaten but was shown compassion by the Good Samaritan. All we have to do is turn to him to be saved This is what many experienced with Jesus when they were healed (Matt. 9:35–36; Mark 3:1–5; 5:25–28; 10:46–52; Luke 17:11–14; 18:35–43). Once converted, we

---

20. L. M. Bateman, "I Will Early Seek Him," Fillmore Bros., 1888, Public Domain, https://hymnary.org/text/i_will_early_seek_the_savior (accessed March 18, 2019). This is a beautiful example of a song that motivates movement toward God by seeking, learning, following, etc. See also the Rend Collective song "Boldly I Approach (The Art of Celebration), " track 11 on *The Art of Celebration*, released March 17, 2014, Integrity Music, 2014, compact disk.

21. The chorus of "Turn Your Eyes upon Jesus" by Helen H. Lemmel (1922) focuses on our movement as turning and looking.

 Turn your eyes upon Jesus,
 Look full in His wonderful face,
 And the things of earth will grow strangely dim,
 In the light of His glory and grace.

 Public Domain. For the lyrics, see https://hymnary.org/text/o_soul_are_you_weary_and_troubled (accessed March 23, 2019).

22. Travis Cottrell, "Just As I Am," by Sue C. Smith, Travis Cottrell, David E. Moffitt, track 6 on *When the Stars Burn Down*, released September 13, 2011, In:Ciite Media, compact disk. For the lyrics, see https://genius.com/Travis-cottrell-just-as-i-am-lyrics (accessed March 23, 2019).

23. See also the GMA Dove Award Song of the Year nominated song, "O Come to The Altar," written by Chris Brown, Mack Brock, Steven Furtick, and Wade Joye (Elevation Worship, 2017).

24. Chris Rice, "Untitled Hymn (Come to Jesus)," Warner/Chappell Music, 2003. For the lyrics, see https://www.streetdirectory.com/lyricadvisor/song/cfwwul/untitled_hymn_come_to_jesus_/. Accessed March 23, 2019.

25. See Lemmel, "Turn Your Eyes Upon Jesus."

must recognize that our burdens are taken away by Jesus when He died on the cross. Obviously now our songs should be directed to him as the One who gives us life itself. The sinful woman and Zaccheus, when forgiven by Jesus, would have new joy and life (Luke 7:36–39; 19:1–10). When we don't know how to live the life He has called us to and we stumble along the way, we are to allow ourselves to fall on Him to be able to live. During times of dark trials we must express our pain to Him in order to live. Because He meets our deepest needs, heals our weaknesses, and hears our prayers, we will be filled with inexpressible joy, and we can very appropriately dance for him. When our life is over and we are about to leave this earth, we celebrate the peace of being at the Lord's side. We can close our eyes to this life and go straight to Him, the One who gives us eternal life. We can hear the apostle Paul's triumphant joy near his end (2 Cor. 5:6–8; Phil. 1:21–23; Col. 1:27; 1 Thess. 4:16–18; 5:9–11). From our conversion to our deathbed, this song calls us all to move close to Jesus at every stage of our Christian lives because He is always present and open to our movement.

A tremendous example of God's movement toward us has come through the Father in the parable of the prodigal or lost son (Luke 15:11–32). We have already seen the significant need for replacing shame as a script with God as our good and intimate Father. The heart of our need is His compassion or mercy. Phillips, Craig, and Dean are well known for performing "Mercy Came Running" (1997), a song that explores the essence of this need from the perspective of the prodigal's return. The sinner recognizes his distance from intimacy with God and his bondage to sin and shame. The first verse provides necessary theology of the separation of God and humans by the veil of the holy of holies in the biblical temple. A blood sacrifice was the only means of freedom. The song harkens back to Christ's crucifixion and the powerful signs of the darkness and earthquake, paving the way for the chorus in which God the Father's mercy is personified in an unmistakable way. Christ emphasized that the Father of the parable did not just wait and watch for and accept His returning prodigal, but, against custom, ran, embraced, and kissed His child (15:20). He was driven by His own feelings of compassion (from *splachnizomai*).

There is so much to commend this song and it has provided help to many throughout its history. My only concern is the confusion that can come from the controversy regarding the theology of Phillips, Craig, and Dean. They are originally from the United or Oneness Pentecostal tradition, which holds to modalism, a denial of the historical and biblical view of the Trinity. According to this view, the God of the Bible is one in essence and person. The references to the Father, Son, and Holy Spirit are simply designations of God's manifestations of Himself at different times and contexts.[26] This is sad, since this view has been considered a heresy by almost the entire Christian Church. It also denigrates the gift of the Father of His own Son, and the Son's voluntary sacrifice to fulfill the Father's will. This would give the song "Mercy Came Running" a questionable meaning at best. Nonetheless, the song is an adequate representation of the God's compassionate movement toward us as sinners.

Intimate Knowledge

Since drawing close to God requires greater personal understanding, believers have expressed their desire for this in many songs.[27] One hymn I grew up with was "Open My Eyes That I May See."[28] Clara H. Scott wrote this in 1895 shortly before her death, out of her desire to be continually receptive to the "Spirit Divine."[29] Each verse begins with the prayer for God to "Open" either eyes, ears, mouth, heart, or mind. It is all centered on our openness to understanding God through His Word (Ps. 119:18). The first verse sets the tone for expressing desire that we "may see glimpses of truth Thou hast for me" that are hidden from the natural human (1 Cor. 2:6–16).

---

26. An earlier online version of the United Pentecostal Churches International's position on the Trinity is clearly in error: "In distinction to the doctrine of the Trinity, the UPCI holds to a oneness view of God. It views the Trinitarian concept of God, that of God eternally existing as three distinctive persons, as inadequate and a departure from the consistent and emphatic biblical revelation of God being one. . . . Thus God is manifested as Father in creation and as the Father of the Son, in the Son for our redemption, and as the Holy Spirit in our regeneration." See Kelly Powers, "Be Aware of Phillips, Craig and Dean (PCD)—United Pentecostal International Church (UPCI), Oneness Theology," https://rootedinchrist. org/2008/01/01/phillips-craig-dean-and-the-united-pentecostal-church-upci-oneness-pentecostals (accessed April 14, 2019). Its present version is, "There is one God, who has revealed Himself as our Father, in His Son Jesus Christ, and as the Holy Spirit. Jesus Christ is God manifested in flesh. He is both God and man. (See Deuteronomy 6:4; Ephesians 4:4–6; Colossians 2:9; I Timothy 3:16.)," https://www.upci.org/about/our-beliefs (accessed April 14, 2019). In 2013, PCD signed a statement affirming the very orthodox Baptist Faith and Message of the Southern Baptist Convention. Matt Privett, "Phillips, Craig and Dean's statement rejecting modalism," http://www.themattrix.com/2014/01/10/phillips-craig-and-deans-statement-rejecting-modalism (accessed April 14, 2019).
27. See Carrie E. Breck and Grant C. Tullar's great hymn "Face to Face," 1898, Public Domain https://hymnary.org/text/face_to_face_with_christ_my_savior (accessed March 18, 2019). This song is based on 1 Corinthians 13:12. See also the simple worship song "Intimacy," by Matt Redman in *The Heart of Worship* (Star Song, 1999).
28. Clara H. Scott, "Open My Eyes that I May See," 1895, Public Domain, https://hymnary. org/text/open_my_eyes_that_i_may_see (accessed March 18, 2019).
29. C. Michael Hawn, "History of Hymns: 'Open My Eyes That I May See," https://www. umcdiscipleship.org/resources/history-of-hymns-open-my-eyes-that-i-may-see (accessed April 14, 2019).

> **"Open My Eyes That I May See"**
>
> 1. Open my eyes that I may see
> Glimpses of truth Thou hast for me;
> Place in my hands the wonderful key
> That shall unclasp and set me free.
>
> *Chorus:*
>
> Silently now I wait for Thee,
> Ready, my God, Thy will to see;
> Open my eyes, illumine me,
>   Spirit Divine!
> 2. Open my ears that I may hear
> Voices of truth Thou sendest clear;
> And while the wave notes fall on my ear,
> Everything false will disappear.
> 3. Open my mouth and let me bear
> Tidings of mercy everywhere;
> Open my heart and let me prepare
> Love with Thy children thus to share.
> 4. Open my mind that I may read
> More of Thy love in word and deed;
> What shall I fear while yet Thou dost lead?
> Only for light from Thee I plead.

Only when God places "in my hands the wonderful key" are we able to "unclasp" that knowledge and be set free. The chorus reiterates our proper posture for receiving understanding of God's very will. Far from presumptuous, we are to wait silently and ready for God to grant it (Ps. 119:81). When He opens our eyes, it is as if He turns on the lights of our minds and hearts (Ps. 13:3). His written Word is "a light unto my feet and a light unto my path" (Ps. 119:105). This illumination has to be given by God's Spirit (Eph. 1:17–18; 3:16–19). The merely human search will only cause "my eyes fail with longing for Your Word" (Ps. 119:82, 123). May our hearts sing and pray for the Lord to open our eyes that we may see Him and His will more clearly.

In the 1970s, one of the most popular songs Maranatha! Music brought to the Church was "Open Our Eyes, Lord" by Robert Cull (1976).[30] This simple song puts into words the desire of every Christian who wants a closer and more tangible relationship with their Lord and Savior. In the 1970s and '80s, when churches added "choruses" to their worship services to supplement or replace the older and less popular music style of hymns, this song was a staple for many churches and youth group worship sets. I am sure just the mention of it transports many middle-aged Christians back to times of intimate seeking of the Lord. Its truth rests in the believer's need and request for illumination. Since Jesus Christ is in heaven, it seems appropriate to ask the Lord, who is either the Father or the Spirit in this case, for spiritual sight in order to communicate with Him. Walking by faith and not by sight (2 Cor. 5:7) does not mean the inability to see anything. It just means we are able to see spiritual realities that the natural person cannot experience.

---

30. Robert Cull, "Open Our Eyes, Lord," Maranatha Music, 1976. For the lyrics, see https://hymnary.org/text/open_our_eyes_lord_we_want_to_see_jesus (accessed March 23, 2019).

While the simplicity of this song is one of its strengths, it can be one of its weaknesses. One must be cautious not to employ a cross-reference approach to connecting its themes to the Bible without care to keep the passages in context and logically connected. A more recent songbook, *Sing With Me*, is based on Psalm 119:18, John 12:21, and Revelation 2:7.[31] It is interesting that in Psalm 119:18 the psalmist asks the Lord to open his eyes in order to "behold wonderful things from Your law," while the song itself just asks to see and touch Jesus. It is true that the primary avenue for seeing Christ is through the Scriptures about Him. However, John 12:21 refers to when a group of Greeks came to the Philip the disciple and asked him, "Sir, we wish to see Jesus." Revelation 2:7 is the first of the recurring phrase "He who has an ear, let him hear what the Spirit says to the churches" used by Christ to the seven churches (2:11, 17, 29; 3:6, 13, 22). What does it actually mean to see Jesus today? He is more than just the Jesus of the Gospels. He is nothing less than that, but much more. When we read the book of Revelation, the visions describing Jesus Christ in 1:12–17, 5:6–14, and 19:11–16 indicate we are to see Him as the great warrior High Priest of heaven and the Son of Man of Daniel 7, the worthy slain Lamb, and the conquering Messiah-Warrior. Furthermore, at the risk of sounding overly picky, while it is so important that we communicate our love to Christ, we should be cautious not to reduce what we communicate to Christ only to that. Nevertheless, this song is a good means of expressing our desire to pursue intimate knowledge of God and Christ.

I need to add one final example of how believers can express their desire for intimate knowledge of God. "I Want to Know Christ," originally performed by Larnelle Harris,[32] is a powerful summary of Paul's desire to know Christ above all else, from Philippians 3:8–11. In the first verse, the believer recounts their current blessings of redemption and the pearl of great price, while in the second verse they recognize the Christian path is one of suffering and loss. In the bridge, the believer carries the theme of the second verse further and uses language very similar to Phil. 3:7–8, 10–11 of laying down all the things of life that are counted as "gain." Yet the end of each verse, they exclaim that they want to know Christ. The chorus builds from the title, "I want to know Christ." Resolute, they list their plan for this by their focus to place Christ before them. Reminiscent of Paul's call to believers in Colossians 3:1–4, they

---

31. Joyce Borger, ed., *Sing With Me* (Grand Rapids: Faith Alive, 2006), #179. This is a songbook of the Christian Reformed Church.
32. Larnelle Harris, *From a Servant's Heart* (Benson Records, 1996). Philip Webb also performs it on his album *He Is King* (The Master's Fellowship, 1988).

lift up their eyes and to be captivated by God's glory. Paul says that this is the glory of God in the gospel and in the face of Christ (2 Cor. 4:4, 6). The song concludes with the believer repeating the simple title "I want to know Christ." This quest of intimate knowledge of Christ is an excellent example of theological clarity, focus, and accuracy.

God's intimate understanding of us is also the grand assumption as well. This is captured well in the words of the Phillips, Craig, and Dean song, "Friend of God" (2005).[33] The believer here asks God why He pays attention to him and hears his prayers. God's mindfulness is the fact that He pays attention not just to the facts of our lives, but to our personal thoughts, cares, and prayers to Him (cf. Pss. 103:14; 115:12). And so they then wonder aloud as to whether God is really thinking about them and yet rightly acknowledge that His intimate loving knowledge of us is amazing. David pondered the same thing in Psalm 139:6 when he admitted, "Such knowledge is too wonderful for me, it is too high, I cannot attain to it" (cf. Rom. 11:33).

God more than knows our suffering: He, in some way, experiences it. Jeremy Camp communicates this in his song "He Knows."[34] This song describes the believer's seemingly insurmountable suffering. The legitimate assumption is that if someone actually knows in a real and intimate way everything we are going through, that will provide us with the strength to carry on. The verses do not describe the actual instances of suffering, but the suffering itself and the feelings that are associated with them. This suffering is not a moment, but is exhausting and seemingly unending. After a while, the pain is hidden from others deep within wounds that no one else has seen hurts too much to show. This aloneness and forsakenness drops us to the point of fainting, sinking, and nearing the very brink. Yet the chorus breaks through all of this suffering, exclaiming that God knows all of our hurts and pains. He knows our feelings because He has walked the path of suffering Himself. All we need to do is recognize that He has personal intimate knowledge of our suffering, let Him release us from their weight that threatens to crush our faith, and keep looking to Him. This is putting Hebrews 12:1–3 into practice. Consider its words:

33. Israel Houghton and Michael Gungor, "Friend of God," Integrity Music, 2004. See the lyrics at https://www.azlyrics.com/lyrics/phillipscraigdean/friendofgod.html (accessed March 22, 2019).
34. Jeremy Camp and Seth Mosley, "He Knows," Capitol Christian Music Group, 2015. For the lyrics, see https://www.lyrics.com/lyric/31235404/Jeremy+Camp/He+Knows (accessed March 22, 2019).

> Therefore, since we have so great a cloud of witnesses surrounding us, let us also lay aside every encumbrance and the sin which so easily entangles us, and let us run with endurance the race that is set before us, fixing our eyes on Jesus, the author and perfecter of faith, who for the joy set before Him endured the . cross, despising the shame, and has sat down at the right hand of the throne of God. For consider Him who has endured such hostility by sinners against Himself, so that you will not grow weary and lose heart.

Not only do we have witnesses who "by faith" endured great suffering, we have our Lord's constant understanding of our sufferings from His vantage point not only from heaven, but also as a fellow-sufferer with us on this earth. We can come to Him with our burdens and follow His ways. Jesus said in Matthew 11:28–30:

> Come to Me, all who are weary and heavy-laden, and I will give you rest. Take My yoke upon you and learn from Me, for I am gentle and humble in heart, and you will find rest for your souls. For My yoke is easy and My burden is light.

He will not always remove our suffering, but He will remove it as a crushing burden upon our souls if we entrust our lives and destinies to Him. "He Knows" is a tremendous anthem of hope in God's intimate knowledge.

There are other songs that communicate God's intimate knowledge of our own names. In our current age, which declares that image is everything, as is our need for acceptance,[35] Francesca Battistelli performs "He Knows My Name."[36] This song centers on the fact that God not only knows our name, but He chose us to be his children even when we aren't perfect and no one else seems to want us. It is apparent that understanding these truths can free us from performing for others to gain their approval. This can also replace the shame script that many live by with one based in God as good Father

---

35. She talks about this in the promo video, "Francesca Battistelli—He Knows My Name (Behind The Song)," YouTube video, 5:17, June 24, 2014, https://www.youtube.com/watch?v=DmR6ZsnfN-w (accessed April 14, 2019). See also Kevin Davis, "#514—'He Knows My Name,' by Francesca Battistelli," New Release Today, http://www.newreleasetoday.com/article.php?article_id=1308 (accessed April 14, 2019).
36. Francesca Battistelli, "He Knows My Name" by Francesca Battistelli, Mia Fieldes, and Seth Mosely, released April 22, 2014, track 3 on *If We're Honest*, Word Music, compact disk. See official trailer for context, https://www.youtube.com/watch?v=jYpBgJHmGmw (accessed April 14, 2019).

who knows us intimately and thus accepts us unconditionally based upon our freedom through Christ's justifying sacrifice (Rom. 8:15–17; Gal. 4:4–7). Her performance and the content of this song struck such a chord with the public that it was nominated in 2015 for the Billboard Music Award for Top Christian Song and GMA Dove Award for Song of the Year. In another popular song with the title "He Knows My Name," Tommy Walker uses the same phrase and also speaks of God as our Maker and Father.[37] Yet God's intimate knowledge is framed similarly to Jeremy Camp's "He Knows"—namely, that it occurs in the midst of our suffering. The chorus beautifully claims that God knows our name, thoughts, tears, and hears us when we call upon Him. Walker notes on his website that John 10:3–4 is a passage that helped inspire the writing of this song.[38] Here Jesus said, "To him the doorkeeper opens, and the sheep hear his voice, and he calls his own sheep by name and leads them out.[4] When he puts forth all his own, he goes ahead of them, and the sheep follow him because they know his voice." This song has become an important worship song for churches because of its truth, simplicity, and straightforward message of God's intimate knowledge of us.

We should mention "Known," performed by Audrey Assad.[39] This song describes God's intimate knowledge of us throughout the seasons of our life. Assad combines references from birth to rebirth, from daybreak to evening, from spring to autumn, all emphasizing God's personal understanding of us as our Creator and Savior. In fact the last verse summarizes the believer's spiritual life span as something that God knows. The verses poignantly capture various ways God knows us like humans and creatures know each other (mothers their baby's face, swallows the sky, a lover his beloved's heart[40]). These are allusions to Psalm 139 where David is not only certain of the Lord's knowledge of his conception and birth (vv. 13–16), but states:

---

37. Tommy Walker, "He Knows My Name," released September 3, 2002, track 12 on *Never Gonna Stop*, Sony, compact disk.

38. Tommy Walker, "He Knows My Name," http://www.tommywalker.net/songstories/?rq=He%20 knows%20my%20name (accessed April 14, 2019).

39. Audrey Assad, "Known," by Phillip Larue and Audrey Assad, released July 13, 2010, track 8 on *The House You Are Building*, Sparrow, compact disk.

40. The only caution I would raise concerning this song is that it has been viewed as a love song to the Lord. One video that puts the music to slides with the lyrics begins with a picture of a heart in the sand and is filled with pictures of romantic images. "Known," YouTube video, 4:36, July 24, 2017, https://www.youtube.com/watch?v=CDWt0N1coWk (accessed May 2, 2019). The lines of the third verse, "As the lover knows his beloved's heart, All the shapes and curves of her even in the dark," is true and meaningful. It is sad that we even need to wonder if it is completely necessary image in our hypersexualized society and the tendency to romanticize one's relationship with Jesus.

You know when I sit down and when I rise up;
You understand my thought from afar.
You scrutinize my path and my lying down,
And are intimately acquainted with all my ways. (vv. 2–3)

Again, the acknowledgment and trust in God's personal understanding of every aspect of our lives should cleanse our hearts from anxiety and sin (vv. 23–24). Jesus reiterates that the Father even knows and cares when a half-cent sparrow falls to the ground (Matt. 10:29–30; Luke 12:6–7) and that His knowledge of and provision for the "birds of the air" should dissipate our worry about tomorrow's troubles (Matt. 6:25–26, 32–34). And so the chorus of "Known" proclaims to God,

Savior, You have known me as I am
Healer, You have known me as I was
As I will be in the morning, in the evening
You have known me, yeah, You know me.

He knows us as ones who not only are saved, but also knew us before He healed us (Isa. 53:4–5, 11; 1 Peter 2:24–25).

Intimate Place/Location

Drawing close to God also requires connecting with Him using language of place or location, and believers have tried to capture this in many songs.[41] The famous hymn "Trust and Obey" written by John H. Sammis in 1887[42] reminds believers that intimate knowledge of God's Word is the means by which we walk with Him. The first verse begins with the recognition that "When we walk with the Lord in the light of His word what a glory He sheds on our way." Then knowing and doing God's will that is revealed there causes Him to "abide with us still." The last verse in summary says that when we obtain sweet fellowship with Christ, "we will sit at His feet, Or we'll walk by His side in the way." All true disciples of Christ know this truth, and as a result "What He says we will do, where He sends we will go; Never fear, only trust and obey." In other words, we do not have to have

---

41. See Cleland B. McAfee, "Near to the Heart of God" (1903); Lelia N. Morris, "Nearer, Still Nearer" (1898); Sarah F. Adams and Hervey D. Ganse, "Nearer, My God, to Thee" (1841).
42. John H. Sammis, "Trust and Obey," words by Daniel B. Towner, 1887. Public Domain.

anxiety because of what Christ may ask us to do for Him. He will walk with us every step of the way.

Christ's abiding presence with us is uniquely characterized as communing with Him by Charles A. Miles' "In the Garden" (1913).[43] Miles recounted:

"In the Garden"
I come to the garden alone,
While the dew is still on the roses,
And the voice I hear falling on my ear
The Son of God discloses.

Chorus: And He walks with me, and He talks with me,
And He tells me I am His own;
And the joy we share as we tarry there,
None other has ever known.

He speaks, and the sound of His voice
Is so sweet the birds hush their singing,
And the melody that He gave to me
Within my heart is ringing.

I'd stay in the garden with Him,
Though the night around me be falling,
But He bids me go; through the voice of woe
His voice to me is calling.

One day in April, 1912, I was seated in the dark room, where I kept my photographic equipment and organ. I drew my Bible toward me; it opened at my favorite chapter, John 20—whether by chance or inspiration let each reader decide. That meeting of Jesus and Mary had lost none of its power and charm.

As I read it that day, I seemed to be part of the scene. I became a silent witness to that dramatic moment in Mary's life, when she knelt before her Lord, and cried, "Rabboni!"[44]

John's description is of a tender moment of the grace of Jesus in the midst of what had to be Mary's darkest hour. On the third day after His crucifixion and burial, she had come to His tomb before dawn (20:1) only to see empty tomb and assume that His body had been stolen. She told the other disciples and later returned to the tomb only to be overcome with grief (20:2, 11). Yet the story turns on John 20:16–18, when Jesus approaches her.

> Jesus said to her, "Mary!" She turned and said to Him in Hebrew, "Rabboni!" (which means, Teacher). Jesus said to her, "Stop clinging to Me, for I have not yet ascended to the Father; but go to My brethren and say to them, 'I ascend to My Father and your Father, and My God and your God.'" Mary

---

43. Charles A. Miles, "In the Garden," 1913, Public Domain, https://hymnary.org/text/i_come_to_the_garden_alone#authority_media_flexscores (accessed March 18, 2019).

44. Kenneth W. Osbeck, *Amazing Grace: 366 Inspiring Hymn Stories for Daily Devotions* (Grand Rapids: Kregel, 1996), 116.

Magdalene came, announcing to the disciples, "I have seen the Lord," and that He had said these things to her.

This intimate time between the two of them in this place would change all of their lives. Because He is alive, our fellowship with Him is unbroken in light of the ministry of the Holy Spirit. No more separation anxiety or deep grief at His death. So we can sing the chorus, "And He walks with me, and He talks with me, and He tells me I am His own; and the joy we share as we tarry there, none other has ever known." Staying in that garden was impossible, but a continued place of intimate fellowship with Christ in prayer is always available.

Another song that catches the significance of our intimate place with God is Michael J. Ledner's chorus, "You Are My Hiding Place."[45] He composed the song in 1980 during the painful separation from his wife. The words came from his meditations from David's Psalms 32 and 56.[46] He focused on Psalm 32:7, when after David acknowledged his sin (v. 5) he could say to God, "You are my hiding place" (cf. Ps. 119:114) and thus, "You preserve me from trouble; You surround me with songs of deliverance. Selah." He also focused on David's words in Psalm 56:3–4:

> When I am afraid,
> I will put my trust in You.
> In God, whose word I praise,
> In God I have put my trust;
> I shall not be afraid.
> What can mere man do to me?

Ledner shared the song with several friends, made a recording of it, and put it aside. Nine months later, while serving in a kibbutz in Israel, he shared the song with friends, who then took it back to California and sang it there. Ledner was contacted by Maranantha! Music to record it.[47] The song reflects

---

45. See also two hymns with the title "Under His Wings," one by William O. Cushing and Ira D. Sankey based on Psalm 17:8, and the other by Barney E. Warren (1897). Both are related to Psalm 91:4.
46. David Cain, "You Are My Hiding Place—Michael Ledner," November 3, 2013, http://songscoops.blogspot.com/2013/11/you-are-my-hiding-place-michael-ledner.html (accessed April 14, 2019). Cf. also, Phil Christensen and Shari MacDonald, *Celebrate Jesus: The Stories behind Your Favorite Praise and Worship Songs* (Grand Rapids: Kregel, 2003), 161–65
47. Michael Boutot, "You Are My Hiding Place," October 27, 2012, http://hishymnhistory.blogspot.com/2012/10/you-are-my-hiding-place.html (accessed April 14, 2019).

that while there may be no place to escape from our problems, the Lord is our hiding place where we can find His rest, healing, and direction.[48]

God's intimate presence and place has become a significant theme in the evangelical worship that has grown out of the 1960s Jesus Movement. Robert E. Webber describes this contemporary phenomena as "praise and worship" that emphasizes "The Temple Sequence."[49] It is a movement from praise to worship "patterned after the Old Testament tabernacle and temple movement from the outer court to the inner court and then into the Holy of Holies." A first stage begins with songs of personal experience or testimony like "We Bring a Sacrifice of Praise into the House of the Lord" by Kirk Dearman (cf. Heb. 13:5), since the people are still outside the fence or gate. A second stage captures the sense of entering into the courtyard of the temple. Songs like "I Will Enter His Gates with Thanksgiving in My Heart" from Psalm 100 by Leona Von Brethorst, and "Come Let Us Worship and Bow Down" from Psalm 95:6 by Dave Doherty,[50] bring people closer to the presence of God. A third stage leads people into the Holy of Holies where they are intimately alone with God in a special place of worship. This is signified by songs like "Father, I Adore You" by Terrye Coehlo (1972), "I Love You, Lord" by Laurie Klein,[51] or "O Lord, You're Beautiful" by Keith Green.

The church has not shied away from songs that employ temple imagery at varying levels of success. For example, "I Am a Temple" by John Mark McMillan[52] uses strange language to coincide with our bodies being the temple of God.

From Paul's words in 1 Corinthians 3:16, "Do you not know that you are a temple of God and that the Spirit of God dwells in you?," songs have emphasized God's filling and cleansing as an important part of this personal temple imagery.[53] However, in this verse Paul is speaking of the church as a

---

48. See also Vernon J. Charlesworth's great hymn "A Shelter in the Time of Storm" (1880; adapted by Ira D. Sankey, 1885) and Fanny J. Crosby and William J. Kirkpatrick's "He Hideth My Soul" (1890).

49. Robert E. Webber, "Enter His Courts with Praise: A New Style of Worship Is Sweeping the Church," *Reformed Worship* 20 (Summer 1991), http://www.reformedworship.org/article/june-1991/enter-his-courts-praise-new-style-worship-sweeping-church. Webber is indebted to Judson Cornwall, *Let Us Worship* (South Plainfield: Bridge Publishing, 1983).

50. Dave Doherty, "Come Let Us Worship and Bow Down," Maranatha! Music, 1980.

51. Laurie Klein, "I Love You, Lord," Brentwood-Benson, 1978. See also Lindsey Terry, "Story behind the Song: 'I Love You Lord,'" http://staugustine.com/living/religion/2015-02-05/story-behind-song-i-love-you-lord (accessed April 14, 2019).

52. John Mark McMillan, "I Am a Temple," released November 29, 2005, track 9 on *The Song inside the Sounds of Breaking Down*, self-released, compact disk.

53. See Janet Morrison, "Temple Restoration" (1996) (1 Cor. 3:16), and Steve Fry, "Oh the Glory of His Presence" (1983),

whole because "you" is plural and could be translated with Southern American English as "y'all." It would be more appropriate to cite 1 Corinthians 6:19–20 where Paul says that our physical body is the temple of the Holy Spirit. Australian Ken Saurajen's "Clear the Temple" communicates this and yet incorrectly uses "it" for the Holy Spirit in the first verse.[54] Others view the temple corporately as God's people.[55] Ron Kenoly sings "(Let Your Glory) Fill This Place,"[56] which leads from the dedication of Solomon's temple to the call for God to fill His church in the same manner. Leeland's "Enter This Temple"[57] prays to God to be among them with his touch. Similarly, the song "Let Your Glory Fill This Temple"[58] focuses on asking God to fill the gathering of believers with His glory as His temple.

At this point, we need to be cautious of indiscriminate use of the temple for the church. While there is support for doing so in certain instances, we have to be careful of bringing too much of the Old Testament temple patterns and practices into our New Testament age. It is certainly true that the Old Testament does shed light on the New Testament's use of the temple concept. Yet the church is not the nation of Israel and its buildings are not replicas of Israel's temple. We are not under the Law and its regulations for temple service and sacrifice. Nevertheless, our God is the same God regardless in which testament He is revealed. Our high priest is Jesus Christ, and the church collectively makes up a new worship center that does not have a veil to separate us from the holy of holies. In other words, we are God's temple, but our churches are not His temples.

---

54. Ken Saurajen, "Clear the Temple," released February 20, 2013, track 4 on *Great and Hidden Things,* self-released, compact disk. See his video "Clear the Temple," YouTube video, 5:14, February 19, 2011, https://www.youtube.com/watch?v=OY0S7tQgRv4 (accessed April 14, 2019).

55. Terry Clark uniquely depicts both aspects of New Testament temple imagery in "These Are the Gates," released January 1, 1990, track 4 on *Live Worship with Terry Clark,* Maranatha! Music, compact disk. While she does not use the term "temple," Francesca Battistelli's "Holy Spirit," by Bryan and Katie Torwalt (recorded 2013–2014, track 12 on *If We're Honest,* Word, compact disk) has the same themes of God's presence and glory filling believers. This song won the Grammy Award in 2016 for Best Contemporary Christian Music Performance/Song.

56. Ron Kenoly, "(Let Your Glory) Fill This Place," released 1995, track 12 on *Sing Out with One Voice,* Hosanna! Music, compact disk.

57. Leeland, "Enter This Temple," released February 26, 2008, track 3 on *Opposite Way,* 2008, Essential Records, compact disk.

58. Andy Smith, Johnny Markin, and Robert Lowry, "Let Your Glory Fill This Temple" (Sovereign Lifestyle Music, 2001).

A final note should be made concerning songs about God's presence with us. The Scriptures inform us that when we are in His presence, we must reckon with Who He really is. We must walk a tight balance between the intimate familiarity that He allows us as His redeemed children and the awesome holiness that separates Him from any being and consumes the slightest impurity. Jared Anderson's "Great I Am"[59] seeks such a balance. The verses seek an intimate place close to the Lord. In the first verse, the believer simply wants to be close to His side. In this case this would be God's dwelling place in heaven where He is surrounded by angels who sing the chorus of this song. The second verse proclaims the believer's intimate loyalty to God's desire to reach unbelievers wanting to be near to his heart that balances love for the world and yet despising its sinful darkness. (see John 3:16; James 4:4; 1 John 2:15–17). Yet the chorus is a majestic reprisal of the heavenly worship in God's throne in Isaiah 6:3 and Revelation 4:8. Drawing close to God also means approaching the presence of the One whom angels worship in awe of His holiness and sovereignty. We see this same balance in Chris Tomlin's "Whom Shall I Fear (God of Angel Armies)."[60] God's intimate knowledge of the believer's troubles causes Him not only to hear their cries, but to provide security and assurance. The chorus connects this intimacy with His ultimate sovereignty.

The location of the God of angel armies in the believer's life is associated with God's omnipresence as a warrior King. He paves our future, guards us from attacks from the rear, and fights for us at our side.[61] This means God's closeness to us is awesomely powerful and intimately caring. Thus it is healthy that many churches have included these songs as a regular part of their musical repertoire.[62]

---

59. Philips, Craig, and Dean, "Great I Am" by Jared Anderson, released March 13, 2012, track 3 on *Breathe In*, Fair Trade Services, compact disk. For the lyrics, see https://www.azlyrics.com/lyrics/phillipscraigdean/greatiam.html (accessed March 22, 2019).

60. Chris Tomlin, "Whom Shall I Fear," by Chris Tomlin, Ed Cash, and Scott Cash, released January 8, 2013, track 3 on *Burning Lights,* Sixsteprecords/Sparrow Records, compact disk. For the lyrics, see https://www.lyricsondemand.com/c/christomlinlyrics/whomshallifeargodofangelarmieslyrics.html (accessed March 22, 2019).

61. The Lord is at the side of a believer to strength them (Ps. 124:1–2; Acts 23:11). He is also at the right hand of certain believers (Pss. 16:8; 73:23; 109:31=of the needy; 121:5; Isa. 41:13). At the same time, a place of blessing is at His right hand (Pss. 17:7; 18:35) where it upholds them (Ps. 63:8; Isa. 41:10).

62. One of the top worship songs of 2015, "Draw Near" by Matt Stinton, performed by Jeremy Riddle on Bethel Music's *The Loft Sessions* (released January 24, 2012, track 9, Kingsway Music, compact disk), is less than adequate in communicating intimacy of place. Drawing near is important, as we have seen from James 4:8, etc. However, this song's romantic

Intimate Contact/Touch

God's intimate contact or touch is not only the last of our elements of intimacy, but it appears to be the most challenging to communicate. It is indeed real and should be celebrated in the way that Bill and Gloria Gaither have helped millions of Christians do since 1964 with "He Touched Me," one of the most famous Christian songs of the last fifty years.[63] Gaither wrote the song while he was accompanying Dr. Dale Oldham's evangelistic crusades. Oldham asked him to write a song that praises Jesus's touch, because a common theme in the stories about Jesus is Him touching and healing people and changing them. Later that week, Dr. Oldham's son Doug began singing it in the meetings and then went on to be the first to record it. That same year, The Bill Gaither Trio recorded it and it became one of their signatures songs. It is gospel-centered and focuses on Jesus's forgiveness and cleansing of the burdens of guilt and shame. Thus the touch from His hand brings joy, wholeness, and unceasing praise.[64]

A more contemporary song, "Forever Reign," performed by Hillsong Worship[65] is a good balance of intimacy of movement, location and touch with the majesty of God. Each verse of this anthem begins with a contrast of the character of God with our human character. God is good when I'm not, he is peace when I'm paralyzed by fear, and so on. All of these declarations of Who God is culminate in the believer's rush toward God in the chorus, in the same way as the prodigal to his Father.

The prodigal came to his Father, who ran (*dramōn* from *trechō*), embraced (literally "fell on his neck" cf. Gen. 33:4; 45:14; 46:29), and fervently kissed

---

overtones and lack of references to God specifically, make it challenging to accept. Is the image of God pulling on our heart strings a biblical image or one simply from Western romance? For the lyrics, see https://www.azlyrics.com/lyrics/bethelmusic/drawnear.html (accessed March 22, 2019).

63. It went on to be recorded by The Blackwood Brothers, Tennessee Ernie Ford, Gaither Vocal Band, Rev. Billy Graham, Guy & Ralna (from the Lawrence Welk Show), The Imperials, The Kingsmen, Hovie Lister & the Statesmen, Mark Lowry, Tom Netherton (also from the Lawrence Welk Show), Preservation Hall Jazz Band, Elvis Presley, Connie Smith, and Kenny Smith. Tori Taff and the editorial staff of *CCM Magazine*, including Christa Farris, *CCM Top 100 Greatest Songs in Christian Music: The Stories behind the Music That Changed Our Lives Forever* (Nashville: Integrity, 2006). They voted the song #38.

64. "A Brand New Touch" by Lanny Wolf (1977) is less adequate. The Lord's touch doesn't seem to have much strength from day to day. Yet the same blessed contact from God is the heart behind the hymn, "Breathe on Me, Breath of God," by Edwin Hatch and Robert Jackson (1878).

65. Jad Gillies, "Forever Reign," by Jason Ingram and Rueben Morgan, released June 29, 2010, track 3 on *A Beautiful Exchange*, Hillsong Worship, compact disk.

(*katephilēsen*) him, all the most intimate of touching motivated by love and compassion. Why would this song reverse the one running? Repentant believers can expect restoration and closeness from God who, according to the Scriptures and this song, is good, love, hope, peace, true, joy, life, more than words can say, Lord, here, and God. This begins when the "wandering" ceases. The final line of the chorus qualifies the One who loves us as also the light of world whose sovereignty is forever. This is as if the believer is still reminded of the balance necessary for approaching their high and holy Father God. One side note is that the only caution I would have about this song is that if someone doesn't know the story of the prodigal son, then the chorus could devolve into unwarranted romantic feelings toward God.[66]

It is difficult for Christians to avoid uniting the biblical theme of God's intimate contact or touch of our lives with awkward imagery. There are aspects of John Mark McMillan's "How He Loves" to be commended, and yet the romantic language of God giving us messy kisses causing us extreme heart palpitations challenges the accuracy of God's love. McMillan gives his impression as to why people have problems with this specific line of the song:

> I think the major problem is that the line makes people uncomfortable. I think the whole idea that God would do anything sloppy seems to bother people. But if they read the Bible I don't see why that would bother them, because I don't think he does anything that isn't sloppy to our human mindset. It's never neat and clean. It's never easy. It's always uncomfortable.

There are some inadequate assumptions here. To claim that God does things in what appears to be a sloppy way to humans is one thing, but to say He never does anything "neat and clean" is quite an overstatement. So to say that God's

---

66. Some songwriters have latched on to the theme of asking God to draw them close to Him. The very popular "Draw Me Close" by Michael W. Smith (released September 11, 2001, track 3 on *Worship*, Reunion, compact disk) expresses the believer's desire to feel God's unconditional acceptance in His drawing them close to Him in a way that He will never let them go. One line has a returning prodigal type tone of them finding their way back to Him. The chorus reflects a seeking heart that only wants and needs God because He's near. However, God is not specifically mentioned, and with lines that speak of warm embraces, confusion with romantic ideas can ensue. See also "Draw Me Close" by Nikki Fletcher, Luke Hellebronth, and Joel Wardle in *Let It Be Known* (Thankyou Music by Worship Central, 2013); "Closer/Wrap Me in Your Arms" by William McDowell in *As We Worship: Live* (2009); and Amanda Cook's "Closer," *Brave New World* (Bethel Music, 2014).

activities are like a sloppy wet kiss of a teenager or large pet dog is not only inaccurate, but not close to any biblical text or precedent.[67]

"He Will Carry Me" performed by Mark Schultz[68] is a very helpful example of God's intimate touch or contact with us amidst our suffering.[69] When the believer is alone, empty, broken, weary, and tempted to give up, the Lord is still with them. This gives them the confidence in the chorus to at least take hold of the Lord's hand of loving comfort. Asaph's Psalm 73 reflects on the presence of the Lord's hand:

> When my heart was embittered
> And I was pierced within,
> Then I was senseless and ignorant;
> I was like a beast before You.
> Nevertheless I am continually with You;
> You have taken hold of my right hand.
> With Your counsel You will guide me,
> And afterward receive me to glory. (vv. 21–24)

Like guiding a child by the hand, the Lord provides the understanding we need to live this life and move on to the next. If we come to be certain of this, then we hold on to God's presence and leading by faith even tighter in order to experience His comfort, which we desperately need. When we are weary and hopeless amidst the wounds we receive in the battles of this life, the chorus then reminds us that we can trust "He will carry us." Isaiah encourages the people of Judah to remember this same truth. Amidst their geopolitical turmoil they should not fear because the Lord is like a gentle shepherd:

> Like a shepherd He will tend His flock,
> In His arm He will gather the lambs
> And carry them in His bosom;
> He will gently lead the nursing ewes. (Isa. 40:11)

---

67. "Worship, Creativity and a 'Sloppy Wet Kiss': An Interview with Worship Artist John Mark McMillan," *Biola Magazine*, http://magazine.biola.edu/article/10-fall/worship-creativity-and-a-sloppy-wet-kiss (accessed March 22, 2019). Later the David Crowder Band covered the song and changed the lyrics to "unforeseen kiss."
68. Mark Schultz, "He Will Carry Me," by Mark Schultz, Sampson Brueher, and Dennis Kurttila, released October 14, 2003, track 8 on *Stories and Songs*, Word, compact disk.
69. See also Elisha A. Hoffman and Anthony J. Showalter, "Leaning on the Everlasting Arms" (1887), based on Deuteronomy 33:27.

Intimately the Lord tends His own flock of people, including the most vulnerable and defenseless. He anthropomorphically reaches down and lifts up His lambs into His arms and carries them close to His chest. This refers to the Lord's promised deliverance when His people are most needy. Jesus is the Good Shepherd (John 10:1–18), and we can receive His comfort and guidance by listening to His voice in His Word and through the Spirit. Ultimately we should have confidence in His impending return, when He will gather us together to be with Him forever (Matt. 24:31; 1 Thess. 4:17).

CONCLUSIONS

The rich tradition of the church's music of intimacy with God cannot be captured in a book, let alone one chapter. At the same time it is clear that believers through their songs have connected with the realities of movement toward or away from intimacy with God, intimate knowledge of God or His knowledge of us, being in an intimate location or place with Him, and experiencing God's intimate contact or touch. However, not all of them communicate the biblical truths and patterns as accurately and precisely as they could. Thus we can see that the adequacy and inadequacy of these songs are like points on a continuum rather than a black-and-white divinely inspired versus heretical perspective. We can take a charitable pastoral perspective. We should be discerning, but nonjudgmental. We should listen to the heart behind the song, and at the same time assess for biblical and theological accuracy, precision, and clarity.

Songwriters must be reminded that their songs often will be sung within a context that may be different than their own. They must write them to be as clear and precise as possible, and provide teaching or even biblical texts with the song lyrics. They have the freedom to make connections with their culture, but they do not have the freedom to foster illegitimate ones. Again, for example, while there is a great love between Christ and His Church, and it has some similar elements of the relationship between a husband and a wife, this does not justify characterizing it as a divine romance.[70] We must not judge people's motives and yet we can advise caution and the need for further theological and biblical reflection. While a song may only take ten minutes to write as it comes out of an

---

70. Phil Wickham, "Divine Romance," released April 25, 2006, track 4 on *Phil Wickham*, Columbia/Ino, compact disk.

experience with God,[71] maybe there could be further reflection with other godly Christians, theological study, prayer, and patience before releasing its contents for public consumption.

As with the students in my class, in the process of writing this chapter I have had many wonderful worshipful moments that bring me closer to the Lord while entering into the lyrics and music. I am indeed grateful to God for His gift of music. It is such a unique instrument for expressing our affections, our consciences, our true and inner selves. Like a magnet of the soul, intimacy with God songs can orient us, start us moving, and bring us to a place where we can see God, hear His voice, and sense His personal work in the secret places of our consciousness. At the same time, these songs allow us to communicate uniquely with the community of believers. We can even join in with St. Dallan Forgaill from sixth-century Ireland and all the cloud of witnesses who have sung and those who continue to sing together these intimate themes from his "Be Thou My Vision":

> Be Thou my Vision, O Lord of my heart;
> Naught be all else to me, save that Thou art;
> Thou my best Thought, by day or by night,
> Waking or sleeping, Thy presence my light.
> Be Thou my Wisdom, and Thou my true Word;
> I ever with Thee and Thou with me, Lord;
> Thou my great Father, I Thy true son;
> Thou in me dwelling, and I with Thee one.
> Be Thou my battle Shield, Sword for the fight;
> Be Thou my Dignity, Thou my Delight;
> Thou my soul's Shelter, Thou my high Tow'r:
> Raise Thou me heav'nward, O Pow'r of my pow'r.[72]

May we be of the same mind in order to glorify God with one voice (Rom. 15:5–6).

---

71. Wickham describes his experience behind writing "Divine Romance," JesusFreakHideout. com, http://www.jesusfreakhideout.com/lyrics/new/track.asp?track_id=4612 (accessed April 14, 2019).

72. Dallan Forgaill, "Be Thou My Vision," translated by Mary E. Byrne, arranged by Eleanor H. Hull (1905, 1912), Public Domain, https://hymnary.org/text/be_thou_my_vision_o_lord_of_my_heart (accessed March 18, 2019).

NOW WHAT?

1. What is your favorite song concerning intimacy with God? What elements of closeness to God does it communicate?

    A. Movement toward intimacy:

    B. Intimate knowledge:

    C. Intimate location or place:

    D. Intimate contact or touch:

2. Why is that song your favorite? Have you examined it further with your Bible in hand and discussed it with other godly Christians?

3. How can you avoid judging the motives of songwriters and performers, and instead hear what they are trying to communicate?

4. How can you avoid simply accepting intimacy-with-God songs because they are musically pleasing and touch you emotionally?

5. What elements of assessing songs do you think are most important for you to practice?

6. How do you think God wants you to share your discerning reflections on songs about intimacy with Him?

AS WE CONCLUDE...

My original question still stands: What does the Bible say about intimacy with God? Hopefully, like me since I made the decision to follow the Lord whole-heartedly as a college freshman, you have grown in your closeness and right-ness concerning intimacy with God. Nouwen describes this as our "development from the magic oneness of the small child to the faithful oneness of the adult Christian."[1] Then as now, I feel an awesome sense of how much there is still to learn and experience of God's closeness. Tozer's assertion continues to resonate: *"God wills that we should push on into His Presence and live our whole lives there."*[2]

My fundamental aim has been to explain intimacy with God in a way that answers fundamental questions about who God is, and how we are to relate to Him. And so we have developed what the Bible says about it as an *affirmation* and an *intervention*. Since it has been a biblical and theological affirmation of its profound themes in the Scriptures, we should have a shared agreement over the basic and most important truths because of the Holy Spirit's work. We should also all have a sense in which God has made an intervention into our lives, ideas, and experience in a holy and affirming way.

So what have we learned? In short, intimacy with God is *the movement of God and Christians toward a place of true knowledge and close contact.* So in Chapter 1, we started to become familiar with these four key scriptural elements of closeness with the high and holy Creator and Redeemer. In Chap-

---

1. Nouwen, *Intimacy*, 149.
2. Tozer, *The Pursuit of God*, 36–37 (italics his).

ter 2 we celebrated God as the source of the indispensible elements for an intimate relationship with Him: our very existence, consciousness and delights,
as well as our specific knowledge of Him personally and in the Bible. We saw
that He is the immanent and transcendent One who is omnipresent, omniscient, and condescending. All this was to show how a believer's presuppositions shape, limit, and expand their view of intimacy with God. In Chapter 3
we began to grasp the radical effects of the fall of humanity and its continuing
barriers to intimacy with Him in our wickedness, satanic opposition, arrogant self-sufficiency, distraction, hiding, and fear. In Chapter 4 we enjoyed
the biblical anthropomorphisms for God's communication of intimacy in the
profoundly rich symbols of His face, eyes, hands and arms, and ears, which
make Him even more personal to us. In Chapter 5 we developed a robust
and grace-filled concept of God the intimate Father who provides relief to
the sufferers of unhealthy shame. In Chapter 6 we interpreted the profound
images of Christ and His people as husband and wife, and bride and bridegroom, to intervene in the church's struggles with these marital images and
point us to their primary message: our intimate faithfulness to Christ and
longing for His return. In Chapter 7 we established the Holy Spirit's intimate
provisions for us as the Paraclete, who as Christ's alter ego brings the Trinity
close to us. We laid a foundation from the Epistles that the main role of the
Spirit is to provide us with intimate knowledge, guidance, and intercession
in our prayers of suffering according to God's will. In Chapter 8 we grappled
with the hiddenness of God amidst suffering and how He not only has intimate knowledge but provides in Himself the necessary intimate place of security and safety amidst suffering. In Chapter 9 we put into practice assessing
the Church's songs that communicate the intimate nature of His movement,
presence, or place, His knowledge, and His contact or touch.

If we were all together, what advice could we now share with each other
about living out our theology of intimacy with God? First, someone would
surely get us started on a key theological truth that would now affirm or set
a new trajectory in their thinking. We could go around and give similar affir-
mations, and write them on a whiteboard so that we can see them all at once.
This might prompt other insights and admissions. Some may be quite vocal and
some may be reticent to share, wanting to sit back and listen first or not wanting
to reveal too much of themselves out of fear of rejection or judgment. Yet some
in the group will sense this and try to gently draw even a general observation
from them. This initial "first impressions" type of discussion would need to have
a follow up later to solidify and deepen the scriptural truths for long-term use.

Second, depending on how close the group is, we could share the most significant barrier to intimacy with God we struggle with. Some may recall an issue from their past. This provides them with admission, but doesn't leave them looking like they are still in that state. Others may speak in generalities, because of the freshness of these issues or because they are still processing the theology to connect it personally and practically. If John Townsend, Christian counselor and author of *Hiding from Love*, was in the group, he might get us to identify a hiding pattern we use. He would help us to see that these could be self-defense mechanisms that cause us to withdraw from connecting with God on a deep and safe level. We could then ask: Are we trying to keep the conversation positive and light to keep our bad parts hidden? Are we seeking to make a good impression with God as an authority figure, in order to gain His approval?[3] Do we do that with the people in the group as well, and thus hide our barriers with God? It is interesting how many "fake" conversation apps are available. Fake texting, fake Facebook, and fake chats may be meant as a joke, but how often do we have fake conversations with God that have walls and lack authenticity? It is time to cultivate relationships that encourage us to be open with God and each other.

Third, this naturally could lead us to move on toward encouraging one another to take joyful responsibility for establishing more biblical and loving patterns of moving toward God rather than away from Him. This could mean identifying an achievable step toward allowing God to meet the very need we seek to meet elsewhere. Perhaps we struggle with shame, and approaching God may cause one or more physiological responses out of fear or anxiousness such as tightness in the chest, increased heart rate, or nausea. Freedom may come, at least in part, through a new settled confidence in the truth in the Scriptures concerning God as a good and intimate Father. This is cultivated through consistent theological reflection, honest conversations with God, worship through songs, and wise counsel from godly believers. Theological reflection and honest conversations with God can be aided by praying through Scripture. Kenneth D. Boa's *Face to Face: Praying the Scriptures for Intimate Worship*[4] is a very helpful tool. He has categorized Scripture texts that can be used when praying to God according to themes of adoration, confes-

---

3. Townsend, *Hiding from Love*, 276.
4. Kenneth Boa, *Face to Face: Praying the Scriptures for Intimate Worship, Volume 1* (Grand Rapids: Zondervan, 1997). His second volume is dedicated to spiritual growth by praying Scriptures concerning God's attributes and character we want to cultivate, etc. *Face to Face: Praying the Scriptures for Spiritual Growth, Volume 2* (Grand Rapids: Zondervan, 1997). For more on the actual mechanics of this practice, see Evan B. Howard, *Praying the Scriptures: A Field Guide for Your Spiritual Journey* (Downers Grove, IL: IVP, 1999).

sion, renewal, petition, intercession, affirmation, thanksgiving, and a closing prayer. Sarah Young's *Jesus Calling*[5] is a best-selling devotional book (so popular that they sell it at Costco!) that words Scripture as if Christ was speaking their concepts directly to us. While the depth of these one-page daily devotionals can be lacking, it is a creative concept. When I ask my students to write something as if God was speaking to them, they either find it helpful, or find it difficult "to put words in God's mouth." Regardless of the reactions, these two types of books should remind us that Christians are not deists, with a Bible that is only to be used to learn theological facts. We hear God's voice through the Bible, and we can intimately converse with Him about what He says.

It can also help some to read and pray through the written prayers of others. Often Christians feel embarrassed or frustrated that they say the same basic words to God. However, God has gifted the Church with not only the ability to write out reflections on God and His Word, but with leaders who are so profoundly gifted that their reflections will be communicated for centuries, even millennia. The Sunday church prayers of the great English preacher/pastor Charles Haddon Spurgeon have been collected.[6] There are also several collections of prayers and poems of significant Christians that the discerning student can use as a guide to moving toward God with fresh language, concepts, and motivation.[7] Care must be taken to make sure that a truly biblical theology of intimacy with God undergirds our use of these prayers. Like our assessment of songs, we must assess all that we read with the goal of cultivating precision in our thinking and interpretations while trusting in the discernment the Spirit of God promises us.[8]

Fourth, we could together make plans to influence our broader sphere of relationships using what we gain from our reflections. Townsend would say, "Learn to give what you have received."[9] As we have drawn near to God,

---

5. Sarah Young, *Jesus Calling* (Nashville: Thomas Nelson, 2004).

6. Charles H. Spurgeon, *C. H. Spurgeon's Prayers*, Forgotten Books Classic Reprint Series (London: Passmore and Alabaster, 1905).

7. Bennett, ed., *The Valley of Vision: A Collection of Puritan Prayers and Devotions*; A. W. Tozer, *The Christian Book of Mystical Verse: A Collection of Poems, Hymns, and Prayers for Devotional Reading* (Chicago: Moody, 1961, 1991); and Dorothy M. Stewart, ed., *The Westminster Collection of Christian Prayers* (Louisville: Westminster John Knox, 1999). A collection from a Catholic perspective may be found in Owen Collins, ed., *2000 Years of Classic Christian Prayers* (Maryknoll, NY: Orbis, 2000).

8. Dallas Willard has some helpful guidance in discerning whether we are hearing God's voice, our own, or Satan's. See his *Hearing God: Developing a Conversational Relationship with God,* updated and expanded by Jan Johnson (Downers Grove, IL: IVP, 2012), 217–52.

9. Townsend, *Hiding from Love*, 281.

the expectation in the Great Commission and Great Commandments is for us to help others do the same. This should be first for those closest to us, for our families and our children. Salvation must not be merely about escaping hell and going to heaven when we die. It must be about the restoration of the Creator-creature relationship[10] that is founded upon the sinner being justified and accepted by faith alone and being adopted into God's family as His beloved children. When we struggle with trials, we must emphasize our trust in our God, who may seem hidden. He is intimately close, seeing and knowing what we are experiencing from the nearest possible position in our lives, and so we are never alone. His arms hold us when we are failing. When we experience the greatest of joys, we should communicate how His face is aglow with pleasure as we turn to Him in deep gratitude for His gifts.

This also means our reflections should influence our ministries. We could discuss our overall church modeling in discipleship and worship. This will require obtaining substantive answers to several questions. Have we understood our congregational gatherings as truly the context in which we as participants draw near to God collectively?[11] How can we provide opportunities for assessing the adequacy of our theology of intimacy with God with our church leaders? How can they build this theology into the existing culture of the church? How can the church cultivate and maintain a balance between God's immanence and transcendence? Are we able to experience the nearness of God amidst our socioeconomic and cultural differences, as Paul describes for us in Ephesians 2:11–22? What are the most appropriate assessment tools that can be used, to understand where the leaders and the church as a whole currently are in their assumptions about intimacy with God? Thus Tozer's challenge to the church more than half a decade ago is still very relevant:

> Were we able to extract from any man a complete answer to the question, "What comes into your mind when you think about God?" we might predict with certainty the spiritual future of that man. Were we able to know exactly what our most influential religious leaders think of God today, we might be able with some precision to foretell where the Church will stand tomorrow.[12]

---

10. See Tozer, *The Pursuit of God*, 83–92.
11. David Peterson, *Engaging with God: A Biblical Theology of Worship* (Downers Grove, IL: IVP, 1992), 250–51.
12. A. W. Tozer, *The Knowledge of the Holy: The Attributes of God: Their Meaning in the Christian Life* (San Francisco: HarperCollins, 1961), 2.

Yes, this should challenge us to reckon with the future of the church. Will we be people with an intimate depth of understanding and relationship with God? Will we underscore the church's necessity to have its leaders consistently lead us close to our God in truth, and experience His fullness together?

At the same time, outside the household of the Church is an unbelieving world that desperately needs to draw near to God in repentance and faith. Their present and ultimate separation from Him is a horrific reality (Matt. 7:21–23; 25:31–46; Rev. 20:11–15). Christ's sacrifice has paved the way for every person of every age and ethnicity to "draw near with the certainty that their sins are forgiven and they have been accepted into the life and fellowship of his coming kingdom."[13] May we continually go "to the main highways, and as many as you find there, invite to the wedding feast" of the King (Matt. 22:9; Rev. 19:7–9). May we passionately perform our role as priests to our God (Rev. 1:6; 5:10) and intercede for the nations with the words of the gospel and our prayers to draw them near to God through Christ.

NOW WHAT?
Concluding Personal Reflections

1. What is the most significant biblical/theological truth that you have learned from this study on intimacy with God?

2. What is your goal for having an intimate relationship with God?

3. How have your assumptions and impressions of intimacy with God changed through this study?

4. What steps will you take to draw nearer to God on a consistent basis?

5. What resources will you pursue in order to move closer to God?

6. With whom will you share the biblical and theological lessons you are learning about intimacy with God?

---

13. Peterson, *Engaging with God: A Biblical Theology of Worship*, 286.

SCRIPTURE INDEX

NAME / AUTHOR INDEX